BEYOND *CALIGARI*

BEYOND *CALIGARI*

✦ ✦ ✦

The Films of Robert Wiene

Uli Jung
Walter Schatzberg

Berghahn Books
New York • Oxford

First published in 1999 by
Berghahn Books

© 1999 Uli Jung and Walter Schatzberg

Library of Congress Cataloging-in-Publication Data

Jung, Uli.
[Robert Wiene. English]
Beyond Caligari : the films of Robert Wiene / Uli Jung, Walter
Schatzberg.
p. cm.
Filmography: p.
Includes bibliographical references.
ISBN 1-57181-156-7 (hb.: alk. paper) ISBN 1-57181-196-6 (pb.: alk paper)
1. Wiene, Robert–Criticism and interpretation. I. Schatzberg,
Walter. II. Title.
PN1998.3.W545J8613   1999   98-31104
791.43'0233'092–dc21   CIP

British Library Cataloguing in Publication Data

A catalogue record for this book is available from the British Library.

Printed in the United States on acid-free paper.

CONTENTS

ACKNOWLEDGMENTS

A study like the one at hand must of necessity be of international scope. Robert Wiene came from the old (now possibly newly developing) central European world, with roots in the former Austrian monarchy. The last years of his life he spent in exile, a fate he shared with many of his colleagues. Thus, the records of his life are scattered all over Europe.

Of the more than ninety films Robert Wiene worked on, about twenty still exist. Copies of these films are stored in archives all over the world. One of the most difficult tasks of this study was to find and screen these copies. The late Fred Junck (1942–1996), director of the Cinémathèque Municipale de Luxembourg, supported us in our efforts with all his competence. He procured almost half of the existing Wiene films for our studies from other archives, and for weeks held them at our disposal. Therefore, our first and foremost thanks goes to the generosity with which he supported our project and the hospitality we enjoyed at his institute at all times.

The German Academic Exchange Service (DAAD) supported our research with a grant, which made it possible for us to study the reception of Wiene's films in the various popular and professional film journals of the time. Because only about one-half of Wiene's films are still available, this was the only way to attain an overview of Wiene's extensive productivity.

Our sincere thanks also go to Viola Haarmann and Ronald A. Waite for their patient and meticulous help in preparing this English-language version of our German publication, *Der Caligari Regisseur Robert Wiene* (Berlin: Henschel Verlag, 1995).

Numerous are the institutions and individuals who assisted us in our years of research and without whom this book would never have been written. Our profound thanks goes to the staff of all archives and libraries, as well as to all individuals who helped us with advice and cooperation.

Film Archives

British Film Institute, London (David Frances, John Gillett); Bundesarchiv–Filmarchiv, Koblenz (Helmut Regel); Bundesarchiv–Film-
archiv, Berlin (former Staatliches Filmarchiv der DDR, Manfred
Lichtenstein); Centre National de la Cinématographie, Bois d'Arcy
(Nicole Schmitt); Ceskoslovensky Filmovy Ustav–Filmovy Archiv,
Prague (Vaclav Mehrhaut, Zdenek Stábla, Eva Kacerová); Ciné-
mathèque Française, Paris (Vincent Pinell, Dominique Brun, Mari-
anne de Fleury); Cinémethèque Royale, Brussels (Jacques Ledoux,
Mme. v. d. Elst); Cinémathèque de Toulouse (Raymond Borde);
Cineteca Nazionale, Rome (Guido Cincotti, Mario Musomechi); Det
Danske Filmmuseum, Copenhagen (Ib Monty); Deutsches Institut
für Filmkunde, Frankfurt (Eberhard Spiess); Deutsches Institut für
Filmkunde, Wiesbaden (Dorothea Gebauer); Filminstitut der Lan-
deshauptstadt Düsseldorf (Klaus Jaeger); George Eastman House,
Rochester, NY (Jan-Christopher Horak, Paolo Cherchi Usai); Gos-
filmofond, Moskow (Mark Strotchkow); Library of Congress–Film
Department, Washington, D.C.; Magyar Filmintezet, Budapest (Ist-
van Nemeskürty, János Varga, Agota Ivanics); Münchner Filmmuseum (Enno Patalas, Fritz Göttler); Museo Nazionale del Cinema,
Turin (Roberto Radicati); Museum of Modern Art, Film Department, New York (Charles Silver); Nederlands Filmmuseum, Amsterdam; Österreichisches Filmarchiv, Vienna (Walter Fritz, Josef
Navratil); Österreichisches Filmmuseum, Vienna (Peter Konlech-
ner); Stiftung Deutsche Kinemathek, Berlin (Gero Gandert, Eva
Orbanz, Werner Sudendorf, Oskar von Törne); Svenska Filminsti-
tutet, Stockholm (Anne-Lena Wibom).

Libraries and Archives

Berlin: Landesbildstelle, Theaterhistorische Sammlung Walter
Unruh der Freien Universität; Boston: Public Library; Budapest:
National-Bibliothek; Cambridge, MA: Harvard University, Wei-
dener Library; Frankfurt a.M.: Deutsche Bibliothek, Universitäts-
Bibliothek, Bibliothek des Deutschen Filmmuseums; Heidelberg:
Universitätsbibliothek, Sammlung Oskar Kalbus; Koblenz: Bundes-
archiv, Nachlass Oskar Messter; Köln: Theaterwissenschaftliche
Sammlung der Universität zu Köln in Wahn (Joseph Garncarz); Los
Angeles: The Cinema-Television Library at the University of South-
ern California, University of California, Special Collection, Paul
Rotha Papers; Marbach a.N.: Schiller Nationalmuseum, Deutsches

Literaturarchiv; Munich: Staatsbibliothek; Neubiberg: Bibliothek der Universität der Bundeswehr (Herbert Birett); New York: Public Library, Theater Collection; Paris: Bibliothèque d'Arsenal (Emmanuelle Toulet); Trier: Universitätsbibliothek; Washington, D.C.: Library of Congress, Motion Picture, Broadcasting, and Recorded Sound Division; Vienna: Nationalbibliothek, Universitäts-Bibliothek, Theaterwissenschaftliches Archiv in der Hofburg, Archiv der Universität, Stadt- und Landesarchiv; Worcester, MA: Clark University, Goddard Library.

Individuals

Rudolf Arnheim, Lizi von Balla, Jan-Pieter Barbian, Helga Belach, Hans-Michael Bock, Géza von Cziffra, Helmut H. Diedrichs, Geoffrey Donaldson, William K. Everson, Hans Feld, Rudi Feld, Elfriede Fischinger, Ludwig Gesek, Kevin Gough-Yates, Herbert Holba, Karl Hölz, Anton Kaes, Marc Kalbusch, Ullrich Kasten, Frank Kessler, Andor Kraszna-Krausz, Stefan Lorant, Eric Rentschler, Deac Rossell, Saskia van Schaik, Aline Scholz, György Tarján.

INTRODUCTION

There can hardly be an international parallel to the way in which *The Cabinet of Dr. Caligari* has been reflected upon for more than seventy years. In no other classic filmic text of international film history has the critical discussion so thoroughly neglected the director of the film as it has with *Caligari*. During the past decades, everything deemed new, pioneering, and artistic in *Caligari* has been attributed solely to the producers, the scriptwriters, the film architects, or the actors. The director, if named at all, is said to have had no part in the creative, artistic process, or worse: his only contribution to the completed film is said to have destroyed the meaningful structure of *Caligari*.

In particular, Siegfried Kracauer's book *From Caligari to Hitler* is responsible for the biased political dimension in which the discussion has been carried since its publication in 1947. The accusation that Robert Wiene took a revolutionary, rousing script and transformed it into the opposite by adding a "link-and-frame" story does not reflect the priority of the film over its screenplay and is responsible, moreover, for Wiene's being discredited as a film director. Consequently, it has not yet been possible to perceive him as an interesting cultural figure in the Weimar Republic.

Thus, two points of departure motivated us in our research on Robert Wiene. On the one hand, Kracauer's thesis – that the study of German film in the Weimar Republic reveals the psychological reasons for German submission to Adolf Hitler – seemed far too daring. We recognized that this thesis was primarily based on a specific political and ideological reading of *Caligari*; and if this reading were assumed to be wrong, Kracauer's intellectual construct would inevitably collapse. On the other hand, we posed the naïve question: Does *Caligari* have a director? We had noticed that research on the films of Wiene's contemporary colleagues – Fritz Lang, Ernst Lubitsch, F. W. Murnau, and G. W. Pabst – had produced an abundance of biographical facts about these directors. In contrast, information on Robert Wiene was extremely scarce, and limited on the whole to entries in film handbooks and dictionaries. The director of what was probably the internationally best-known German film was an unknown.

In the course of our work, we soon discovered a series of filmographical studies on Wiene. As early as 1960, the Danish journal *Kosmorama* had printed an incomplete filmography of Robert Wiene,[1] which had been previously amended and corrected by Gerhard Lamprecht.[2] Considerably more extensive was the documentation already compiled by Helmut Regel and Heinz Steinberg at the University of Cologne in 1963–64 for a seminar on "German Silent Film."[3] On more than thirty pages they had not only listed the majority of Wiene's films, but also summarized most of them and commented on their contemporary reception.

In February 1969, the journal *Filmkundliche Mitteilungen* of the Deutsches Institut für Filmkunde (DIF) published a "Documentation (for analysis) Robert Wiene." This documentation managed to list sixty films attributed to Wiene as a scriptwriter and director. Again, information on the staff and cast as well as on the content and contemporary reception were included. The author, Jürgen Labenski, had obviously made efforts to contact those contemporaries of Wiene who were still living, but he did so "without enlightening results." In the subsequent issues of the journal, this documentation was expanded – letters and further material about contemporary reception were reprinted.[4] In France as well there had been a first attempt at a study of Robert Wiene. Francis Courtade published a "Biofilmography of Robert Wiene" in the journal *L'Avant-Scène du Cinéma* in 1975.[5] The biographical information did not go beyond brief notes, however; the filmography was limited to information on the individual staff and cast. This filmographic research documents no more than an occasional budding interest in Robert Wiene and his work. They obviously remained fragmentary attempts, however, and Robert Wiene's reputation remained doubtful, even among some of the experts. As late as the summer of 1986 in a German film archive, at the beginning of our own research, we were asked incredulously why we wanted to study a "third-rate" director.

Until well into the 1980s, the study of German silent film was limited primarily to the viewing and interpretation of a standard set of classics, which consisted of the films by Lang, Murnau, and Pabst, as well as several pieces by other directors: Karl Grune's *The Street*, Arthur Robison's *Shadows*, Paul Wegener's *Golem*, Paul Leni's *Waxworks*, and of course Wiene's *Caligari*. Not even the work of Ernst

Lubitsch was studied comprehensively in German before 1984. Since then much has changed. German silent film has become the object of extensive research. Directors like Paul Leni, Reinhold Schünzel, Richard Oswald, Joe May, E. A. Dupont, Harry Piel, and Max Mack have long since been studied to the extent that the survival of their films allows. Scriptwriters like Thea von Harbou, Hans Heinz Ewers, and Carl Mayer have been covered in monographs. Producer Erich Pommer has been the subject of two recent monographs; moreover, a book series has been launched that publishes the original screenplays of influential films of the Weimar period, thus documenting a deep academic interest in Weimar film culture. Today a study on Robert Wiene no longer has to be justified before the expert public in the field.

It is not difficult to outline the reasons for this development. The standard set of German silent films, established primarily through the writing of Kracauer and Lotte Eisner, largely reflected the artistic production of the German film industry, while the overwhelming majority of the films produced remained unnoticed. While researchers convinced themselves that they were studying film as a part of popular culture, they ignored the popular films of their field. It was probably with the international appreciation of the so-called New German Cinema of the late 1970s and early 1980s that a new interest in other periods of German film history emerged. Especially in the United States, where the college culture was diverse and innovatively inclined, the study of German film was rapidly integrated into the standard set of German classes. Since then, publications on German film are no longer a marginal phenomenon in the United States, and they affect research in Germany.

Research conditions have also improved considerably over recent years. The leading German professional journals of the silent film era – *Der Film-Kurier, Die LichtBildBühne, Der Film,* and *Der Kinematograph* – are now accessible on microfilm in a number of libraries. Internationally, film archives have increased their efforts to provide "valid" versions and good copies of early films through restoration and reconstruction. This offers research much greater opportunities to study the films of the Kaiser period and the Weimar Republic. German silent film history, held just within the field of researchers' awareness by Kracauer's and Eisner's books, increasingly became an "active" field of study, discovery, and reevaluation.

With respect to Robert Wiene, this provided an opportunity to document the work of a versatile and extremely productive director and scriptwriter of German silent film history, free of any classic association. Of the approximately ninety films Wiene took part in, in

varying capacity between 1912 and 1938, at least twenty have survived. Unfortunately, their copies are dispersed over several countries. It is equally unfortunate that Wiene's work before *Caligari* has
to be assumed to be almost entirely lost. These films can be
described based only on the contemporary reviews. Nonetheless,
these reviews already provide valuable insights into Wiene's subject
preferences, which continued in the Weimar film period.

Fortunately, also, Wiene's work has been included in the film
archives' restorations and reconstructions. The reconstruction of
Caligari through the Federal Film Archive (Bundesfilmarchiv) in
1984 seems to have opened doors for further efforts with respect to
Wiene. Since the beginning of our research in 1986, no fewer than
six films of the director have become accessible again; previously
these could be viewed only in fragmented form or were stored in
archives as endangered nitro-copies. The former Soviet film archive
Gosfilmofond added German and Russian titles to their nitro-copy of
A Woman's Revenge – the only surviving print – and did not hesitate
to recopy it for us. The Cineteca Nazionale owned the only print of
Wiene's *The Mistress* and upon our request produced a back-up print
of the film. The Federal Film Archive acquired the nitro-copy of
Folly of Love and recopied the film for us. Finally, the Czechoslovakian film archive bought a privately owned print of *The Famous
Woman* and produced a back-up print. All of these are examples of
how film researchers and archives work together and support each
others' pursuits.

In addition, the German Kinemathek Foundation (Stiftung
Deutsche Kinemathek) reconstructed a film serial by Karl Gerhardt,
The Hunt for Death, on the occasion of the 1992 Berlinale Retrospective "Babelsberg." Wiene was the scriptwriter for the first two parts
of this film. The last reconstruction of a Wiene film that came to our
attention was *Raskolnikow*. The Nederlands Filmmuseum produced a
more than two-hour-long version of the film based on several
archive copies. Upon publication of our book in Germany, Matthias
Knop of the Deutsches Institut für Filmkunde (DIF) provided an
integral version of *Orlacs Hände* (*Orlac's Hands*) in 1995; it has been
touring in European cities with live accompaniment by the avant-
garde trio "Metropolis Projekt," which provided a new musical score
for the film. Finally, the umbrella organization "Lumière Project" of
the European Union provides the organizational platform for the
Cinémathèque Royale in Brussels, the Munich Film Museum, and
the Cineteca del Comune di Bologna to join forces in yet another
reconstruction of *Caligari*, which drew on "three tinted nitrate copies
that were not consulted for the previous restorations"[6] and which dif-

fers from the 1984 restoration in the quality of tinting and toning. Also in 1995 the Federal Filmarchive and the Cineteca del Comune de Bologna teamed up to restore *A Scandal in Paris*, which premiered at the seventh annual UCLA Festival of Preservation. Moreover, the restoration of *Genuine* was approved as an official Lumière Restoration project in late 1995. The project, involving five European archives, is apparently still underway.[7]

All these improvements in the resource base have enabled us to produce a Robert Wiene filmography that is more complete than any other published previously. This filmography, of course, does not reflect a director on the order of a Lang or Murnau; this was clearly not our intention. Modern film history writing does not look for previously unnoticed genius, but attempts to reconstruct film history as an everyday phenomenon. In this sense, Wiene's work is an example of film production that had to appeal to mass audiences while at the same time trying to establish the cultural value of the medium as an art. So Wiene comes across as a competent, versatile, and sought-after director, who again and again had to balance the commercial and artistic aspects of his work. As far as we can gather from the surviving films and the contemporary reviews, Wiene's commercial films from the 1920s are tasteful mass products – undemanding and uncomplicated in structure, but offering an unlimited array of roles with which the spectator could identify.

Wiene's ambitious films, however, aim to combine both literary aspirations with great dramatic art, and modern lifestyles with complex psychology. Some films are still waiting to be rediscovered and made accessible to a larger audience. The often-heard accusation that Wiene constantly tried stylistically and commercially to imitate his sensational *Caligari* success during the course of his career is no longer reasonable. Even the "expressionistic" films *Genuine* and *Raskolnikow*, irrespective of their "artistic success," follow their own stylistic and directing concepts, which are only superficially connected to *Caligari*. *Caligari* did not occur at the beginning of Wiene's career; nor does the film mark the height of Wiene's work. It was not until the mid-1920s, during his Vienna period, that Wiene was unequivocally treated as a star director, both by the contemporary press and by his colleagues.

In terms of the different periods of Wiene's career, this actually makes for a surprise: even though *The Cabinet of Dr. Caligari* does represent a turning point in his career – which justifies the distinction in his work between the "pre-*Caligari*" and the "post-*Caligari*" periods – a finer structure is necessary for the time after 1920. Our book takes this into account. A broad evaluation of Wiene's career between 1912

and 1920 and a comprehensive discussion of *Caligari* is first followed
by the presentation of a group of films Wiene directed immediately
after *Caligari*. The years 1920–1921 mark Wiene's transition from a
more-or-less employed director to a freelance director and scriptwriter. This period led to the founding of Wiene's own company,
Lionardo. In this period, 1922–1923, Wiene was his own producer,
but on three occasions he also sought out a powerful partnership
with the newly established Neumann Film. In 1924, he was hired as
head director by the Viennese Pan Film, and by 1926, he had made
six films for this company. This was the period of his highest recognition in the German-language film industry.

The last two periods in Wiene's work are defined more by the
standard period distinctions made in German film history. The seven
films that we discuss under the heading "The Last Silent Films,"
however, are also clearly connected thematically: almost all of these
films position strong female figures in the center of the stories. With
the sound films, however, Wiene seemed to be more interested in
gathering experience at first. He experimented with a number of
standard genres – from crime drama to operetta, from the psychological drama to the spy melodrama.

Robert Wiene 1926 (?)

With this book, based on the intense study of the available resources, we have tried to document and describe the extensive and versatile work of Robert Wiene that has up to now remained largely unknown. The picture that emerges is not one of a newly discovered classic, exceptional director; with his dual orientation toward both art and commerce, Robert Wiene is much more a typical representative of early German film history.

Notes

1. The filmography was published in two parts in *Kosmorama* 5, no. 46 (1959) and vol. 6, no. 48 (1960).
2. Lamprecht's manuscript – partly typed with handwritten notes, partly handwritten – is archived in the Stiftung Deutsche Kinemathek in Berlin.
3. Helmut Regel and Heinz Steinberg, *Der deutsche Stummfilm* (Cologne: Arbeitsgemeinschaft für Filmfragen at the University of Cologne, Winter Semester 1963/64), mimeographed, Deutsches Institut für Filmkunde (DIF), Frankfurt.
4. *Filmkundliche Mitteilungen* 2, nos. 1–4 (1969).
5. Francis Courtade, "Biofilmographie de Robert Wiene," *L'Avant-scène du Cinéma*, nos. 160–161 (1975): 28–30.
6. Catherine A. Surowiec, ed., *The Lumière Project: The European Film Archives at the Crossroads* (Lisbon: Associaçáo Projecto Lumiere, 1996), p. 31.
7. Ibid., 108, 242.

Chapter 1

❖ ❖ ❖

WIENE'S LIFE AND FILM CAREER

The few available photos of Robert Wiene show a man of about fifty years of age. His round face reveals a slight, restrained smile. Thin, round metal-rimmed glasses give him the appearance of a friendly but reserved man of his times. His scarcely visible, blonde moustache reinforces this impression. His hair has already become thinner, occasionally he chews on a cigar, and frequently a cigarette dangles from his lips. This is no aesthete; there is no Babelsberg glamour about this man. A photo taken during the filming of *Der Rosenkavalier* shows him in the background, in shirtsleeves, smoking, while Richard Strauss, Michael Bohnen, and Friedrich Féher pose for the camera. Wiene, the director, seems to have stolen into the picture, as if to countermand their self-promotion.

He is often described as friendly and forceful, yet he also appears to have been a reticent, retiring person. Almost twenty years older than colleagues such as Lang, Murnau, or Pabst, he avoided the hubbub of the Berlin film metropolis. There are few interviews with him, and publicity articles about him are a rarity. He was a man who did his work but talked little either about his work or himself.

Wiene's birthday has usually been cited in the film dictionaries and encyclopedias as 16 November 1880 or 1881. His place of birth, if specified at all, is given as Saxony or Dresden. As it seems, even Wiene's contemporaries did not know the exact date or place. Presumably, Wiene did not let the public know too much of his private life. The official documents we have obtained provide nothing more exact, but they at least allow reasonable conjectures about time and place of birth. When he enrolled at the University of Vienna for the first time on 20 October 1894, he claimed to be twenty-one-and-a-half years of age, which indicates that he was born in the spring of 1873. For place of birth he named Breslau (today Wroclaw, Poland). On the matriculation form for his second semester at the University of Vienna he added Neutra (Hungary) as his place of origin *(Zuständigkeitsort)*.[1]

A Viennese *Meldezettel* – a registration form to establish residence – dated 5 January 1909 and filled out in Wiene's own hand, gives 27 April 1873 as the date of birth and Breslau as the place of birth. As place of origin and nationality, Wiene claims Neutra in Hungary. (The spelling of the town varies from document to document: Neutra, Nitra, Nytra, Nyitra.) Evidently, before World War I Wiene was a Hungarian citizen despite his Silesian place of birth, and possibly he wanted to make this clear to the authorities of the Viennese university. During the multinational Austro-Hungarian monarchy, a distinction was made between the place of birth and the family's place of origin. Since Wiene's father was born in Neutra, Hungary, Wiene apparently held Hungarian citizenship at this time.

Throughout his life, Wiene came to stay in Vienna several times. The archive of the city of Vienna holds seven different *Meldezettel* filled out by him from 1909 through 1925.[2] His date of birth is always the same, namely, 27 April 1873, except on one form where the date is given as 27 April 1872. Wiene spent the last few years of his life in Paris, where he died on 15 July 1938. On documents obtained from the Préfecture de Police in Paris, we find as birth dates 27 April 1875 and 27 April 1879.[3] Although we cannot explain these variations in the year of his birth on official documents, 1879 is difficult to believe because it would have made Robert Wiene fifteen years old as a second-semester student at the University of Vienna. Indeed, 1875 is more believable. However, since we have ten separate documents – mostly in his own handwriting – that state 27 April 1873 as the date of his birth, we consider that date the most credible.

The place of birth is even more problematic. On the four University of Vienna matriculation forms, he states Breslau in Silesia as the place of his birth. On his seven residence registration forms, we find Breslau listed four times, Berlin twice, and Bratislava in Czechoslovakia once. Several times he declares Neutra, Hungary, and after 1918, Nitra, Czechoslovakia, as his place of origin, undoubtedly referring to his father's birthplace. Neutra or Nitra lies on the border between Hungary and Czechoslovakia, and after the breakup of the Danube monarchy it became part of the new Czech republic. This may account for the variation in his declaration of citizenship, which is sometimes Hungarian and sometimes Czechoslovakian. Twice in

1924 he lists his citizenship as German, although he had a Czech passport in 1925 that had been issued in Vienna. The later French documents add to the complication because there we find Bratislava repeatedly given as the place of birth and the nationality as Czech. Bratislava, situated fifty-five miles from Nitra, was his mother's birthplace. In the 1930s Wiene still had a Czech passport, which had been issued in Berlin. In our view, he was likely born in Breslau, because that is where his family lived when he was born. Presumably, as an émigré in France in the late 1930s, he preferred to be seen as a native of Czechoslovakia rather than of Nazi Germany.

Carl Wiene, place and time unknown

Wiene's Family Background

According to one source, Robert Wiene's grandfather on his father's side was a goldsmith, first in Vienna and then in Budapest.[4] Robert's father, Carl, was born on 5 May 1848 in Nontra (yet another spelling for Neutra), Hungary, according to some reference works and on 5 May 1852 in Vienna according to others. A 1985 theater reference book lists both dates and places of birth without taking a position.[5] We maintain that Nontra is Carl's most likely place of birth because both his sons, Robert and Conrad, list Nontra as their family's place of origin.

Carl Wiene, place and time unknown

As a child, Carl came to Budapest with his parents. It was the parents' wish that he be an engineer, but his first encounter with a theater performance inspired him to become an actor.[6] His highly successful acting career began in 1871 with regular engagements in Breslau, Hannover, Vienna (Burgtheater), Stuttgart, and finally Dresden where he was appointed an actor in the Royal Saxony Court Theater – a post that he held for eighteen years until 1907. At that time his reputation was good enough to allow for starring performances in other large cities. In 1895 and 1896, for example, he appeared in Vienna while his son Robert was a student of law at the University of Vienna.[7]

Conrad Wiene, place and time unknown

Carl Wiene was considered one of the finest actors of his day, both in respect to the wide range of classical and modern roles he could play and the unique quality he brought to each part. He was especially known and praised for his successful interpretations of roles from the contemporary theater. His contributions to the theater also included translations of contemporary works, in which he had a personal interest. Most notable among these is his translation of José Echegaray's *Wahnsinn oder Heiligkeit (Insanity or Sainthood)* from the Spanish. In the preface to the translation, he indicates his interest in this play about a man who gradually succumbs to insanity, a role he himself interpreted on the stage.[8] In his last years Carl himself suffered a nervous condition and a loss of memory, which forced him to retire in 1907.[9] He died in Berlin on 10 February 1913.

Little is known about Carl's private life except that he was married to Pauline Loevy from Bratislava and had two sons, Robert and Conrad. The latter was born in Vienna on 3 February 1878. As in the case of his brother Robert, Conrad's place of origin was Neutra, Hungary, which gave him Hungarian citizenship up to World War I and Czech citizenship thereafter. Following his father, Conrad began a fifteen-year acting career in 1900, spending the last ten with the Schiller Theater in Berlin. From 1915 on he was active in the film industry as a director and scriptwriter in Berlin and Vienna. Throughout their film careers, Robert and Conrad occasionally worked together, with Robert providing film scripts for his brother's films. Conrad was married to Lily Josephine Radamsky, born in Vienna on 26 June 1876. Little else is known about him.

Wiene's Law Studies at the University of Vienna (1894–1896) and Law Practice in Weimar (1901–?)

Nothing is known about Robert Wiene's early childhood and upbringing. According to records of his father's various positions in German theaters, he most likely attended elementary school in Stuttgart and high school in Dresden. This is probably where he earned his diploma. Whether he had to do military service is not known. Wiene then must have taken up his university studies in the spring term of 1894 at the Humboldt University in Berlin, apparently choosing to study law. When he enrolled at the University of Vienna on 20 October 1894, he indicated that this was his second semester and that he had taken a previous semester at the University of Berlin.

His subsequent three semesters of law studies at the University of Vienna include intensive courses in the history of law, civil law, and canon law. In addition to this he registered for one class of cultural studies each term: one hour per week in the winter semester 1894–1895 on German literature in the nineteenth century, and two hours per week in the summer semester 1895 on the question of immortality. In the winter semester 1895–1896, he restricted himself to four courses, all of them in the law.

In the summer semester 1896, however, we find indications of a crisis. Although he continued to be enrolled in law, Wiene did not register for any law classes. He registered for only two courses in cultural studies, amounting to no more than four hours per week altogether. He selected a course in "Psychology and Aesthetics of Richard Wagner's Works of Art" (Psychologie und Aesthetik der Kunstwerke Richard Wagners) and a course in "The Problem of Form in the New Fine Arts" (Das Problem der Form in der neuen bildenden Kunst). After this semester Wiene left the University of Vienna. The university archives give no hint as to where he might have gone.[10]

We have no information about Wiene's activities from 1896 to 1901. In the official records of the city of Weimar, Wiene is listed in 1901 with the title "cand. jur.," which could mean that he continued his law studies there; it could even mean that he had a limited authorization to practice law. In 1902 and 1903 the records list him as "Jurist" (attorney), which implies that he had completed his law studies and most likely had earned his doctorate.[11] It has not been possible to confirm the date or place of Wiene's doctorate, nor do we know the theme of his doctoral dissertation.[12]

Although he apparently practiced law in Weimar at this time, there are some indications he continued his cultural interests. In a letter to the well-known German composer Engelbert Humperdinck dated 21 April 1903, Wiene requested permission to send the composer his recently completed libretto of a popular opera in three acts. Since it is one of the very few available statements of Robert Wiene's views on art, we quote the passage at length:

> I have tried to create what, I think, is the essence of a modern popular opera: a chain of pure psychological moments, bound by just enough dramatic action as is necessary to hold the *observer's* attention without distracting the *listener* too much from the music. I have tried gently to strike chords resonating in everyone, at least every German, to connect with things familiar and alive in us, and otherwise give the music the widest play possible. So much so, that I concentrated on a particular idea in each of the three acts, molding each into a musically independent – I would like to say symphonic – whole.[13]

Unfortunately there is no evidence that Humperdinck received the libretto, or if so, what his response was. Apparently Wiene did live in Weimar for a considerable period of time practicing law and cultivating his artistic interests before he became actively involved in the film industry. In 1926, a biographical note about Lil Dagover (Jane in *Caligari*) states that she came from Weimar to the film business through Robert Wiene.[14]

Wiene and the Neue Wiener Bühne (1908–1909)

We do not know how long Wiene stayed in Weimar after 1903 or whether he was there only intermittently. It is clear, however, that he was back in Vienna in 1908. His first residence was in the Alserstraße 47, which he then exchanged for a residence in the Kinderspitalgasse 1/11, where he stayed from 5 January through 26 November 1909. It was the theater world that brought him back. According to the *Fremden-Blatt* of 7 August 1908, Wiene had taken over the directorship of the Kleines Schauspielhaus at Johannesgasse 4. Soon thereafter the ensemble needed a new location and Wiene negotiated the rental of a theater at Wasagasse 33, the former Danzers Orpheum, which had been a vaudeville theater. The *Fremden-Blatt* furthermore reports that the new theater would be called the Residenztheater and would continue the programs of the former Kleines Schauspielhaus. We also learn that Wiene had plans for developing a theater with a modern repertoire.[15] At the same time he intended to stage classical plays such as Schiller's *Kabale und Liebe (Intrigue and Love)*.[16]

Wiene obtained a ten-year lease on the Danzers Orpheum and was prepared to manage the theater together with co-manager Adolf Steinert, the experienced director of the Berlin Lessing-Theater. The *Fremden-Blatt*, which kept its readers well informed of developments in the Viennese theater world, notes on 6 October 1908 that Wiene's new theater would open on 31 October under the name of the Neue Wiener Bühne. Its repertoire was to consist of some of the best modern plays as well as valued pieces from the more traditional canon.[17] However, the partnership between Steinert and Wiene did not last long. As early as 28 May 1909 the *Neues Wiener Journal* printed a letter to the editor by Steinert in which he gave notice that Robert Wiene had left the management of the theater, but that the theater nevertheless would carry on as usual. The tone and style of this letter are very harsh and convey a bitterness that gives the reader the impression that the two partners did not part on good terms.[18]

It is not known precisely why Wiene left the Neue Wiener Bühne after only one season. As it seems, his involvement with the Kleines Schauspielhaus and the Neue Wiener Bühne were his only professional involvements with the theater. No evidence exists that he ever acted or that he was engaged as a dramaturge by the Lessing Theater in Berlin, as is claimed by numerous film encyclopedias and handbooks. In contrast to his younger brother Conrad, Robert's involvement with the theater was in a managerial and administrative role, for which his legal training may be responsible.

Wiene's Transition from Theater to Film (1909–1914)

Although little is known about Wiene's life in the first decade of the new century, we can venture some reasonable conjectures. He began to practice law in Weimar early in the decade and presumably continued to do so at least intermittently throughout the decade and possibly even beyond. At the same time, we have good reason to believe that he maintained his cultural interests – especially in the theater – throughout this time. There is his libretto for a popular opera mentioned in his letter to Humperdinck in 1903. We also have a letter by his father to the dramatist Ernst Hardt, dated 21 November 1902, in which the father cites Robert's opinion about a play that had been sent to the famous actor for his evaluation. Apparently, father and son had discussed the play in detail, and it is clear from the letter that Robert himself had been in contact with the playwright.[19] There is an even earlier letter from 1899, which Robert wrote on behalf of his father, where it is evident that Carl considered him competent to deal with theater-related matters.[20]

It is likely, therefore, that through his father's fame in the theater world and his contact with writers, actors, and agents, Robert would have a continued association with that world. It is even reasonable to speculate that with his legal training and his father's contacts, Robert may have functioned as an agent for theater people. Then, of course, there is the above-described venture by Robert to manage a theater in Vienna from 1908 to 1909. This complex and expensive project presupposes that he had continued links to the theater.

Wiene's transition to the film industry cannot be traced in the surviving documents. It is generally known that by 1913 theater people were flocking to film. Wiene's letter to Humperdinck and his plans for the Neue Wiener Bühne suggest that he was oriented toward popular culture and contemporary plays. The widespread interest to raise the artistic level of film at this time may also have induced him to turn his focus to the new and developing medium.

As far as we know, Wiene's first contribution to film was in 1912 with his script for *Die Waffen der Jugend (The Arms of Youth)*. It was a

two-reeler, which passed censorship in December 1912. According
to one source, it was also his debut as a film director.[21] By 1914 we
find him engaged by the Messter Company in Berlin, for which he
worked on thirty films either as a scriptwriter or director before he
made *Caligari* in 1919/1920. At the same time, he worked for two
other prestigious companies, namely, Deutsche Bioscop in Berlin
and Sascha Film in Vienna, as well as for a few other companies.
During this time he acquired a reputation as a scriptwriter, especially through his collaborative work with Walter Turszinsky,[22] with
whom he wrote five scenarios. The scripts he wrote for fourteen very
popular films directed by Rudolf Biebrach, in which Henny Porten
had the starring role, also brought him attention.

At this time, Henny Porten was by far the most popular star on
the German screen, and since Wiene participated in so many of her
films, his name became known to a wider movie-going public.
Porten's appreciation for her working relationship with Wiene was
voiced when she explained her hesitation about shifting to a new
director, Ernst Lubitsch: "I was so used to working with Rudolf
Biebrach, and I also had such a strong personal and artistic relationship with Robert Wiene with whom I have made many films."[23]

Wiene's expertise as a scriptwriter was apparently well known in
the pre-*Caligari* period. For example, his friend Emil Lind had
requested Wiene's evaluation of a film script by a Mr. Friedmann.
On 15 September 1915, Wiene responded with a devastating critique
of the script, which allows us to perceive Wiene's strong commitment to the art of scriptwriting:

> The matter isn't altogether that easy. A little more intellectual exertion is
> surely required. And even in the worst script there is more fantasy, more
> motivation, and more dramatic impact than one believes and usually
> realizes once the thing is done and one sees the final product pasted
> together by some fly-by-night director.[24]

Another request for his expert opinion pertaining to a film script
came from Rudolf Meinhard, one of the directors of the Meinhard-
Bernhauerschen Bühnen. From Wiene's letter of 10 May 1919, we
gather that Meinhard had asked his advice about preparing a film
version of Strindberg's *Miss Julie*. Wiene warns against the project
as follows:

> As agreed, I have attentively reread *Miss Julie*, and I have come to a quite
> unexpected result. I am really sorry to have to say this, but I have come
> to the firm conclusion that the play is little, indeed very little suited for an
> adaptation into film. The subtlest and profoundest elements of content,
> characterization, and psychology are bound to be lost in the translation

into film. Nothing will remain but a solid, unartistic, and prosaic movie piece that must lack any literary and artistic value. As embarrassing as I am finding this in more ways than one, in good conscience I can only advise you to give up this idea.[25]

For the Smile of a Woman, a non-realized project (1919),
an advertisement caricature from *Die LichtBildBühne*

Although this letter does not reveal the precise obstacles that militate against a film adaptation, it becomes clear that Wiene advocates a high degree of artistic and literary value for a film. His attitude here should be understood within the framework of the debate over the respective merits of theater and film that was raging at this time. Advocates of film – and Wiene by this time was one – contended that film should not merely be theater for the masses but should be seen as a unique medium whose artistic qualities must be developed.[26] Interestingly, Wiene maintains this just a few months before he begins shooting *Caligari*.

It is thus clear that from 1915 to 1919 Wiene had quickly established himself as a highly competent scriptwriter and film director, which undoubtedly played a role in his being chosen to direct *Caligari*. It should be pointed out that in 1919 Wiene was forty-six years old and thus belonged to an older generation of film people. In contrast, Murnau began his film career in 1919 (Wiene was the "artistic supervisor" for Murnau's *Satanas* in that year) and Pabst not until 1922. While they were just at the beginning of their careers, Wiene was already sufficiently well known before *Caligari*, as is suggested by a caricature of him that appeared in *LichtBildBühne* as early as 16 August 1919. In a double-page announcement of a forthcoming Stuart Webbs film, *Um das Lächeln einer Frau (For the Smile of a Woman)* – an unrealized project – we see sketches from left to right of the cameraman, Karl Freund, followed by the director, Robert Wiene, and the film's star, Stella Harf. Wiene is shown with clenched fists in a dynamic pose that characterized his directorial style.[27]

Wiene spent a part of his pre-*Caligari* film career in Vienna, where he wrote two scripts and directed two films for Sascha Film in 1918/1919. At that time Sascha Film was the dominant film company in Austria, having been founded by the famous film pioneer Count Alexander "Sascha" Kolowrat. There are two possible reasons as to why Wiene made films for Sascha at this time: On 4 April 1916, possibly because of the war, Messter and Sascha founded a film company, Sascha-Messter Filmfabrik, for the purpose of increasing the production of films for German-language lands.[28] Or, Robert Wiene might have followed his brother Conrad, who had worked for the Sascha Film Company since 1917.[29]

While in Vienna, Wiene was involved in yet another activity on behalf of the Viennese film industry in which his legal training must have been of value. According to the film pioneer Heinz Hanus, he and Robert Wiene took the initiative in establishing a film directors' guild for Vienna in 1919. Among the membership we find Conrad Wiene, Joe May, Michael Kertesz, Fritz Freisler, Friedrich Féher, and others. The leadership of the guild stayed in the hands of Hanus and Robert Wiene until 1922.[30] Since Wiene was back in Berlin in September 1919 for the shooting of *Caligari* and since he directed five films in Berlin in 1920, he must have made a number of trips between Berlin and Vienna for the Viennese directors' guild.

When Wiene arrived in Vienna on 22 May 1918 and rented an apartment on Blechturmgasse 26, he was accompanied by his wife, Henriette (née Trinks) who was born on 28 April 1894.[31] It is not known when they married, nor is any biographical information about his wife available except for the fact that she was twenty-one years younger than her husband. Thus, the union likely took place during World War I at the earliest. They had no children, and the marriage lasted until Wiene's death in 1938.

The enormous success of *The Cabinet of Dr. Caligari* was certainly a turning point in Wiene's career. He started shooting the film toward the end of 1919, the premiere taking place on 27 February 1920 in the Berlin Marmorhaus. The *Caligari* reception is a story by itself. Among film scholars the film has provoked lively interest,

Robert Wiene during the shooting of *I.N.R.I.* (1923)

which continues unabated to the present. The account of the making of *Caligari* given in Siegfried Kracauer's *From Caligari to Hitler* has been a continued source of controversy. We will deal with this crucial issue at length in our *Caligari* chapter.

The Post-*Caligari* Period (Berlin, 1920–1923)

In his post-*Caligari* period, we find Wiene writing relatively few film scripts for other directors and concentrating instead on his own directorial work. He made fewer films but some of them became more ambitious, more expensive, and more daring. Undoubtedly, the success of *Caligari* allowed him to be more independent and to attract both funding and major stars for his film projects. At the same time, he ventured some highly interesting film experiments: in 1920 he again collaborated with scriptwriter Carl Mayer to make the strikingly eccentric *Genuine;* he directed the Moscow Art Theater Players (the Stanislawsky ensemble) in their first film appearance in *Raskolnikow* (1923); and in his monumental biblical film, *I.N.R.I.* (1923), he assembled the outstanding stars of the day.

Another characteristic feature of Wiene's post-*Caligari* period is that he began to participate in the production aspect of his films. Between 1922 and 1924, three of his films were produced by the Lionardo Film Company in Berlin, which according to Gerhard

Lamprecht belonged to Wiene.[32] *Die höllische Macht (The Infernal Power* [1922]) and *Der Puppenmacher von Kiang-Ning (The Doll Maker of Kiang-Ning* [1923]) were produced by Lionardo Film, which indicates that Wiene produced those two films independently. *Raskolnikow* (1923) was produced as a "Lionardo Film of the Neumann Produktion." It is not clear precisely what that meant in terms of Wiene's financial risk and decision-making power. What we can conjecture is that Wiene had negotiated a contract with Neumann as an independent producer in which he retained more independence than he would have had as a director for a large film production firm like Ufa. Indeed, Wiene never made a film for Ufa.

Wiene in Vienna (1924–1926)

The next significant stage in Wiene's career was back in Vienna during the years 1924 to 1926 when he made five films for Pan Film, Vienna. It is important to note that he made these films for Pan at a time when there was such a crisis in the Austrian film industry that its annual film production had sunk to five.[33] At Pan Film Wiene obtained the position of *Oberregisseur* (senior director),[34] which suggests that again he had negotiated a situation where he maintained maximum participation in the direction and production of his films. Moreover, with three of his films he was his own producer with the "Robert Wiene Produktion der Pan Film": *Orlacs Hände (Orlac's Hands* [1924/25]), *Der Rosenkavalier* (1925/26), and *Die Königin vom Moulin Rouge (The Queen of Moulin Rouge* [1926]). The first two attained international acclaim, proving that the Austrian film crisis was not just a crisis of finances but also of talent.

During this period in Vienna, Wiene was at the peak of his film career. Certainly in Vienna he was the dominant film personality at this time. Accordingly, we encounter him in some rare interviews, which give us eye-witness accounts of him in the film studio. After observing Wiene at work on *Die Königin vom Moulin Rouge* at the Vita studios, a journalist for *Die Bühne* wrote an entertaining account of his restless, intensive, driving work tempo, which left Wiene hardly any time to answer even the simplest of the journalist's questions:

> Above all, everywhere and nowhere Robert Wiene's glittering eyeglasses. Soon he sinks, tired, into a Louis XV chair, then he clambers up the scaffolding, casts a glance down, back in a flash and out holding a meeting, and when he rushes back in he catches the ladder he dragged with him when he was running out, like once upon a time Mohammed during his conferences with Allah.[35]

This article is provided with a caricature of Wiene by J. Kapralik, who indicates with a few strokes the familiar Wiene traits – the moustache, the cigarette butt, and the round eye-glasses.

Robert Wiene, Lil Josyanne, Lily Damita, André Roanne, and Paul Olivier at the time of the shooting of *Die Königin vom Moulin Rouge (The Queen of Moulin Rouge)* 1926

In contrast to the above image of Wiene, there is his brief appearance in Friedrich Porges's documentary *Der Film im Film (The Film in the Film* [1923]), in which a number of directors are at work in their Berlin studios. Wiene is filmed on the set of *I.N.R.I.*, the gigantic Staaken studio and the former Zeppelin hangar. He is introduced with the intertitle, "… another, who usually achieves much with patience (Dr. Robert Wiene)";[36] and indeed in the film we see him standing next to the camera – obviously aware that he is being filmed – calm, gently smiling, watching, and guiding the action without histrionics.

Another striking characterization of Wiene on a film set occurs in connection with *Orlacs Hände*, which he made in Vienna in 1924. In an interview that Alexandra Sorina, the female lead, gave to the popular Viennese journal *Die Filmwoche*, she spoke enthusiastically about Wiene's artistic skill and human sensitivity:

> Robert Wiene is a director with subtle artistic feeling, who unflaggingly searches for artistic problems, a director who knows the innermost souls of his actors and knows how to create a hypnotizing atmosphere during shoots.[37]

Robert Wiene

A caricature of Robert Wiene by J. Kapralik

Wiene received by far his widest publicity through the making of *Der Rosenkavalier*, a film version of the well-known Viennese opera. The collaboration of Richard Strauss and Hugo von Hofmannsthal, two established stars of the Viennese art world, generated an enormous interest in the film and, by extension, in the director. Numerous photos appeared in the journals showing Wiene with Richard Strauss either on the set or at the premiere.[38] On the occasion of the Viennese premiere of the film on 30 March 1926, *Mein Film* printed a short biographical sketch of Wiene, illustrated with a caricature highlighting his characteristic features: the round face, the glasses, the cigarette, and the wily smirk. The biographical note concludes with a laudatory description of Wiene's contributions to the Viennese film world:

Robert Wiene is among the few representatives of Viennese film art today. He has succeeded in creating internationally significant and acclaimed films at a time when the Viennese film industry was going completely to waste. In a way, he has newly discovered Vienna as film terrain and with that alone he has acquired lasting merit.[39]

A most interesting report about Wiene's film career appeared in an American theater journal, *The Billboard*, in November 1925 while Wiene was at work on *Der Rosenkavalier* in Vienna. According to an editorial note introducing the article by Barnet Braverman, "The writer when in Vienna had considerable first-hand contact with Dr. Wiene."[40] He gives the following description of Wiene:

Wiene, the cinema fanatic, is about 45, amiable but matter of fact in manner, over medium height and sturdily built, and has keen features indicative of a man who has overcome resistance. At his home in Berlin his sympathy with new efforts are represented in drawings and paintings belonging to the experimental in form and color. Before he undertook movie directing 10 years ago he had been regisseur at the Neue Wiener Bühne, Vienna and at the Lessing Theater, Berlin. In Germany, Italy, France, England and Switzerland as well as Austria, regisseurs invariably show the highest regard for the name of Wiene.[41]

The Last Berlin Years (1926–1933)

During the last years of the silent film era, Wiene – back in Berlin – wrote one more film script for his brother, a biographical film about Johann Strauss, and directed six more films. They were society melodramas and comedies using major film stars with attractive outdoor shots in Barcelona, Paris, the French coast, and Vienna. We can perceive a continuity from the Viennese to the Berlin years in the titles of his films: *Die Königin vom Moulin Rouge* (*The Queen of Moulin Rouge* [1926]), *Die Geliebte* (*The Mistress* [1927]), *Die berühmte Frau* (*The Famous Woman* [1927]), *Die Frau auf der Folter* (*The Woman on the Rack* [1928]), and *Die grosse Abenteuerin* (*The Great Adventuress* [1928]), which intimate that the plot of each film is dominated by a strong female protagonist.

The time for film experiments such as *Orlacs Hände* and *Der Rosenkavalier* seemed to have passed by then. Wiene's major achievement with his last silent films consisted of high-level entertainment films. He drew on scripts based on popular plays by dramatists such as Georges Feydeau, Alexander Brody, and Melchior Lengyel. His directorial style was light-handed, uncomplicated, subtle in working out details, and sometimes successful in conveying a Lubitsch touch.

Independent as always as a film businessman, Wiene signed separate contracts with different film companies for each film, a strategy consistent with his entire post-*Caligari* career.

The year 1929 must have been a year of transition from silent to sound films for Wiene as well as for the entire German film industry. He did not make a single film during that year, but in the subsequent few years he directed four sound films that reveal a conscious attempt to integrate sound in the film narrative. As was characteristic of his entire film career, here too he experimented with a variety of genres: a psychological thriller, *Der Andere* (*The Other* [1930]), a love and adventure comedy, *Der Liebesexpress* (*The Love Express* [1931]), a gangster milieu film, *Panik in Chicago* (*Panic in Chicago* [1931]), and an espionage melodrama, *Taifun* (*Typhoon* [1933]). Once again he signed separate contracts with different film companies for each film and for *Taifun* established his own company, Camera Film Productions G.m.b.H.[42] The films were effective as popular entertainment with big name stars such as Fritz Kortner, Heinrich George, Liane Haid, Victor De Kowa, Olga Tschechowa, Veit Harlan, and Valeri Inkischinoff.

Exile and Death (1933–1938)

The last film Wiene was able to complete in Germany after the Nazi rise to power in January 1933 was *Taifun*, which, however, was never screened in Germany because it was banned on 3 May 1933.[43] The next piece of news comes from the Hungarian film journal *Filmkultura*, which reports that Wiene arrived in Budapest on 26 September 1933 to begin shooting *Eine Nacht in Venedig (A Night in Venice)*.[44] At this time Hunnia film studios, where Wiene made his film, was inviting German directors to film in its studios on the condition that Hungarian versions be made along with the German films. Wiene did precisely that with both a German and a Hungarian cast of actors and with the assistance of the young Géza von Cziffra, who translated Wiene's script for the film and co-directed the Hungarian version.[45]

Upon completion of the shooting, Wiene apparently did not return to Germany. It is most likely that he was pursued for "racial reasons." On all the University of Vienna matriculation forms between 1894 and 1896, as well as on the Viennese residence registration forms between 1909 and 1925, Wiene states his religion as protestant. After his death, however, an obituary in the Berlin journal *Der Film* states: "To the last he denied being Jewish, even though there can be no doubt about it."[46] Moreover, in an official list of the Reichsfilmkammer (Reich Film Chamber) of 26 July 1938, that is, after his death, Wiene is mentioned with the designation, "nichtarisch" (non-Aryan).[47] Wiene spent a part of his exile in London, but it is not known when he arrived there. During the filming of *Eine Nacht in Venedig* in 1934, he allegedly had plans to move on to London according to one of the actors, György Tarján.[48] First, however, Wiene must have been in Paris where he had apparently established a temporary residence, as we learn from a letter to Janowitz dated 20 July 1934 about his plans for a sound remake of *Caligari.*[49] Whatever his plans in Paris may have been, he spent the years 1935 to 1936 in London. There is a note in *World Film News* in April 1936 stating that Wiene had, "formed his own company in England."[50] According to Andor Kraszna-Krausz and Hans Feld, who knew him personally in London at this time, he had an office with Concordia Films, Ltd. on Regent Street and was a highly paid consultant for the filming of Friedrich Féher's *The Robber Symphony* (1936).[51] In *The British Film Catalogue* Wiene is listed as a producer of that film.[52]

Hans Feld, who had himself arrived in London only in 1935, met with Wiene frequently, and in a letter on 27 March 1987 he painted a most vivid portrait of him:

> He was the center of a small circle and we met once a week in the afternoon at his comfortable flat in Maida Vale. There was Viennese coffee, cakes, and stimulating conversation. Not to mention the Havanna cigars – for us a dreamed of luxury. Wiene and his wife offered a home away from home. He took personal interest in the daily lives of his guests and with his smiling skepticism he created some balance. His art collection – mainly Benin sculptures – was a reminder of a world which most of us had forgotten.[53]

One of Wiene's film projects at this time, dating back a number of years, was a sound remake of *Caligari.*[54] Already in Paris in 1934 he had undertaken vigorous preliminary steps to acquire the film rights for his own company, Camera Film Productions, as well as to find backing to realize the project.[55] As a partner he found Rex Films in London at 14 St. James's Place, which guaranteed him the right to direct the film. In his letter to Oskar Fischinger on 7 January 1936, he says of his *Caligari* plans, "In case you are interested, I myself will be going into the studio in the middle of March with a big Caligari film; and will be making an equally interesting film after that." Apparently, Wiene was well established in London at this time; not only was he ready to start shooting his *Caligari* remake, but, as noted in the following letter, he offered Fischinger help in distributing his films in England: "I am very interested in your films, for which I could do something in England, I think. So please let me know whether they are free for release in England and how you think they might be promoted in England."[56]

Robert Wiene with an unidentified woman in Budapest 1933

It is striking that Wiene showed interest in Fischinger's avant-garde short films; moreover, he was considering them for a soon-to-be-established company for modern films. We see a most optimistic Wiene in London with plans for new and risky film ventures. It is all the more astonishing, therefore, to find him in Paris at least five months later.[57] We have no idea why he left London so suddenly and what happened to his ambitious plans, especially for the sound remake of *Caligari.* The Cinémathèque Française in Paris preserves a shooting script in French of a sound remake version of *Caligari.*[58] The author is not named, but Concordia Films, Ltd., London is cited as the owner of the text. The French-language script might suggest that Wiene came to Paris in the hope of completing his project there. Why his plans faltered in London as well as in Paris remains unknown.

Almost no documents have survived regarding the last two years of Wiene's life. All that remains is an essay he wrote for the émigré journal *Die Neue Weltbühne* on the occasion of the Paris World Fair in 1937. Most striking is his description of Picasso's *Guernica* at the Spanish Pavillon. Wiene expressed empathy for the sufferings of the Spanish people, but it is clear that his sympathies lay with the Republicans and their struggle for freedom.[59] In view of his experienced writing style, it would not be surprising if more of Wiene's journalistic pieces might be found in the future.

Wiene completed only one more film during his last two years in Paris before his death. The film, *Ultimatum*, is ostensibly a melodramatic spy story, but it is also much more than that. On the eve of World War II Wiene refers back to the tense situation in Central Europe preceding World War I. The plot involves the conflict between Austrians and Serbs, and the struggle between the two peoples is presented more humanistically than nationalistically.

A few days before the completion of the film, Wiene collapsed on the set and had to be hospitalized. He had already been seriously ill for some time, and he undertook this last film production against the advice of his physician. He was brought to the Maison de Santé Rémusat at 21 rue Rémusat, a hospital close to his home at 6 rue Corot, Paris 16. He died in that hospital on 15 July and was buried the following day.[60] During the next few weeks Wiene obituaries appeared all over the world, but the one that captured the man's spirit best was by Alexandre Arnoux, who had written the dialogues for *Ultimatum* and grown close to Wiene during the shooting of the film. In Arnoux's moving obituary, one paragraph captures Wiene, the film fanatic, best:

> He was a conscientious worker deeply committed to his work. With stubbornness and patience, he gave himself to his work without restraint. He expressed himself in every image, in every detail. He consumed his life's last flame with a tragic heroism because he knew the end was near. He wanted to complete his film. He did complete it except for a few details – at the expense of his life.[61]

Robert Wiene was survived by his wife. She went to Czechoslovakia after his death and was known to have been there at the outbreak of the war. We do not know what became of her.[62]

Notes

1. These matriculation forms are at the archive of the University of Vienna.
2. The seven residential registration forms for Wiene are available at the Wiener Stadt- und Landesarchiv, Vienna.
3. We owe thanks to Frank Kessler for making these documents available to us.
4. Ludwig Eisenberg, *Grosses Biographisches Lexikon der deutschen Bühnen im 19. Jahrhundert* (Leipzig: P. List, 1903), 1121.
5. Paul S. Ulrich, *Theater, Tanz, und Musik im Deutschen Bühnenjahrbuch*, vol. 2 (Berlin: A. Spitz, 1985), 1663.
6. From Carl Wiene's own report as quoted in Bodo Wildberg, *Das Dresdner Hoftheater in der Gegenwart: Biographien und Charakteristiken* (Dresden and Leipzig, 1901), 115–20.
7. Eisenberg, *Grosses Biographisches Lexikon*, 1121 f., and *Neuer Theater-Almanach* 25 (1914): 165.
8. José Echegaray, *Wahnsinn oder Heiligkeit*, trans. Carl Wiene and Gustavo Kirem (Leipzig: Reclam, n.d. [1889]).
9. *Neuer Theater-Almanach* 25 (1914): 165. Hans Janowitz later reported: "I must add that Robert Wiene, the director, was also familiar with the workings of the deranged mind; his father, a famous actor, had gone slightly mad when he could no longer appear on the stage. He forgot his identity, and wandered aimlessly through the streets of Berlin." "*Caligari*: The Story of a Famous Story," unpublished manuscript, New York Public Library, Theater Collection, 16.
10. Nationale der Juridischen Fakultät der Universität Wien, 1894–1896, Archive of the University of Vienna.
11. City Directories of the city of Weimar, 1901–1903; we owe thanks to Ullrich Kasten for this information.
12. Throughout his career, his name appears in the newspapers as Dr. Robert Wiene or Dr. Wiene. The earliest citation of this sort that we have been able to locate is dated 1908. The Viennese *Das Fremden-Blatt* of 7 August 1908 lists him with this title.
13. Letter to Humperdinck, 21 April 1903, University Library, Frankfurt a.M. All translations are our own, unless otherwise noted.
14. *Die Filmwoche*, no. 16 (1926): 371. This is confirmed by Lil Dagover herself in her autobiography, *Ich war die Dame* (Munich: Schneekluth, 1979), 54–59, where she describes her encounter with Robert Wiene as having taken place in Weimar in 1917.
15. *Das Fremden-Blatt*, 23 August 1908, p. 14.
16. *Neues Wiener Journal*, 11 August 1908, p. 3.
17. *Das Fremden-Blatt*, 6 October 1908, p. 15.
18. *Neues Wiener Journal*, 28 May 1909, p. 9. A more detailed account of the Neue Wiener Bühne is given by Gotthard Böhm in "Geschichte der Neuen Wiener Bühne" (Ph.D., University of Vienna, 1965).
19. Carl Wiene, in a letter to Ernst Hardt, Dresden, dated 21 November 1902, Deutsches Literaturarchiv Marbach, Handschriften-Abteilung. Apparently, father and son had a close relationship as is indicated by an earlier letter to Hardt, dated Vienna, 3 July 1902, in which Carl relates that he was in Vienna on a visit to his family in the company of his two sons and that he was about to leave on his summer vacation in Tyrol with Robert.
20. Robert Wiene, in a letter to a director Guttenbrunn, dated 19 April 1899, Stadtbibliothek, Vienna.
21. Ilona Brennicke and Joe Hembus, *Klassiker des deutschen Stummfilms, 1910–1930* (Munich: Goldmann, 1983), 240. Lamprecht in his filmography cites Friedrich Müller along with Robert Wiene as possible directors of the film.
22. Turszinsky was a successful and widely accepted scriptwriter for films. Before writing scripts, he had acquired a reputation as a literary journalist. Wiene's col-

laboration with him was terminated by Turszinsky's untimely death at the age of forty-one on 21 May 1915.

23. Quoted from Helga Belach, *Henny Porten: Der erste deutsche Filmstar, 1890–1960* (Berlin: Haude & Spener, 1986), 57.
24. Robert Wiene, in a letter to Emil Lind, Berlin, dated 15 September 1915, Freie Universität Berlin, Theaterhistorische Sammlung Walter Unruh.
25. Robert Wiene, in a letter to Ludwig Meinhard, Berlin, dated 10 May 1919, Theatermuseum der Universität zu Köln.
26. See Anton Kaes, ed., *Die Kino-Debatte: Texte zum Verhältnis von Literatur und Film 1909–1929* (Tübingen: Niemeyer, 1978). See also Rudolf Kurtz, "Film und Kultur," *Illustrierte Zeitung* 159, no. 3975 (1919), special issue on "Der deutsche Film."
27. *Die LichtBildBühne* 12, no. 33 (1919): 119f. At this time it was quite usual to advertise films even before they were shot. Frequently, the funding for a film could be secured only through such announcements. However, what applied to caricatures then, applies now; only what is well known through other contexts can be caricaturized.
28. *30 Jahre Sascha-Film: Festschrift der Sascha-Film Verleih- und Vertriebs-G.m.b.H.* (Vienna: Sascha, 1948), 11.
29. Walter Fritz, *Die österreichischen Spielfilme der Stummfilmzeit: 1907–1930* (Vienna: Österreichische Gesellschaft für Filmwissenschaft, 1967), lists Conrad for the first time as author and director of *Dem Frieden entgegen.*
30. Heinz Hanus, *50 Jahre österreichischer Film* (Vienna, 1958), unpaged brochure. For a more detailed account, see Herbert Edler, "Heinz Hanus – Filmschaffender und Begründer einer Berufsvereinigung für Filmschaffende in der ersten Republik: Ein Beitrag zur (Sozial-) Geschichte des österreichischen Films" (Ph.D., University of Vienna, 1983).
31. Residence registration forms *(Meldezettel),* Wiener Stadt- und Landesarchiv.
32. Gerhard Lamprecht, *Deutsche Stummfilme,* vol. 7 (Berlin: SDK, 1970), 491.
33. See Friedrich Porges, ed., *Mein Film-Buch: Vom Film, von Filmstars und von Kinematographie* (Berlin: Mein Film-Verlag, 1928), 254f; see also Ludwig Gesek, *Filmzauber aus Wien: Notizblätter zu einer Geschichte des österreichischen Films* (Vienna: Österreichische Gesellschaft für Filmwissenschaft, 1965), 41f, 51f. For a better account of the Viennese film crisis, cf. Armin Loacker, "Die österreichische Filmwirtschaft von den Anfängen bis zur Einführung des Tonfilms," *Maske und Kothurn* 39, no. 4 (1993): 75–122.
34. See Anonymous, "Meister der Filmszene: III. Dr. Robert Wiene – Ober-Regisseur der Pan-Film A.G.," *Mein Film,* no. 15 (1926): 2.
35. Leonard, "Paris in Wien: Bei Robert Wiene im Vita-Atelier," *Die Bühne* 3, no. 92 (1926).
36. Quoted directly from the 16mm fragment, which is preserved by SDK, Berlin.
37. Anonymous, "Ein Besuch bei Alexandra Sorina," *Die Filmwoche,* no. 39 (1924): 9.
38. The earliest photo we found is in *Der Filmspiegel* 6, no. 7 (1925): 112; it shows Richard Strauss sitting at the piano and accompanying Richard Bohnen, the opera star. Wiene is in the background, leaning against the piano, cigarette in his mouth and in shirtsleeves watching the scene. Another photo shows Robert Wiene, Richard Strauss, and Pan Film representatives T. Bachrich and Ludwig Nertz on their way to the Dresden opera house premiere *(Mein Film,* no. 4 [1926]: 10); *Der Film-Kurier* 8, no. 14 (1926) shows Wiene, Strauss, and Bachrich at the same location.
39. Anonymous, "Meister der Filmszene."
40. Barnet Braverman, "Courage in the Movies: Concerning Dr. Robert Wiene, Creator of the Famous Film, *Dr. Caligari's Cabinet,*" *The Billboard,* 14 November 1925, p. 49, and 21 November 1925, p. 49. Selections of this article appeared in German in *Die LichtBildBühne* 19, no. 1 (1926): 22–27.
41. Ibid. According to what we have been able to verify, Wiene was fifty-two at that time. We have not been able to obtain any verification that he was ever engaged by the Lessing Theater.

42. Alexander Jason, *Handbuch des Films, 1935/36* (Berlin: Hoppenstedt, 1936), 216 lists "Camera-Film-Prod. G.m.b.H., Berlin SW 68, Kochstr.18" as a firm founded in 1931 with a capital of 20,000 RM and jointly managed by Robert Wiene and Adolf Noé; according to this reference work the firm was now no longer in existence.

43. Minutes of the decision by the Film-Oberprüfstelle, no. 6593, are dated 3 May 1933, Deutsches Institut für Filmkunde, Frankfurt. The dates given by Alfred Bauer in *Deutscher Spielfilmalmanch, 1929–1950* (Berlin: Filmblätter Verlag, 1950), 252, are apparently false.

44. *Filmkultura* 6, no. 9 (1933): 9.

45. Conversation with Geza von Cziffra on 16 December 1987.

46. "Zum Tode Robert Wienes," *Der Film*, no. 33 (1938); Hans Feld, who knew Wiene personally, included him in his essay, "Jews in the Development of the German Film Industry: Notes from the Recollections of a Berlin Film Critic," *Leo Baeck Institute Yearbook 27* (London: Secker & Warburg, 1982), 344.

47. Reichsfilmkammer–Abstammungsnachweis: Liste der Juden, Mischlinge und jüdisch Versippten vom 26.7.1938, Berlin Document Center. We owe thanks to Jan-Pieter Barbian for making this document available to us.

48. Tarján had played the role of Antonio Crivelli in the Hungarian version of the film. In a conversation on 22 October 1987, Tarján claimed that Wiene had invited him to join him in London for a film venture.

49. This letter is quoted in a legal statement by Hans Janowitz in 1945, Janowitz Papers at the Stiftung Deutsche Kinemathek, Berlin.

50. *World Film News*, no. 1 (1936): 28. We owe thanks to Kevin Gough-Yates for this information.

51. Conversations with Kraszna-Krausz and Hans Feld in 1987. The former had been editor of *Die Film-Technik* in Berlin and the latter was editor of and film and theater critic for the Berlin *Der Film-Kurier*.

52. Dennis Gifford, *The British Film Catalogue 1895–1970: A Guide to Entertainment Films* (Newton Abbot: David & Charles, 1973), no. 10031.

53. Letter from Hans Feld to Walter Schatzberg on 27 March 1987. In a letter to Oskar Fischinger on 7 January 1936, Wiene gave his full address: 66 Maida Vale, London W9. This letter has been published in *DIF-Mitteilungen* 2, no. 3 (1969).

54. Recent research has discovered more material related to the sound film remake of *Caligari*. We will return to this in Chapter eight.

55. This as well as other details about acquisition of the legal rights to the remake of *Caligari* are found in the Janowitz Papers at the Stiftung Deutsche Kinemathek, Berlin. Wiene's company, Camera Film Productions, with which he had produced *Taifun* in Berlin in 1932/33, was apparently reestablished by him in Paris in 1934 at the following address: 56, rue de Laborde.

56. Wiene's letter to Fischinger, 7 January 1936.

57. On 27 June 1936, Wiene applied for an identification card for alien residents; original application form from the Préfecture de Police, Paris, for which we owe thanks to Frank Kessler.

58. The Cinémathèque Française has a receipt for the document signed "Escoffier" (that was Lotte Eisner's pseudonym during the Nazi occupation). The document had been given to the Cinémathèque by Leo Gergely in 1946.

59. *Die Neue Weltbühne* 33, no. 37 (1937): 1171 f.

60. Information confirming Wiene's death is found on his death certificate. We owe thanks to Frank Kessler who obtained it from Paris.

61. Alexandre Arnoux, *Du Muet au Parlant: Mémoirs d'un Témoin* (Paris: La Nouvelle Édition, 1946), 159.

62. The solicitor Julius B. Salter in a letter to Ernst Matray dated 1 June 1946, Janowitz Papers, Stiftung Deutsche Kinemathek, Berlin.

Chapter 2

✦ ✦ ✦

WIENE'S PRE-*CALIGARI* FILM CAREER

Wiene's pre-*Caligari* film career falls into a stage of German film history that Siegfried Kracauer condescendingly calls the "archaic period insignificant in itself."[1] Wiene, who was only one of many scriptwriters and directors at work at that time, participated in at least forty-three films in the five years prior to *Caligari*. The *Illustrierte Zeitung* of September 1919 gives us an overview of the German film industry at the time, and the facts are startling:

> Today, more than a hundred companies produce films in Germany, which are shown to audiences in about three thousand theaters. It has to be considered more of an underestimate than an overestimate when one assesses that one million people a day flock to the movie theaters. This is evidence of how large the group is that film addresses and reaches.[2]

Already by 1910 the German film industry began to unfold and then to flourish during World War I, when it dominated the domestic market without competition from abroad. Between 1913 and 1919, 2,315 films were produced in Germany, with peaks in 1915, 1918, and 1919.[3] During this time – 1915 to 1919 – Wiene and so many others started to work intensively in the German film industry. In addition to Wiene, the following people began their film careers during this period: Max Mack, Joe May, Carl Froelich, Paul Wegener, Ernst Lubitsch, Emil Jannings, Paul Leni, Richard Oswald, Fritz Lang, Henrick Galeen, Fritz Kortner, Werner Krauss, Reinhold Schünzel, Arthur Robison, Conrad Veidt, Ernst Deutsch, Lupu Pick,

Hans Albers, E. A. Dupont, and Lotte Reiniger – to name only the best known. They began during a time of German film history that was not at all "archaic" and laid the foundations for the developments in the 1920s.

Before he came to make *Caligari,* Wiene had written at least thirty-seven film scripts, eighteen of which were for Henny Porten films. Engaged by the Messter Film Company, he worked closely not only with Henny Porten but also with Rudolf Biebrach, who directed fourteen of those films. Wiene himself directed three Porten films, all in 1916/17. By the time Wiene began to work with Porten, having spent ten years in the industry she had become established as a movie star, a celebrity in the modern sense. She was the first German *prima donna* of the screen, and she became a model for generations of women.

Wiene's apprenticeship began with Walter Turszinsky, an accomplished writer with whom he co-authored five film scripts in comedy, tragedy, and melodrama – the genres to which he returned again and again throughout his career. The eighteen scripts he wrote for Porten films deal with these same genres. Undoubtedly, the star's versatility provided rich opportunities for Wiene to exercise his own talent. Needless to say, her star status enhanced his standing in the profession. By 1919 Wiene's reputation as "the author and director of the Henny Porten films"[4] was established. The Messter years also placed Wiene in close cooperation with a number of highly capable film people, all of whom undoubtedly contributed to his professional training: the actress Henny Porten, the actor and director Rudolf Biebrach, the film composer Giuseppe Becce, the cameraman Karl Freund, and the art director Ludwig Kainer.

Most German pre-*Caligari* films have to be considered lost. This applies, of course, also to Wiene's films of that period. However, film journals, film programs, stills, and censorship decisions provide at least some idea of the content and style of many of the films. During this time, films became diversified along certain precise genres, such as detective films, adventure films, biblical films, nonfiction travel films, and the major narrative genres of comedy, melodrama, and tragedy. The films that Wiene wrote and directed during his pre-*Caligari* period can be divided among those three narrative genres, though comedies outnumber the others by far.

The Comedies

ER RECHTS, SIE LINKS (He This Way, She That Way) [1914]   A physician and his wife have marital problems, which they try to solve by having extramarital adventures. After a series of humorous episodes, all complexities are resolved and a general feeling of well-being prevails.[5]

DER SPRINGENDE HIRSCH *(The Jumping Stag)* [1915]   There is no precise information available about this plot. It is referred to as a patriotic war comedy about the Russian occupation of an East Prussian town during the early days of World War I.[6]

DER LIEBESBRIEF DER KÖNIGIN *(The Queen's Love Letter)* [1917] Love and jealousy combine to complicate the lives of the Queen of Illyrium (Henny Porten) and her husband. After a number of humorous episodes involving high affairs of state, the two are happily reconciled. One critic granted Wiene "the great insight of [an] author and director." Moreover, he is said to have achieved "portrait and head shots which prove once again that film allows for the creation of more detailed and impressive pantomime than the stage."[7]

DER SEKRETÄR DER KÖNIGIN *(The Queen's Secretary)* [1916]   A young queen (Henny Porten) is secretly married to the commandant of her military guard. The arrival of a Viennese operetta company complicates the commandant's life because his former sweetheart is now that company's leading star. The opera star, dressed in a man's disguise, becomes the queen's secretary, and this leads to a number of deliciously comic situations that are only resolved through the intervention of an American millionaire who falls in love with the masquerading singer. The film, which is not a sequel to *Der Liebesbrief der Königin*, was described in superlatives in terms of the plot, directing, the acting, and the cinematography.[8]

DER SCHIRM MIT DEM SCHWAN *(The Parasol with the Swan)* [1916] A complex comedy of multiple mistaken identities is ultimately resolved through the marriage of the rich American widow Gisela Bark (Henny Porten) to Count Wolf zu Bretz.[9]

DIE RÄUBERBRAUT *(The Robber Bride)* [1916]   A romantic young woman (Henny Porten), just out of school, is required by her father to enter into an arranged marriage. She will have none of this; instead her romantic fancies assure that her future husband will be a gentleman bandit who wins her hand in battle against the gendarmes. The parents cater to her fancies by staging a grand masquerade. According to plan, she falls in love with the bandit (Friedrich Féher), and though she discovers the plot, love wins out in the end.[10]

LEHMANNS BRAUTFAHRT (Lehmann's Honeymoon) [1916]   The befuddled high school teacher Emanuel Lehmann, who is supposed to marry his cousin Röschen, misses the engagement feast due to his elation over a recently awarded grant for study in his beloved Greece. He awakes from a dream in which he has had a number of adventures in ancient Greece so vivid that he does not quite return to reality. The family humors him and, dressed as ancient Greeks, induces him to marry Röschen after all.

DER STANDHAFTE BENJAMIN (Steadfast Benjamin) [1917]   One reviewer described the film as "a new movie farce by the skillful and successful poet-director Robert Wiene."[11] Benjamin Nickmüller, a clerk in a shoe store, unexpectedly inherits a large sum of money. His boss, with prior knowledge of the inheritance, binds him to a ten-year contract, which Benjamin unwittingly accepts. Benjamin steadfastly abides by his contract, but at night lives the life of a cavalier. Moreover, with comic wit and clever strategies he manages to convince his chief to drop the contract and make him a partner.

DIE PRINZESSIN VON NEUTRALIEN (The Princess of Neutralia) [1917]   Henny Porten plays Ethel Vandergolt, a multimillionairess who has rejected 115 suitors. They form a club to seek revenge and as their standardbearer choose Dick Robinson, a congenial bohemian actor of uncertain repute whose mission is to woo and win the lady, only to reject her to teach her a lesson. His compensation for this mission impossible is to be $100,000. Unexpectedly, Ethel and Dick fall in love with each other; his newly emerged moral principles induce him to withdraw from his task. Used to designing strategies to discourage her suitors, Ethel now arranges to have Dick believe that she has lost her wealth. The trick works, Robinson appears, marries her, and as a wedding gift discovers that his wife is a millionairess after all.[12] The title itself remains a mystery.

VEILCHEN NR. 4 (Violet No. 4) [1917]   This film, which Wiene probably directed, is once again a comedy of mistaken identities. Part of the film's humor includes the vanquishing of a tiger in a hotel and the presence of a black prince who decorates the hero.[13]

GRÄFIN KÜCHENFEE (Countess Kitchenmaid) [1917/18]   In this film, Henny Porten plays the dual role of the countess Gylleband and her maid Karoline Blume who delights in amateur acting. While the count is abroad, the countess takes advantage of the opportunity by likewise traveling, but in the company of her three suitors. The local prince arrives at their estate while they are gone, expecting to be received. Blume impersonates her mistress and the entire house staff impersonate aristocratic guests and entertain the prince. In the meantime, the countess lands in jail where she pretends to be her maid. Timely confessions on all sides provide a happy ending.[14]

AUF PROBE GESTELLT (Put to the Test) [1918]   In this film, Henny Porten plays an impoverished, widowed countess who is supposed to marry an imbecile millionaire (played by Reinhold Schünzel). Granted seven days to reflect on her decision, she seeks amusement in the bohemian quarter where she meets a painter. She brings him back to her castle and by means of masquerade and impersonation she puts him to the test. The resolution of the comedy is that she drops the rich imbecile and marries the painter.[15]

AGNES ARNAU UND IHRE DREI FREIER (Agnes Arnau and Her Three Suitors) [1918]   Two rich fathers have decided to have their children – who have not yet met – marry each other. Tony, the son of the one father, is supposed to come to the castle of the other to meet his intended bride, Agnes (Henny Porten) who – always ready with pranks – converts their home into an inn where she plays a waitress. The expected guest arrives, but it is Hans, Tony's older brother. In short, due to a number of masquerades and impersonations, Agnes is finally confronted with not one but three suitors without knowing the

Auf Probe gestellt (Put to the Test) Director: Rudolf Biebrach (1919) –
Henny Porten, Rudolf Biebrach, Hermann Thimig (from left to right)

Agnes Arnau und Ihre drei Freier (Agnes Arnau and Her Three Suitors)
Director: Rudolf Biebrach (1918)

true identity of any. In the comedy's resolution, Agnes, of course, chooses the right one.[16] One reviewer praised "the charming, humorous script by Robert Wiene" with its Biedermeier background.[17]

DIE HEIMKEHR DES ODYSSEUS (The Homecoming of Odysseus) [1918] This film satirizes a familiar Homeric story. Josepha, a rich innkeeper's daughter (Henny Porten) marries the accomplished mountaineer Hans on the condition that he will abandon his dangerous profession. Prior to the wedding feast, Hans violates his promise by climbing the highest peak to pick some extra large edelweiss for his bride. She, however, rebuffs him for his apparent disloyalty and he leaves. Ten years later Josepha, a modern Penelope, is beset by obnoxious suitors. To discourage them she wears men's clothes, but to no avail. As a last device, she announces that she will accept the man who brings her edelweiss from the highest peak. Only a bearded stranger can meet the test, and fortunately it is Hans himself.[18]

DIE DAME, DER TEUFEL UND DIE PROBIERMAMSELL (The Lady, the Devil, and the Model) [1919]   Henny Porten stars in this "charming comedy of exchanged identities, delightfully written and beautifully filmed."[19] In the film, written by Wiene and directed by Rudolf Biebrach, she becomes obsessed with a beautiful ermine coat, which she displays as a model. One day a noble gentleman buys the coat and in a subsequent dream appears to her as the devil who offers her the coat as a temptation. Fearless as ever, our heroine defies the devil and awakens. Almost as a fulfillment of the model's secret wish, a baroness, who had tried on the yearned-for coat earlier, appears and offers her an exchange of identities for eight days. In the resulting confusion, the gentleman appears with the coat, which he claims to have bought for Henny. In the meantime, the baroness herself, living in Henny's modest quarters, meets and captivates her boyfriend, Fritz. The two pairs encounter each other at a nightclub and a happy end is established when the couples are realigned. Porten was celebrated for her role as a natural, healthy Berlin girl who triumphs over the temptations of the devil and high society. Alfred Abel was praised in the reviews for playing a dual role as devil and baron with his usually cool professionalism.[20]

Die Dame, der Teufel und Die Probiermamsell (The Lady, the Devil, and the Model)
Director: Rudolf Biebrach (1919) – Henny Porten, Alfred Abel

The Federal Film Archive in Berlin has taken over from the former GDR National Film Archive a forty-five-minute fragment of this film with the original tinting intact. Since Wiene's script is not available, we cannot really evaluate his share in the film version. Nevertheless, we observe a number of situations that must have been clearly outlined in the script. Several motifs belong to the familiar inventory of Wiene's comedies: The temporary exchange of roles between the socialite and the model vividly recalls the network of exchanged and assumed identities in earlier films Wiene wrote for Henny Porten. Beyond that, the elaborately developed dream sequence with its descent into the underworld and three tests of courage and fortitude, satirized by a playful Henny Porten, introduces fairy tale and mythological motifs that are new for Wiene. The passion for the ermine coat at the beginning of the film is the discordant element which becomes an obsession for the model and the occasion for her dream. However, in the dream sequence all the elements that are usually attributed to hell are given a new interpretation. Hell loses its terror for the aspiring and goal-oriented Henny: she has no fear of snakes, at a heat of 9,000 degrees she does not need to remove the ermine coat, and she can even kiss the devil – though with some effort, to be sure. Nevertheless, she still does not get the coat.

Ihr Sport (Her Sport) Director: Rudolf Biebrach (1919)

The confusion between dream and reality, which occurs several times, contributes to the comedy's humor. As if Henny's character could bring some of her dream qualities into the real world, she rubs her ring whenever she wants a wish to come true. Since chance actually does bring wish fulfillment, her faith in her own power over the realities of life increases. At the end two things bring her down to earth again: after ten days her rich customer brings the exchange of identities to an end and Henny's character never receives the coat. Humbled and "cured," she now contents herself with her own normal life with Fritz at her side.

DER UMWEG ZUR EHE (Detour to Marriage) [1919]   Harry Walden, a popular Viennese actor, plays the lead role in this comedy about an impoverished nobleman who is sought by an American millionaire as a husband for his daughter. The baron's sense of honor forbids such an arrangement, and he instead seeks independence through employment as a waiter, a servant, and finally as a manager of his former estate. The rich American father pursues him relentlessly, using his wealth to ruin the baron's efforts at employment. The yearned-for resolution of the comedy is achieved only when the daughter – using her father's wealth, to be sure – takes matters into her own hands.[21]

IHR SPORT (Her Sport) [1919]   The plot revolves around man-hating Adelina von Gentz (Henny Porten), who wants to disrupt the recent marriage of her good friend Helga to Rudi Walters. A letter warning Helga about the unworthiness of all men succeeds in alienating the newlyweds. Moreover, Adelina disguised as a servant wants to spy on them during their honeymoon in the Alps. There she meets a vacationer, also by chance named Rudi, who has learned the whole story and accepts the challenge of curing Adelina. He overcomes her resistance with his manliness and wins her love. At the conclusion of the comedy, there are two happy, loving couples.[22]

SCHUHPUTZSALON ROLF G.M.B.H. (Shoe-Shine Parlor Rolf, Ltd.) [1919]   This two-act, low-budget comedy, written by Robert Wiene, was praised for elevating this genre to a higher level.[23] No plot summary is available.

The Melodramas

DAS WANDERNDE LICHT (The Wandering Light) [1916]   This film, based on a novella by Ernst von Wildenbruch, revolves around a private, young nobleman who is said to be unbalanced. Breaking out of his isolation, he attends a high-society ball, meets a young woman with whom he falls in love, and decides to marry. The bride (Henny Porten) receives warning letters before the wedding but ignores them. During the festivities after the wedding, the condition of the groom (Bruno Decarli) deteriorates suddenly, and during the ensuing scene his wife leaves and seeks refuge with her uncle and guardian. The young count's old servant, who really is insane, suggests to him that his wife has died. The bereaved count now spends day in, day out in melancholy, wandering with a candelabra from room to room in memory of his beloved. Tragedy is avoided when the young woman returns to the castle and discovers that it is not her dear husband who is mad, but the old servant. The latter is dispatched to an institution and the young couple is reunited and happy. This was Wiene's first film with madness as the central theme. A reviewer said the following about this subject: "We have here literature as film and the proof that psychologically interesting processes can indeed be portrayed in film."[24]

GELÖSTE KETTEN (Unchained) [1916]   A young widow, Lisabeth Blenke (Henny Porten), is engaged to be married to count Harro. She endears herself to the count's family, but the count's cousin, judge Joachim von Trautendorff, opposes the marriage because, years before, he had had to sentence her to jail for theft. To prevent the union, he visits the home of Lisabeth's foster-mother, where he encounters Lisabeth herself. She tells him about the sufferings and deprivations of her youth and wins the judge's sympathy and trust. Her future husband, however, upon receiving incriminating letters from the foster-mother, creates a scene. Lisabeth leaves him and marries Joachim.[25] It is worth noting that with this script Wiene turned to a legal subject matter for the first time.

Das Wandernde Licht (The Wandering Light)
Director: Robert Wiene (1916) – Bruno Decarli, Henny Porten

FEENHÄNDE (Fairy Hands) [1916/17]   Helene (Henny Porten), a poor orphan, lives in the house of her uncle, Count Föhrwald. The impoverished count has two hopes – first that a projected railroad will run through his property and second that his son Georg will marry rich. Because Georg is in love with Helene, she must leave. The resourceful Helene makes her fortune independently by building up a fashion business, which is frequented by the wives of the very industrialists whose support her uncle needs for the railroad venture. Helene uses her influence to save her uncle and then marries Georg.[26]

DIE EHE DER LUISE ROHRBACH (The Marriage of Luise Rohrbach) [1916/17]   The film features high school principal Luise Taden (Henny Porten), who should have been warned about her betrothed, factory owner Wilhelm Rohrbach (Emil Jannings), since he has recently beaten a worker and he received a three-day jail sentence for it. In fact, on the wedding day he reveals his brutal nature when he beats a man to death for pestering his wife. He is sentenced again, this time to three years in jail, but the sentence is remitted to ten months through the efforts of his wife and his lawyer Rüting. Never-

Die Ehe der Luise Rohrbach (The Marriage of Luise Rohrbach) Director: Rudolf Biebrach (1917) – Emil Jannings, Henny Porten

theless, Luise no longer loves her brutal husband, and after his release from jail, Rohrbach rapes her when she refuses him. Soon thereafter the struggle over their child begins. To keep the child, Luise confesses that she has committed adultery, though she has not. The child is returned to her after she serves a three-day sentence, and she then marries a man more suited to her temperament, namely, the lawyer Rüting.

Wiene's script uses the classic plot design of a triangular relationship involving a refined and sensitive woman, a brutal insensitive husband, and a civilized gentleman who comes to her defense both as a defense attorney in court and as a devoted, loving man. One of Wiene's favorite themes, the justice system, is represented here in a threefold way: in dynamic scenes before the court, in prison, and in the lawyers' offices. However, the legal system deserves little praise. It is more in spite of than because of a number of flawed legal decisions rendered by the court that Louise Rohrbach gains her freedom from her husband, is united with her child, and marries a worthier man. A large fragment (four reels) of this film is available from the Federal Film Archive in Berlin.

Gefangen Seele (Imprisoned Soul) Director: Rudolf Biebrach (1917) –
Henny Porten, Paul Bildt

GEFANGENE SEELE (Imprisoned Soul) [1917]   The unscrupulous Baron van Groot has Violetta (Henny Porten) under his hypnotic power, which he uses ruthlessly. The young physician, Stefan Rainer, tries to help her, falls in love with her, and wishes to marry her. Shortly before the wedding, Violetta receives a letter from her master, the baron, forcing her to come to him. Since all attempts to liberate herself from his diabolical, hypnotic power have failed, she goes to him but takes along a revolver. The next day the baron is found shot to death, with Violetta lying unconscious next to him. She believes she has committed the murder, but in court the true murderer is found and convicted.[27] In this film there is not only another court scene but also a psychological drama, anticipating the diabolical, hypnotic relationship between Caligari and Cesare. It is significant to note that the script for this film with all the above-mentioned themes was authored by Robert Wiene two-and-one-half years prior to *Caligari*.

FRANK HANSENS GLÜCK (Frank Hansen's Fortune) [1917] Two friends, Frank Hansen (Viggo Larsen) and Georg Balker (Lupu Pick), find a huge and precious diamond in the Mexican diamond fields. Two scoundrels get Frank drunk to find out the location of the buried diamond. While stealing the diamond they shoot and wound Georg. Upon awakening from his drunken stupor, Frank suspects their perfidy and steals the diamond back. He returns to Georg's hut, where he takes his friend for dead. Frank becomes a millionaire banker, marries a beautiful, understanding woman, and becomes a philanthropist; but nothing can still his doubts about the rightfulness of his fortune. Old Georg in the meantime is still alive but is no longer of sound mind. One day he recognizes Frank's photo in the newspaper, and believing him to be the diamond thief goes forth to take revenge. Georg and the two scoundrels find Frank at the same time, but Georg comes to his senses and recognizes Frank's innocence.[28]

DAS LEBEN EIN TRAUM (Life Is a Dream) [1916/17] A young baroness on a vacation meets and marries a man who turns out to be a scoundrel. Under blackmail threats from an accomplice, he exhausts his wife's fortune and even attempts to steal her jewelry after she rejects him. During the attempted theft, his accomplice murders him, and the poor baroness is suspected of the crime. These crises bring her to the verge of insanity. She is cured of her illness by the intervention of physicians who experiment with the power of suggestion. She is put to rest in her old bed and upon awakening is told that her vacation with her father is about to commence. The experiment is successful and she believes that her dreadful experiences were nothing but a bad dream.[29] A reviewer described *Das Leben ein Traum* as, "a Messter film, totally devoted to psychological experimentation as a means of exploring human motivation."[30]

EDELSTEINE (Precious Stones) [1917/18]   Wiene's script provides a complicated, romantic plot about a young woman's pathological desire for jewelry. Maddalena (Henny Porten), the daughter of an antique dealer, meets Count Forrest in her father's shop when the young nobleman pawns a precious family heirloom. Her passionate yearning to be the only one to wear the unique jewel leads her to engage in a variety of intrigues. After her own father's death, she enters the count's house by serving as his wife's nurse. Soon the wife dies, and after a year of mourning the count offers Maddalena his hand. On the wedding day – the day on which she can properly, according to family custom, wear the jewel – she dies.[31]

Das Geschlecht derer von Ringwall (The Ringwall Family)
Director: Rudolf Biebrach (1918)

DAS GESCHLECHT DERER VON RINGWALL (The Ringwall Family) [1918]   This script by Wiene belonged to a series called "Seltsame Menschen" (Unusual People). No further information about the series could be obtained. A curse seems to hang over the von Ringwall family. A temperament easily aroused to wild rage leads members of the family to their doom. The father, in a fit of rage, murdered their mother on the false suspicion of infidelity. The two remaining family members, Magdalena (Henny Porten) and her brother Argad, live isolated in a solitary house in the mountains. Argad's hot blood, true to the family curse, soon leads him into a dispute in which he is killed. Magdalena, the most temperate of the clan, swears revenge. Fortunately, she is distracted from becoming yet another victim of the curse by the presence of an ailing young man in her house whom she nurses back to health and begins to love. According to some accounts, he was responsible for her brother's death. Nevertheless, love is triumphant and the family curse is overcome.[32]

In the press reports of the time, this film was criticized for its plot's convolutedness. One critic considered the dramatic development of the first half of the film quite acceptable but, "then ... Wiene, one of the best minds among screenwriters, drops the thread and walks the rutted paths of the movie drama."[33]

EIN GEFÄHRLICHES SPIEL (A Dangerous Game) [1919] No sufficient information for a plot summary is available. It seems that the melodrama deals with an innocent attempt to test the criminal justice system, and the challengers are involved in more than they bargained for.[34]

The Tragedies

ARME MARIE (Poor Marie) [1915] The saleslady Maria Weber turns to theft when her father is threatened with eviction. Because she will not yield to her manager's advances, he exposes her to the owner, who investigates the matter and forgives her upon learning the truth. When the manager insults her, he is dismissed, and soon thereafter Maria becomes the owner's wife. However, the dismissed manager tries to blackmail her, and to conceal her past she attempts secretly to take money from her husband's business. She is caught in the act and suffers a stroke. She dies, but not until her husband has forgiven her.[35]

FLUCH DER SCHÖNHEIT (The Curse of Beauty) [1915] A beautiful young woman, Vera, married to an elderly aristocrat, Count von Selbitz, sets the stage for this tragedy. Vera suffers under her husband's rigid formality. She takes some solace in her son Otto, who loves her dearly. When her husband sends the son away to a military academy, Vera becomes susceptible to the passionate attentions of a young painter who has been engaged to paint her portrait. When the count discovers the two in a liaison, his anger and grief drive him to suicide. Vera does not pretend to mourn and soon opens her house to a number of admirers; all this is held against her by high society. Young Otto returns and spends a few happy weeks in his mother's presence, in no way questioning her virtue. She realizes, however, that with her habits her home is no place for her son, and she sends

him away. Ten years later he returns as a full-grown man with a successful career, about to make a good marriage. He is once more
enchanted by his mother, still believing in her goodness and innocence, when he discovers her in a liaison with a former classmate of
his. Shocked, he rejects her pleas for forgiveness, rushes into his
father's study and shoots himself. Vera finds a suicide note with the
words, "Now I know why my father died." Vera collapses and dies
next to the body of her beloved son.[36]

DIE BÜSSENDE MAGDELENA (Penitent Magdalena) [1915]   A brief
note in *Die LichtBildBühne* describes the film as a tragedy that takes
place in musical circles.[37] No other information is available.

FRAU EVA (Mrs. Eve) [1916]   The plot revolves around a poor girl
who yearns for a life of luxury. She marries a decent man (Emil Jannings, in his film debut) who has by dint of hard work become the
co-owner of a factory. Eva, who thinks only of luxury and pleasure,
involves her husband's business partner in wasteful expenditures.
When the business is on the verge of financial ruin, her trusting husband discovers what had been going on behind his back. Eva regrets
her destructive life and commits suicide.[38]

DER MANN IM SPIEGEL (The Man in the Mirror) [1916]   Bruno
Decarli plays the role of a man whose sister was seduced by a young
prince. On the occasion of the prince's wedding, he murders him.
The prince's widow had seen him only once in the mirror, but her
intuition convinces her that he was her husband's assassin. To bring
him to justice she charms him until he declares his love. However,
when he confesses his guilt she cannot expose him because by then
she too is in love. Hopelessly caught between her passion for
revenge and her love, she commits suicide.[39] The reviewer commenting on Wiene's contribution to the film says, "The material as
such is not exactly new ... but it is presented with extraordinary skill
here, staged by Robert Wiene with refined taste and taking full
advantage of the rich artistic means at his disposal."[40]

FURCHT (Fear) [1917]   Count Greven (Bruno Decarli) returns to his
castle from a journey around the world in a melancholy, disturbed
condition. Soon we learn that during a visit to a temple in India he
stole a Buddha statue for which he had developed a consuming passion. He now lives in fear and dread of being pursued by Indian
priests. According to a vision, he has only seven years left to live and
will then be killed by the hand dearest to him. He now leads a tumul-

tuous life of pleasure and distraction. Toward the end of the seven years, consumed by fear, he dies by his own hand. The priest (Conrad Veidt) who had appeared in his vision comes to the castle and takes back the fateful icon.[41]

The Swedish Film Institute in Stockholm owns a fine and fairly complete print of this film. What is immediately most impressive from a screening of the film is the outstanding performance of Bruno Decarli, then one of the leading theater actors in Berlin. He plays Count Greven, who experiences a wide range of emotional states from extreme depression to manic excitement, from a desolate fear to the utmost hysteria. The count's subjectivity – his psychological distress – is at the very center of the film, as indeed the title of the film makes clear. What heightens the tension in this psychological drama is the ambiguity about whether the count's fears are based on fact or on paranoid fantasy. His flashback narration makes it clear that he did indeed steal a sacred Buddha statue from an Indian temple and thereby commit an act of desecration. What is not clear, at least from the Stockholm print and from the plot summary in the program booklet, is whether there really is an Indian priest pursuing him to punish him, as he has come to believe. At any rate, that belief becomes his *idée fixe* and dominates his subjectivity to his death.

As a result of his encounter with the Indian priest, be it fact or fantasy, he believes that as part of the curse he has been granted seven years to learn to love life. This belief transforms him and he decides to live life to the fullest. He begins with lavish festivities at his mansion involving wild dancing, carousing, and gambling. Although he sponsors these activities, he always remains at their periphery, quickly satiated and always in search of novel experiences. Next, he turns to scientific research in a laboratory in which he works day and night. He discovers a new way of producing artificial protein to conquer famine. However, at the celebration in honor of his discovery, he himself in the presence of all destroys the scientific equipment that contains his secret formula, ostensibly because it amuses him. Still driven by a thirst for novelty, he leaves his festivities and his research and temporarily finds solace in love. However, as the end of the appointed time approaches, he reverts to his fearful, paranoid behavior, expecting any moment to die by "the hand that is dearest to him" as was prophesied by the Indian priest.

From a Western, rational perspective his occult experiences would be interpreted as psychological, that is, as motivated by feelings of guilt and fears of persecution. He himself, of course, is convinced of the presence of occult powers in his house, as demonstrated by the following events that he experiences: first, there is the Indian priest's commanding gesture in front of his house, which wakens him; then, the count fires a full round of ammunition at the priest at close range without wounding him; next, the priest utters a curse according to which the count has seven years left to take pleasure in life, but will then die by the "hand dearest to him"; thereafter, the count finds a mysterious note, apparently from the priest, pinned to the well-hidden Buddha statue; and, finally, the count throws the statue into a pond but immediately thereupon finds it back in its place of concealment.

These experiences can be seen either as nourishing his fears or as expressions themselves of his growing madness. Even during the seven years of life granted him by the curse, his pleasures are repeatedly undermined by his expectation of the eventual fulfillment of that curse. The count dies by his own hand and it seems clear that it was his own madness that drove him to his death. However, Wiene subverts that conclusion by leaving the final scene of the film to the Indian priest, who appears as a ghostlike apparition to reclaim the sacred statue and put an end to the desecration of the Indian temple by the foreign intruder from the West. This scene is achieved by a series of skillful double-exposure shots that create an eerie, haunting conclusion to what seems to be no more than a psychological thriller.

In *Fear* Wiene creates an environment that is consistent with the subjectivity of the protagonist. He confines Count Greven to his huge castle, letting him wander through the vast chambers at night with a candelabra casting ominous shadows from room to room. He has the windows boarded up whenever the count is overcome by his fears in an attack of madness, so that the count is shrouded in darkness in a dual sense. With close and medium-close shots, Wiene underlines Bruno Decarli's masterly representation of phases of madness through body language and facial expression. This is not the first time Wiene selected madness as a theme for a film script, nor, of course, is it the last time. In fact, the exploration of subjectivity and of psychological states is one of the recurring themes in Wiene's oeuvre, as it is in the modernist tradition. We will examine this aspect of Wiene's films in Chapter Eight.

Am Tor des Todes (At the Gate of Death) [1918]

Count Arnold Galeen (Harry Walden), given only a few more weeks to live by his physician, returns to his ancestral castle to await death. He has lived fully and extravagantly but feels that the best is yet to come. Death personified grants him the wish for a new life, and the count plunges into the vicissitudes of a passionate way of life, which leads him into the same errors and disappointments as before, just as death had prophesied.[42]

OPFER DER GESELLSCHAFT (Victim of Society) [1919]   A critique of society and its criminal justice system is the subject of this film. The public prosecutor Chrysander (Conrad Veidt) prosecutes a woman, Martha Bellina, who is charged with murder, and succeeds in convicting her to a long-term sentence without considering extenuating circumstances. He maintains that society must be freed of such elements. Chrysander's success in this case advances his career and social status. He becomes engaged to the daughter of the presiding judge *(Gerichtspräsident),* but before a marriage can take place he discovers Martha's diary, which proves to him that it is not society that must be protected from people like Martha, but quite the reverse. In her youth, Martha had been seduced by a student who left her with a child. Martha inherited a small fortune from an elderly man whom she had nursed for years. She then married to give her son a father and a name. Once again, the man turned out to be a scoundrel who exploited her. After giving her son what was left of the inheritance and leaving him in the care of a private academy, she left her worth-

Die lebende Tote (The Living Dead Woman)
Director: Rudolf Biebrach (1919) – Henny Porten, Carl Ebert

less husband and attempted to make her way as a dancer. By chance their paths crossed again and when her wretched husband attempted to blackmail her she shot him.

Chrysander is so moved by reading her diary that he withdraws from society to write a book entitled *Victims of Society.* His solitude is disturbed by the unexpected arrival of his former fiancée. Chrysander, not knowing that she had married in the meantime, responds to her desire to continue their previous relationship. Her husband intervenes and in a physical altercation Chrysander kills him. Chrysander's statement under oath that he had not known of the marriage is viewed by the court as perjury and he is sentenced to death. Martha tries to rescue him by revealing his identity to the minister of justice. The minister himself had been the student who had taken advantage of her and left her with an illegitimate child, namely, Chrysander. The death sentence, however, cannot be rescinded and Chrysander goes to the scaffold, a victim of society and its moral principles.[43] This was the second film Conrad Veidt made with Wiene before *Caligari*. Once again Wiene turned to the justice system, including two significant court scenes in the film. As before, the justice system is not portrayed favorably. The courts turn out to be incapable of ascertaining the truth, and they pass judgments accordingly. The highly constructed plot involves a strict prosecuting attorney who is involved in a case that transforms his entire sense of justice. More than ten years later Wiene returned to this theme in *Der Andere* (1930).

DIE LEBENDE TOTE (The Living Dead Woman) [1919]   Henny Porten plays Eva, a young woman married to the distinguished professor von Redlich. Although she is deeply devoted to him and loves her

Die lebende Tote (The Living Dead Woman)
Director: Rudolf Biebrach (1919) – Henny Porten, Paul Bildt

daughter dearly, her life is unfulfilled. She turns to her former lover, Karl von der Tann, who renews their relationship at the first opportunity. Supposedly going to visit her sister, Eva spends the night with her lover. When the train with which she was supposed to visit her sister is derailed, she is declared one of the many who perished in the wreck. Filled with shame and guilt, Eva never returns to her family. Instead, she acts in a variety show and, with the help of cocaine, fills her empty existence with dreams of her former family happiness. She grows desperate in her need for the drug, and von der Tann offers to provide it in exchange for another night of love. She promises to grant his wish, but in her yearning for release from her present life she takes an overdose and when he appears for the promised embrace he finds her dead.[44]

Gosfilmofond (the National Film Archive of the former Soviet Union) has preserved a fifty-minute fragment of this film. Unfortunately, the sequences in this print are not in the proper order, making it difficult, but not impossible to analyze the film. The narrative is apparently divided into the two spheres of Eva's life before and after the train wreck. Before, she is excluded from the public sphere occupied by her husband who also neglects her in her private life. Afterwards, she occupies a public sphere in the theater as an actress and in high society, where in turn her private life becomes victimized by a dependency on cocaine supplied by her exploitative lover. Before she dies, she dreams of the ideal home with a husband who cares for her and shares her private sphere.

SATANAS (Satan) [1919/20]   This was one of several episodic films of the time, such as Griffith's *Intolerance* (1916) and Lang's *Der müde Tod* (*Tired Death* [1921]). In the announcements for the film, Wiene's name was highlighted as artistic supervisor, rather than that of the director F. W. Murnau who was not yet well known. Some advertisements also featured Conrad Veidt, who starred in all three episodes. The plot revolves around Satan's yearning for salvation. God will grant him his wish, but only under the condition that he find human beings who will requite good for evil deeds. Satan (Conrad Veidt) journeys through three thousand years of human history searching for such people. First he is at the court of Pharaoh Amenhotep (Fritz Kortner), then at the palace of Lucrezia Borgia, and finally in modern times he is with the communist revolutionary, Hans Conrad. On these three, Satanas had placed his hope, but in vain. Their iniquity is evident and thus the condition for his salvation remains unfulfilled.

The reviews of this film were mixed. Some were critical of the pretentious undertaking of representing the history of humankind in episodes from antiquity to the present. However, one review is noteworthy because *Satanas* was to be Wiene's last film before *Caligari*. The reviewer seems to put forward *Satanas* as evidence that the film medium needs a new style:

> The heyday of naturalism in film seems to be over. No new style corresponding to the nature of the medium has been found yet. But the presentation of Robert Wiene's film *Satanas* proves that powerful effects can be achieved through purposeful stylization ... Conrad Veidt is Satanas in all his transformations. He has acquired a form of dramatic expressionism for this role, which he executes with success.[45]

The above quotation formulates in a few words – as part of a larger theoretical discussion – the inadequacy of films in the naturalist style. Apparently, there was a demand for something new in cinematic style. That Conrad Veidt's expressive or expressionist style of acting is cited by the critic as an example of this new style may explain why *Caligari* was not laughed out of court a few weeks later. Apparently, *Caligari* belonged to the trend of the time.

Thematic Overview

In addition to the eighteen comedies, ten melodramas, and ten tragedies summarized above, there are five other Wiene films about which we could find no plot summaries:

DIE WAFFEN DER JUGEND (The Weapons of Youth) [1912], written and possibly directed by Wiene.

LOTTEKENS FELDZUG (Lotteken's Campaign) [1915], written by Walter Turszinsky and Wiene and directed by Bruno Ziener; this film is possibly a comedy about a peasant's love for his horse.

FRÄULEIN BARBIER (Miss Barbier) [1915], written by Walter Turszinsky and Wiene and directed by Emil Albes.

DIE KONSERVENBRAUT (The Canned Bride) [1915], written by Walter Turszinsky and directed by Wiene.

DIE VERFÜHRTE HEILIGE (The Seduced Saint) [1919], a film Wiene wrote and directed for Stuart Webbs Film Company, Munich.

What is striking about the comedies that Wiene wrote and/or directed is the recurrence of classical comic situations involving mistaken identities, masquerades, disguises, and impersonations. Of the eighteen films we listed under the rubric "Comedies," twelve revolve around these themes. In *Der Sekretär der Königin*, there is a singer disguising herself as a man to impersonate the queen's secretary, thereby creating many delightfully comic situations. In *Gräfin Küchenfee*, the maid impersonates her absent mistress and the entire house staff masquerade as aristocratic guests to impress the visiting prince. In *Agnes Arnau und ihre drei Freier*, there is a hilarious helter skelter around three suitors, each of whom claims to be the same person – a certain Tony – who is supposed to wed Agnes. *Die Dame, der Teufel und die Probiermamsell* presents a deliberate exchange of identities between a model who works in a fashion shop and a wealthy customer weary of her way of life.

The social milieu in most of the comedies is the monied aristocracy and high society. Occasionally a middle-class character appears, like the teacher in *Lehmanns Brautfahrt* who is quite content with his social class, but simply dreams of experiencing the glories of ancient Greece, which he has studied so passionately. Circumstances place Benjamin Nickmüller in *Der standhafte Benjamin* in the position where he must continue to be a clerk by day but has the means to share the life of high society by night. By the end of the film he succeeds in climbing to the higher class, whereas the model in *Die Dame, der Teufel und die Probiermamsell* is content to return to her social class after eight days of high living. Just as successful social climbing is rare in these comedies, so also is the impoverished aristocrat who must earn his living among the middle class to protect his honor. The baron in *Umweg zur Ehe* prefers to work as a waiter – even as a servant – rather than accept the American millionaire's offer of his daughter, until she takes matters into her own hands.

Since Ernst Lubitsch's name is so closely identified with early German film comedy, it might be instructive to compare Wiene's comedies with those Lubitsch did before 1920. First of all, it seems that Lubitsch's humor is derived from different sources. The dominant social milieu in Lubitsch's comedies is not high society as is the case in Wiene's films but the lower middle class and the middle class. Lubitsch's best-known characters, many times played by himself, are clerks, sales people, and the like. His stories involve complications that frequently led to a significant rise in social class, usually through a marriage. Comic situations revolving around masquerades or exchange and/or confusion of roles appear rarely in Lubitsch's films but frequently in Wiene's films. Yet it is doubtful that these comic devices constituted a unique and unmistakable stylistic pattern for Wiene's authorial and/or directorial practice. However, there has been so little research in the pre-1920 German film comedy that it is difficult to identify personal comedy styles at all. Nevertheless, from all the possible pretexts for comic action, Wiene displayed a marked predilection for those we described above.

It seems to have been Henny Porten who shared responsibility for the relative predominance of comedies in Wiene's oeuvre before *Caligari*. She starred in ten of Wiene's eighteen comedies. Most of her comedies were made in collaboration with him as scriptwriter and/ or as director. Before Wiene came to the Messter Film Company, Henny Porten had hardly played in any comedies at all, and after he left the firm, she rarely did one. Apparently, the collaboration with Wiene encouraged her to try her skill in this genre more frequently.

In Wiene's melodramas, by contrast, there is not one dominant set of themes or situations as in the comedies. To begin with, there are fewer melodramatic films in his repertoire (ten compared to eighteen comedies). However, a considerable interest in psychological and related problems is discernible in the melodramas. In *Das wandernde Licht*, an insane servant almost succeeds by power of suggestion in driving his master insane. In *Gefangene Seele*, a young woman stands under the hypnotic power of the diabolic Baron van Groot. *Das Leben ein Traum* shows a heroine who is cured of her traumatic experiences by hypnotic suggestion. *Edelsteine* revolves around a woman's pathological desire for jewelry. Other recurring themes are a rise in social status through marriage *(Gelöste Ketten, Die Ehe der Luise Rohrbach),* the sudden acquisition of wealth *(Frank Hansens Glück),* or legal subject matter such as dramatic courtroom scenes *(Gelöste Ketten, Die Ehe der Luise Rohrbach, and Gefangene Seele).*

In Wiene's ten tragedies the distribution of themes is quite broad. Again there are instances of social climbing, which, however (unlike in the melodramas) ends in death and disaster *(Arme Marie, Frau Eva, Opfer der Gesellschaft).* The motif of insanity *(Furcht, Satanas)* is as frequent as the legal themes so typical for Wiene *(Opfer der Gesellschaft).* Many protagonists are driven to suicide *(Fluch der Schönheit, Frau Eva, Der Mann im Spiegel, Furcht).* Moreover, there are unfulfilled women yearning to live fully *(Frau Eva, Fluch der Schönheit, Die lebende Tote).* In general, the theme of "living life to the fullest," marks Wiene's entire work prior to *Caligari*; he incorporates variations of it in his comedies *(Auf Probe gestellt, Die Dame, der Teufel und die Probiermamsell),* as well as in his melodramas *(Frank Hansens Glück),* and tragedies *(Am Tor des Todes, Furcht).*[46]

Notes

1. Siegfried Kracauer, *From Caligari to Hitler: A Psychological History of the German Film* (Princeton, N.J.: Princeton University Press, 1947), 15.
2. Prof. Dr. Leidig, "Die Filmindustrie in der Volkswirtschaft," *Illustrierte Zeitung* 153, no. 3975 (1919): 6.
3. Ilona Brennicke and Joe Hembus, *Klassiker des deutschen Stummfilms, 1910–1930* (Munich: Goldmann, 1983), 241–45; we do not know whether nonfiction films were included in these figures.
4. *Der Film* 4, no. 29 (1919): 32.
5. *Der Kinematograph* 9, no. 419 (1915): 24.
6. *Die LichtBildBühne* 8, no. 49 (1915): 39.
7. *Der Film* 2, no. 14 (1917): 88.
8. *Der Kinematograph* 10, no. 484 (1916): 8; *Die LichtBildBühne* 9, no. 14 (1916): 44.
9. Helga Belach, *Henny Porten: Der erste deutsche Filmstar, 1890–1960* (Berlin: Haude & Spener, 1986), 192.
10. *Der Kinematograph* 10, no. 510 (1916): 15f; *Der Film* 1, no. 37 (1916): 50, 52.
11. *Der Film* 2, no. 16 (1917): 66.
12. *Die LichtBildBühne* 10, no. 22 (1917): 63; *Der Film* 2, no. 23 (1917): 56.
13. *Paimanns Filmlisten* 2, no. 73 (1917–18): 255 gives a brief, confusing plot summary.
14. *Der Kinematograph* 12, no. 577 (1918), quoted from Belach, *Henny Porten*, 198; *Paimanns Filmlisten* 2, no. 103 (1917–18): 371.
15. *Der Kinematograph* 12, no. 585 (1918): 28; *Paimanns Filmlisten* 3, no. 121 (1918–19): 14.
16. *Der Kinematograph* 12, no. 595 (1918): 26.
17. *Der Film* 3, no. 22 (1918): 69.
18. *Der Film* 3, no. 44 (1918): 109; *Paimanns Filmlisten* 3, no. 143 (1918–19): 105.
19. *Der Film* 4, no. 4 (1919): 36.
20. *Der Kinematograph* 13, no. 629 (1919): 39.
21. *Paimanns Filmlisten* 3, no. 148 (1918–19): 123; "Hausprogramm" des UFA-Theater Kurfürstendamm, Berlin.
22. *Paimanns Filmlisten* 4, no. 181 (1919): 261; Belach, *Henny Porten*, 202.
23. *Der Kinematograph* 13, no. 666 (1919): 26.
24. Ibid.
25. See Belach, *Henny Porten*, 194.
26. Ibid.
27. *Die LichtBildBühne* 10, no. 36 (1917): 80; *Paimanns Filmlisten* 2, no. 77 (1917–18): 271; Belach, *Henny Porten*, 196.
28. See the original film program of the Messter Film Company, *Der Film* 2, no. 34 (1917): 43. *Paimanns Filmlisten* 2, no. 81 (1917–18): 287 lists the film under the title *Frank Hansen*, apparently the distribution title for Austria.
29. *Die LichtBildBühne* 10, no. 8 (1917): 38.
30. *Der Film* 2, no. 9 (1917): 32.
31. *Der Film* 3, no. 8 (1918): 45; *Paimanns Filmlisten* 2, no. 105 (1917–18): 378; Belach, *Henny Porten*, 198f. The sources give deviating accounts of the plot.
32. *Der Kinematograph* 12, no. 590 (1918); *Der Film* 3, no. 17 (1918): 61.
33. Ibid.
34. *Paimanns Filmlisten* 4, no. 176 (1919–20): 242.
35. *Der Kinematograph* 9, no. 437 (1915), as found in Hans Helmut Prinzler and Enno Patalas, eds., *Lubitsch* (Munich: C. J. Bucher, 1984), 202.
36. Original film program, Deutsche Bioscop Gesellschaft; the film is reviewed under the title *Seine schöne Mama* in *Die LichtBildBühne* 8, no. 22 (1915): 22.
37. *Die LichtBildBühne* 8, no. 38 (1915): 22.
38. *Der Kinematograph* 10, no. 477 (1916): 10; the reviewer also gives credit to Art.

Berger (Arthur Bergen?) as co-author of the script.

39. *Der Kinematograph* 10, no. 512 (1916): 26, 29; *Der Film* 1, no. 40 (1916): 46 names Konrad Wiener [sic] as director.
40. *Der Kinematograph* 10, no. 512 (1916): 26, 29.
41. Original film program of the Messter Film Company; *Paimanns Filmlisten* 2, no. 81 (1917–18): 287.
42. *Österreichischer Komet*, no. 446 (1918): 26 f; *Paimanns Filmlisten* 3, no. 143 (1918–19): 105 lists this film under the title *Am Tor des Lebens*.
43. *Der Filmbote*, no. 45 (1919): 32.
44. *Der Film* 4, no. 36 (1919): 36 f; *Film-Tribüne*, no. 11 (1919), as quoted in Belach, *Henny Porten*, 203.
45. Clip from a review of *B.Z. am Mittag*, as found in an advertisement of Phoebus-Film Verleih in *Der Film*, no. 6 (1920): 125.
46. From 1910 to 1919 Porten played in 106 films. Only seventeen of them were comedies, of which ten were made in collaboration with Wiene; see the plot summaries in Belach, *Henny Porten*, 171–232.

Chapter 3

✦ ✦ ✦

THE CABINET OF DR. CALIGARI

When approaching critical studies about *The Cabinet of Dr. Caligari*, one is confronted with the unusual discrepancy between
evaluations of the film as a classic from the silent film era – a masterpiece of the early avant-garde, a forerunner of international art
cinema – and an estimation of the film's director as mediocre, an
evaluation that neglects Wiene's contribution to the film's acknowledged success. We take issue with that judgment and wish to trace
the negative image of Robert Wiene to its source. Wiene's reputation
in the making of *Caligari* is crucial to his reputation as a director altogether. The denial of Wiene's share in this film's artistic and commercial success led to a diminishment of his image as a filmmaker in
every respect.

It is important to note yet another paradox. The shift in opinion
about Wiene's film work took place a few years after his death. During the Weimar period, Wiene received constant praise as a
scriptwriter and as film director both before and after *Caligari*. This
is confirmed by numerous references in the film journals of the time.
Only since World War II has he been seen as a film director of
mediocre quality whose one single success was accidental.

Kracauer's Critique of *Caligari*

Since the war, the single most influential history of Weimar film has
been Siegfried Kracauer's *From Caligari to Hitler*, in which the chapter
on *Caligari* is crucial to the book's thesis. For Kracauer, Wiene as a

director is of no interest at all. He views him as the man who transformed a revolutionary film into a conformist one by constructing a frame.[1] This view stigmatized Wiene as a reactionary for years to come. Since the publication of Kracauer's book in 1947, interpreters of *Caligari* have been induced to see the film within a specific framework. This framework is based both on Kracauer's overall thesis that the German film reflects the mentality of the German people and on

Das Cabinet des Dr. Caligari (The Cabinet of Dr. Caligari)
Director: Robert Wiene (1919/20) – Friedrich Féher, Werner Krauss

his unquestioning reliance on a single source, namely, Hans Jano-witz's manuscript "*Caligari*: The Story of a Famous Story,"[2] which even today has not been published completely.

With his overall thesis, Kracauer wants to demonstrate that the films of the Weimar period indicate a readiness among the German people to submit to a tyrant. With his analysis of these films, his pur-pose is to explore the deeper levels of the German soul – the collec-tive unconscious of the German people – to find an answer to the question, why did the Germans choose to follow Hitler:

> Thus, behind the overt history of economic shifts, social exigencies and political machinations runs a secret history involving the inner disposi-tions of the German people. The disclosure of these dispositions through the medium of the German screen may help in the understanding of Hitler's ascent and ascendancy.[3]

Kracauer wishes to examine the "history of the German collective mentality." He believes this can be done best with film since it "more than any other medium offers an access to the inner dispositions of broad strata of the population."[4] While there is some justification for using popular media such as film or pulp literature, in his book he does no such thing. The films he selects for examining the collective mentality are the highbrow films which – with the exception of *Cali-gari* – were seen only by very few people. There were hundreds of popular films with no special expressionist or artistic pretensions to which thousands of people flocked. Kracauer might be justified in using a highbrow film to study the *Zeitgeist*, but he is after the collec-tive mentality (and moreover *Zeitgeist* is itself a highbrow concept).

Kracauer's thesis, as stated in his introduction, is really not pre-sented until the fifth chapter, the chapter on *Caligari*. His "psycho-logical history"[5] of the German film begins with *Caligari*, which he characterizes as the "archetype of all forthcoming postwar films."[6] If his thesis is correct, then the collective mentality of the German people must also be recognizable in German films before 1918. Yet for Kracauer, early German film history from 1895 to 1918 is "an archaic period insignificant in itself."[7] Thus, in his first four chap-ters, he summarizes the German film of this period only in terms of a periodization.

Kracauer grants that the German film industry prospered during World War I, but without attaining a cultural self-sufficiency: "One would think that under such auspicious circumstances Germany might have succeeded in creating a cinema of her own, of truly national character. Other countries did."[8] However, a contemporary of the German film industry at the time paints a different picture:

*Das Cabinet des
Dr. Caligari
(The Cabinet of
Dr. Caligari)*
Director: Robert
Wiene (1919/20) –
Werner Krauss

Today over a hundred film companies in Germany produce films which are screened for the public in about three thousand theaters. One doesn't assume too much by maintaining that daily a million people attend movie theaters. This is surely evidence that film is reaching a wide audience.[9]

Of course, it is difficult to judge whether the films of this time were culturally self-sufficient productions, but until very recently this early period has not been researched at all. In any case, Kracauer is interested in only four films of this era: *Der Student von Prag* (*The Student of Prague* [Paul Wegener, 1913]), *Der Golem* (*The Golem* [Paul Wegener and Henrik Galeen, 1914]), *Homunculus* (Otto Rippert, 1916), and *Der Andere* (*The Other* [Max Mack, 1913]). Once again, these were ambitious films that were accessible primarily to a small educated stratum of the population. In other words, all German films with the exception of the four named above do not belong to Kracauer's thesis. This approach permits him to begin his psychological history of the German film with *Caligari*.

Kracauer maintains that he must write this psychological history of the German film and, by extension, of the German people because economic and social causes do not suffice to explain the rise of Hitler. His methodology is then understandably not sociological, and consequently he will not draw on "the statistically measurable popularity of films" but, instead, on the "popularity of their pictorial and narrative motifs."[10] Once he has made this point, he can now concentrate on any sample of German films he pleases, whether they were popular, box-office successes or not. He can, for example, focus on the studio-made art films among the many so-called *Kammerfilme*, without taking into consideration that these films had only a small audience in Germany. His method of selection is especially dubious in the chapter following *Caligari*, entitled "Procession of Tyrants." How many films does he cite as personifications of the tyrant archetype? Just four: *Nosferatu* (F. W. Murnau, 1922), *Vanina* (Arthur von Gerlach, 1922), *Dr. Mabuse, der Spieler* (*Dr. Mabuse, the Gambler* [Fritz Lang, 1922]), and *Das Wachsfigurenkabinett* (*The Waxworks* [Paul Leni, 1924]).

Kracauer's method is confused. He wants to explain a mass phenomenon, but he wants to do it without reference to statistical analysis. However, a thesis like his could be demonstrated only by a statistical analysis of distributed films – all distributed films, including foreign films. By limiting himself to a selection of films produced in Germany without reference to their popularity, he presupposes an entirely different methodology. The selection of motifs from a limited number of "art" films is neither sociology nor psychology. This method seems to hark back to a traditional bourgeois conception of the artist as mediator for the spirit of the times. Kracauer surely would not deliberately espouse such a view; nevertheless, it is concealed in his confused methodology.[11] This questionable method, which has not been seriously challenged until recently, leads Kracauer to select *Caligari* as the central text in support of his thesis. For Kracauer, the addition of the frame means the transformation of a revolutionary into a conformist film, whereby at the same time his thesis about Weimar film and the Germany of the Weimar Republic is illustrated. He sees a dichotomy between rebellion and submission that can be clarified through the film version of *Caligari* because in this version the director deprived a film of its revolutionary content by transposing the primary plot into the subjectivity of a madman. From Kracauer's perspective, the primary plot still carries this revolutionary content but the frame puts "the original into a box." This symbolized for him the general withdrawal of the Germans into their shell, that is, into their submission to authority.

The Story of a Famous Story

Since Kracauer's argument about the function of the frame story is essential to his project, we must inquire about its legitimacy. In a footnote to his *Caligari* chapter, Kracauer reveals the source of his thinking:

> The following episode, along with other data appearing in my pages on *Caligari*, is drawn from an interesting manuscript Mr. Hans Janowitz has written about the genesis of this film. I feel greatly indebted to him for having put his material at my disposal. I am thus in a position to base my interpretation of *Caligari* on the true inside story, up to now unknown.[12]

The manuscript by Janowitz to which Kracauer refers here is a 105-page unpublished typescript entitled, "*Caligari*: The Story of a Famous Story." Apparently, this manuscript was written from 1939 on in New York City where Janowitz lived since his emigration from Prague. We have reason to believe that Janowitz worked on this essay for some time. In the Janowitz Papers, which are now held by the Stiftung Deutsche Kinemathek in Berlin, there is an early draft in German entitled, "*Caligari*: Die Geschichte eines berühmten Filmes" (*Caligari*: The Story of a Famous Film), as well as several later drafts in English. There is an English-language fragment consisting of Chapter One in the Film Library of the Museum of Modern Art in New York. This sixteen-page fragment is identical in content with the first chapter of the above mentioned 105-page manuscript, which was given to the New York Public Library by Janowitz's widow in 1955.

This "true inside story" of the making of *Caligari* is nothing more than Janowitz's recollection – twenty years after the fact – of the circumstances that led to the creation of this classic German silent film. It could also be considered a document written by an exile of Nazi Germany who was trying to capture his share of *Caligari*'s fame. One of his main reasons for telling this story was to establish for the scriptwriters the true authorship of the film *Caligari*. This becomes clear in the third chapter, when he makes the following startling pronouncement: "To us a picture-story-script had to be a straight-jacket for the director, a very tight, precise and balanced straight-jacket, with strong belts and fasteners, so that nothing could escape in any way from our instructions."[13] No professional scriptwriter would subscribe to such a point of view – one that sees the work of art in the script and not in the film. Ironically, Carl Vincent – the Franco-Belgian film historian whose *Histoire de l'art Cinématographique* Kracauer frequently cites throughout his book as an authoritative source – describes Janowitz's credentials as follows: "Hans Janowitz, from Czechoslovakia like Wiene, is an amateur script writer. His main activity is trading in oils."[14]

Once Janowitz has established the scriptwriter's authority, he can turn to his chief lament, namely, that Wiene distorted the original script by the addition of the frame. In contrast to Kracauer, however, Janowitz does not see this in political, revolutionary terms:

> Dr. Wiene, a man in his early fifties, of an older generation than ours, was afraid to venture in this new form of expressionist art. Therefore, to excuse the story, the oblique angles of the roofs and rooms of the scenery, the stylized masks of the actors, the askew painted world, the "Caligaric world," the "crazy world of 1919," he intended to change our script on a very important point: at the end of the film our symbolic story was to be explained as being a tale told by a mentally deranged person, thus dishonoring our drama – the tragedy of a man gone mad by the misuse of his mental powers – into a cliche, in which every incident was to be explained in a cheap manner, in which the symbolism was to be lost.[15]

Janowitz maintains here that Wiene, in his opposition to the expressionist décor, wanted to explain it as a representation of madness. It is known from others sources, however, that Wiene had immediately accepted the plans of the set designers.[16] Notably, Janowitz describes his story as a symbolic tale about a man's tragic circumstances without any reference to a political theme. It is Kracauer who embeds Janowitz's ire against the frame into his political ideology.

Janowitz repeatedly returns to the issue of the frame with which, according to him, Wiene transgressed the true intent of the script. To be sure, he grants that not even this pernicious frame could totally destroy the impact of their narrative:

> This dramaturgic somersault, hazardous as it was, did not interfere with the gripping fascination, aroused in the audience by the story of our invention, the tragedy of a psychiatrist gone mad by misuse of his mental powers; nothing could interfere with that fascination, because once the mood of an audience has reached such a state of tenseness, no blunder is foolish enough to break this fascination. At any rate Dr. Wiene's "box within a box" framework was not foolish enough to do so. Actually it was clever enough to explain the unknown expressionism (the expressionism of writing, of painting and of acting) in such a way as to bring it within the grasp of the audience. Nevertheless, it was the nucleus of the tragedy of a psychiatrist who had lost his mind, the gripping story of a man whose *idée fixe* compelled him to "become Caligari" in order to learn, whether murder through commanding a hypnotized medium was possible... .[17]

Janowitz grants that the frame he considers foolish serves at least to make the film's expressionism palatable to the audience. However, his main point continues to be that the primary purpose of the script is to tell the tragic story of a psychiatrist who has lost his mind. Symbolically, this becomes for him a story that reveals the madness implicit in authority. Caligari's victimization of Cesare stands for the ruthless exploitation of the common man by authorities gone mad: "… our Dr. Caligari, the great authority, was mad, mad with the lust to kill, mad with lust to force his brutal instincts on innocent subjects!"[18]

The Screenplay

Ever since the publication of Kracauer's book, there has been a heated debate about the function of Wiene's frame. Kracauer and Janowitz in his essay both claim that without the frame the film would have been more powerful, more honest, more revealing. It is time that this claim be challenged, and we wish to begin to do so by drawing on a source that was not available to Kracauer: the original film script of *Caligari*.[19] Janowitz, of course, knew the script but inexplicably fails to mention that it too had a frame.

In this frame Francis and Jane can be seen on the terrace of an upper-middle-class dwelling, where as a married couple they entertain guests. The atmosphere is festive until Francis and Jane notice a group of gypsies pass before the house. They become pensive and quiet and, after being urged by their friends to explain their change of mood, Francis begins to tell their story: "Yes, my friends you don't know that gruesome tale of Holstenwall which made Jane and me so melancholy when those gypsies passed by." He continues, "Yes, my friends, it has been twenty years now … at that time I lived as a private tutor in Holstenwall, an idyllic old town …"[20] And here begins the well-known story of Dr. Caligari.

In the original frame story, twenty years after the events Francis and Jane live as a married couple in comfortable circumstances. Here no revolutionary intent is possible; nor is there even any social criticism involved. The social standing of the narrator, the acceptance of bourgeois conventions (their marriage), the twenty-year detachment from the events, and the accidental occasion for their recollections hardly serve as an effective frame for a tale with revolutionary force. Moreover, this story is told from a first-person narrative point of view, which is present in the titles quoted above and throughout the text. This aspect of the script makes it clear that the story being told is not necessarily objectively true but is being narrated by the person who experienced it and is how he experienced it.[21]

By drawing on the original screenplay and Janowitz's memoirs, we are in a position to evaluate the screenplay and Kracauer's reliance on it as the "true inside story." First, his uncritical acceptance of

Janowitz's account of the making of *Caligari* twenty years later under the alienating circumstances of exile in New York is surprising. Second, Janowitz's claim that the film would be better without the frame is a value judgment, but Kracauer embraces it as belonging to the "true inside story"; however, an author's assertion cannot become the scholar's truth. Third, Janowitz's contention that the inner story of *Caligari* continues to carry the true message of the film even with Wiene's frame[22] is accepted by Kracauer: "Even though *Caligari* had become a conformist film, it preserved and emphasized this revolutionary story... ."[23] This is by no means self-evident. In fact, no film critic up to the publication of *From Caligari to Hitler* ever suggested that the film had a revolutionary message, with or without the frame. Janowitz himself in his "The Story of a Famous Story" grants:

> It was years after the completion of the screen-play that I realized our subconscious intention, and this explanation of our characters, Doctor Caligari and Cesare, his medium, that is: The corresponding connection between Doctor Caligari, and the great authoritative power of a Government that we hated, and which had subdued us into an oath, forcing conscription on those in opposition to its official war aims, compelling us to murder and to be murdered.[24]

Kracauer accepts this explanation and does not question the validity of a subconscious intention discovered many years after the fact. For a film historian to privilege the alleged intention behind a script over the film in its final form is insupportable. Not only does Kracauer deliberately accept Janowitz's claim for the authorial primacy of the scriptwriter over the film's director, he furthermore chooses to base his argument on Janowitz's recollections about the script twenty years after the fact instead of analyzing the film itself, which is after all an original. In other words, this personal memoir becomes the "true inside story" for Kracauer's interpretation of *Caligari*, which in turn inspires the thesis of *From Caligari to Hitler*.

Kracauer's influential book in no way damaged the reputation of *Caligari*. Kracauer's argument about the political function of the frame notwithstanding, the film has continued to be a favorite international film classic from generation to generation. Wiene's reputation, which had remained intact throughout his lifetime, however, suffered immeasurable damage from the book's influence as the leading history of Weimar film in the postwar period. Wiene was labeled a political reactionary and a mediocre film director who could not grasp the true meaning of a daring script and who contributed nothing to the film beyond the mere addition of a frame that dishonored the original intent of the scriptwriters.

Wiene's Contribution

A comparison between the original scenario and the finished film may clarify the function of the frame and the reasons that may have induced Wiene to employ it. The implication from Kracauer and Janowitz is that, when confronted with the script, Wiene decided for commercial and cowardly reasons to impose a frame where there was none before to make it more palatable to the public. It is clear, however, that there was a frame to begin with and that Wiene replaced it with another frame that he apparently found more suitable. With the new frame, Wiene removes the main story from the realm of personal nostalgia and makes it more likely that the viewer will identify with the deeds and sufferings of the main character. By contrast, the frame as found in the screenplay also puts the audience at a constant distance from the action because they are repeatedly reminded of the frame by the titles of the first-person narrator who tells his tale after a twenty-year hiatus.

In the original script at the SDK, the closing frame unfortunately is missing and as a result we cannot contrast it with Wiene's closing frame. It is this concluding frame that so aroused the ire of Kracauer and Janowitz. However, it is this very conclusion that heightens the film's complexity, problematizes the entire story, and adds to the contours of the film as a work of art. For example, by extending the expressionist décor into the concluding frame, Wiene avoided a sharp break between fantasy and reality and thereby heightened the tension and maintained a hermeneutic openness.[25]

The extension of the expressionist décor into the concluding frame provides the iconographic link to the final scene. The expressionist distortion of the environment in which the psychiatric work takes place makes the viewer question whether he or she has finally figured out what is real and what is fantasy. In that last scene Caligari appears as a benign psychiatrist, a pillar of society. But at the very end Wiene has him look directly into the camera and closes in an iris around his head. Iconographically, the viewer is reminded of the first appearance of Caligari when he is introduced in his guise as mad mountebank. Then too Wiene had closed in an iris around his head. That association should induce the viewer to question the solidity of citizen Caligari and his promise to cure Francis.

It is not only the frame that permits insight into Wiene's dramaturgic adaptations of the script for his film version. Although the main plot follows the script faithfully, there are several interesting directorial interventions. To begin with, it must be remembered that both Mayer and Janowitz were novice scriptwriters; in fact, the *Cali-*

gari script was a debut for both.[26] There is ample evidence for their lack of experience. One out of several examples might suffice. At the beginning of act 4, the two authors present a lengthy narrative title: "While we hurried to the police station to interrogate Jakob Straat, Jane was very concerned about our long absence and went to look for us at the festival grounds."[27] The following five images show exactly what is stated in the title. Wiene, however, as an experienced scriptwriter and director avoids the practice of using titles that simply duplicate the action.

A different example of Wiene's intervention to enhance a scene's effectiveness is the way in which he presents the first appearance of the somnambulist. In the script, the box containing Cesare is delivered to Caligari's booth at the fairground. Caligari opens it at once and we immediately see Cesare with his eyes open.[28] By contrast, in the film the first representation of Cesare to the public and to us is at the fairground in front of Caligari's booth, where Caligari is exhibiting a life-size poster of the somnambulist and inviting the crowd and us to enter his tent and see the real thing for ourselves. Inside the tent the camera gradually moves closer to the stage and finally moves to the famous close-up when Cesare reluctantly opens his eyes and stares at us, one of the most dramatic and unforgettable moments in

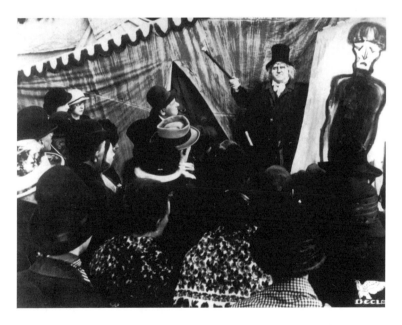

Das Cabinet des Dr. Caligari (The Cabinet of Dr. Caligari)
Director: Robert Wiene (1919/20) – Werner Krauss

the film.[29] To be sure, this scene was suggested by the script.[30] It is Wiene, however, who recognized that our first encounter with Cesare should not be casual as it was in the script, but startling as it is in the film.

Another difference between script and film is the representation of the relationship between Francis and Allan. In the script Francis is a private tutor (he is referred to as Dr. Francis in the credits) and Allan is a young student; thus, a significant age difference can be taken for granted. In the film, however, they are of equal age, which makes them both suitors for Jane and competitors for her affection. In other words, the film problematizes the relationship between the two men and invites additional interpretive possibilities.

Linked to this relationship is, of course, the relationship between Jane and Francis, which is stable in the script but not in the film. Mayer and Janowitz let the two discover their intimate emotional affinity through Allan's death. Most specifically, after the funeral the two share a momentary vision of Allan's spectral appearance, which brings them ever closer.[31] Keeping the frame in mind, at this point we can already anticipate that this liaison will eventually lead to their marriage. Here the scriptwriters seem to adhere to fairly conventional and bourgeois expectations for stable relationships. By contrast, Wiene eliminates the above scene and leaves the relationship much more open ended. Furthermore, by omitting the ghostly apparition of Allan altogether, Wiene intended to adapt the script to the modernist sets. The appearance of spooks may be appropriate in a neoromantic atmosphere but not within the context of a modernist setting, such as the one proposed by the architects and eagerly accepted by Wiene. The last image of the extant script (presumably the last image of the inner story) shows Jane and Francis standing in front of a plaque with the following inscription:

> Here stood the Cabinet of Dr. Caligari
> Peace to his victims ~ Peace to him!
> The City of Holstenwall[32]

This happy ending is, thus, irreversible in its finality. More than that, the inscription creates a distance that removes the protagonists – while they are still in the inner plot – from the tragic events they just experienced.[33] The last line of the extant script suggests a return to the frame and a confirmation of Caligari's demise as final and absolute. By contrast, the concluding frame of the film unexpectedly reverses the happy ending of the inner story and problematizes the entire plot. The traumatic events that we thought were resolved have us in their grip once more until the concluding scene, which, however, does not provide a conclusive resolution. This indeterminacy that the controversial frame adds to the film, and which must be considered part of Wiene's narrative strategy, was completely misunderstood by Janowitz. It is furthermore a part of the director's strategy to obscure the first-person narration of the script and create the illusion of a third-person narrative. That is why the concluding frame, wherein the audience is reminded that it has been witnessing Francis's tale, is so stunning and provocative.

Because Wiene's contribution to the making of *Caligari* is neglected and because the film is often criticized for being too theatrical, we wish to select several examples as evidence of the director's hand that at the same time reveal the cinematic qualities of the film. This is also supported by a letter from a contemporary, Rudolf Kurz, to Lotte Eisner: "I consider my friend Robert Wiene to be the key creative person in the making of the *Caligari* film, which I know from numerous conversations with him during the making of the film. I think it is ridiculous to believe that his directorial style could be determined by external matters such as the set designs."[34]

The originality of the editing technique of *Caligari* was hailed as early as 1956 by C. Dennis Pegge in his article "*Caligari*: Its Innovations in Editing." He indicated that the film consisted of 378 separate

Das Cabinet des Dr. Caligari (The Cabinet of Dr. Caligari)
Director: Robert Wiene (1919/20) – Friedrich Féher, Lil Dagover

shots and maintained that "*Caligari* must be recognized as a pioneering effort in editing, but also as a demonstration of that affinity between filmic expression and the thought process that Eisenstein and many others later dwelt upon."[35] Indeed, in *Caligari* numerous examples of cross-cutting, parallel action, irises of various shapes, high- and low-angle camera shots, flashbacks, lettering, and split screens can be found, as well as a few panning shots.

In one set of parallel actions, Francis and Dr. Olfens, Jane's father, are examining Cesare while the criminal, Jakob Straat, is attempting a murder that leads to his immediate arrest. As soon as they learn about this, they leave for the police station while Jane, wondering about her father's absence, looks for him at the fairground and comes to Caligari's tent. At the very same time, Francis and Jane's father are at the police station participating in the cross-examination of Jakob Straat.[36] In the film script, the parallel action is introduced by lengthy titles that describe what is happening simultaneously. Wiene reduces the titles to a bare minimum and instead makes the point through cross-cutting.

An example of thought process can be found in the shots of the sleeping Caligari while Francis and several physicians examine the director's office. The first shot is taken from a high angle, representing the point of view of the older physician who has been keeping Caligari under observation.[37] The second and third shots of the sleeping Caligari[38] cannot be identified as anyone's point of view but could be clearly read as visualizations of the physicians' anxiety about being disturbed in their plot against their chief.

A significant scene is the transition at the very beginning of the film from the opening frame to the inner plot. The frame focuses on the seated Francis, who begins to tell his story to a companion.[39] The frame concludes with a curtain iris that closes in and opens again with a panoramic shot of Holstenwall: the inner plot begins. Twice there are cuts back to the narrator[40] to remind the viewer that the story about to unfold is a story told by Francis. This happens at the very beginning but never again; only at the very end of the inner story does the film cut back to the narrator.[41] This is in distinct contrast to the script, where the first-person narration in the titles never lets the viewers forget that they are observers of a tale of past events being told in the present. In Wiene's film the audience forgets that it is a story and experiences it as a real-life event that reveals the main character's ordeal and his shock in the surprising reversal during the closing frame.

A fine example of Wiene's conversion of the scriptwriters' ideas into film is his representation of the three murders.[42] The first murder is initially reported in a title, followed by the police investigation in the official's bedroom. The second – that is, Allan's, murder – is seen through the pantomime of shadows reflected on the wall, so that the crime – even the murder weapon – is perceived but the criminal cannot be identified.[43] Cesare's attempted murder of Jane raises the horror even further because the attempt takes place face to face in carefully designed segments:[44] Cesare's stealthy entrance through the window; his approach to the victim with measured steps, a dagger in his hand; and finally his outburst into a vicious, lustful rage at Jane's resistance. From a filmic point of view, these three instances constitute an early example of the iconography of crime in which the gradual transition from concealment to revelation creates the dynamics of the horror story.[45]

The above exemplifies a network of references, forward and backward, a directorial strategy on which Wiene relies throughout the film. Another example of the use of this device takes place after the criminal, Jakob Straat, is arrested. Francis is present while Straat is being cross-examined and although his guilt seems to be proven, Francis continues to observe Caligari in his cabin. Why does he do this? The only reason given is a gesture at the end of the cross-examination, when Francis puts his left hand to his brow suggesting strenuous thought. An iris closes in around Francis, underlining the significance of the move and, at the same time, referring the viewer to a previous similar gesture. Once before Francis had put his hand to his brow; he was standing at the corpse of his friend Allan, thinking back to the somnambulist's prophecy, as a title indicates. Thus, it becomes clear now that Francis, while listening to Jakob Straat, still harbors suspicions about Caligari's and Cesare's involvement. For that reason he returns to spy on Caligari.

Yet another example lies in the two straightjacket scenes. After Caligari's identity has been revealed in the inner plot, he lunges in mad rage at the older physician. Why does he not attack Francis who, after all, is responsible for his demise? Possibly the answer is revealed in the reversal of this scene in the closing frame. Francis's attack on the director reveals his persecution complex: the straightjacket is inevitable. But at the same time this scene refers back to the earlier action: the Caligari of the inner plot also suffers from a persecution complex regarding his older colleague whom he apparently suspects of plotting against him to usurp his own position.

Although these two scenes are separated by the boundary between the inner story and the frame story, they are evidently linked and reinforce one another. The *appearance* of madness in both stories is identical, but who is really mad and who is really sane? If Caligari is sane in the outer story, then Francis's insanity is beyond question. If Francis is insane in the outer story, then he is clearly insane in the inner plot; but this implies nothing definitively about Caligari's sanity in the outer plot. Ostensibly, by dress and appearance, Caligari is shown to be sane. However, there is reason to have some doubts. In the final shot of the film, as indicated above, an iris closes in around the director's head, underscoring his ambiguous gaze at the camera. Just as important is the other figure in this iris. Immediately behind the director, but seen in deep focus, is the second psychiatrist whom Caligari had attacked in the inner frame, presumably because he suspected him of wanting to usurp his position as director. Thus, it is not the clear-cut reversal according to which only Francis is insane. The last shot of the film clearly stands outside of Francis's narration; it could not be a part of his fantasy. Therefore, the suspicion it arouses refers back to the inner story, posing new questions about what is real and what is not.

The Academic Discussion

What we have been trying to do is to move the discussion about *Caligari* away from the alleged intentions of the scriptwriters, to look at Wiene's participation in the making of the film, and in general to turn to an analysis of the film itself as we have it. We are not alone in attempting to move beyond Kracauer's influential but biased reading of *Caligari*. Barry Salt, with his contentious, but sharp and precise reaction to Kracauer's book, led the way. In his article "From Caligari to Who?" Salt takes issue with the crucial points of Kracauer's thesis. He denies that expressionism is characteristic of Weimar films, he disputes that a few "art" films give us "access to the depths of national psychology," and he notes that Kracauer avoids films that are "incompatible with the 'psychological paralysis' that [he] dreamed up." Salt asserts that German audiences wanted to see American films, crime thrillers, Harry Piel adventure films, comedies of all sorts and, of course, Lubitsch films. The Germans, according to Salt, got the films they wanted, but "Kracauer refuses to investigate them." The only films that were uniquely German and popular, maintains Salt, were the films about Frederick the Great, but the message there was so obvious that Kracauer's "'psychological' interpretation of plot details" was not needed. Salt's conclusion is simple and striking: "Don't make generalizations about film history or history in films without taking into account all the films, and also without seeing a representative and sizeable sample of them."[46]

An even more fundamental rejection of Kracauer's thesis can be found in Thomas Elsaesser's essay, "Social Mobility and the Fantastic":

> What seems to me not permissible, if we are to understand the manner in which history has entered into these films, is the double reduction which Kracauer operates upon his material. In order to establish the homology between German cinema and German history on which his thesis rests, he first of all has to "narrativize" German history in a particular fashion, by which I do not primarily mean the inevitability he posits, whereby all events are seen to lead up to Hitler and Fascism: what is problematic is the process and selection of the forces and determinants he deems as pertinent to our understanding of history. That he has to narrativize, even personalize these forces is evident if we look at the protagonist he creates: the "German soul," the national character, who becomes the plaything of instinct, sex, fate, destiny, tyrants and demons. The history he thus constructs is itself an expressionist drama, and while he makes it clear that the categories he employs are those that the films themselves suggest, the tautologous nature of the reasoning seems inescapable: the films reflect German history, because this history has been narrated in terms and categories derived from the films.[47]

We share Elsaesser's criticism in regard to the narrativization of Weimar history, in which Kracauer constructs this history as expressionist with expressionist protagonists. We are not willing, however, to grant that Kracauer selects his categories for his historical perspective from the films themselves. Quite the contrary: we maintain that their origin is an external, ideological model.

Michael Budd has written a number of articles about *Caligari* in which he asserts that what is unique about the film is its mixture of classical narrative and modernist expressionism. He is familiar with Janowitz's memoirs and knows about the original *Caligari* script at the SDK, but he draws no conclusions from these sources that lead him to dispute Kracauer's thesis. He does criticize Kracauer for failing to "situate the writers' work within the literary history of Expressionist style and form, ..."[48] For Budd, a number of themes in the film – for instance, insanity and the uncanny – represent literary expressionism, and from this he concludes:

> the tensions of literary Expressionism were mediated by Mayer and Janowitz's narrative ... At this moment when the unbearable isolation of the modernist artist was being rejected by most Expressionists, Mayer and Janowitz helped make possible the movement's transformation from an avant-garde into a mass-cultural phenomenon... .[49]

If *Caligari* helped at all to popularize expressionism, then it was through the sets and the completed film and certainly not through the film script, which was published only in 1995. The themes of *Caligari* were widespread in both German film and literature both before and after the war. Moreover, let us not forget that we now know that Mayer and Janowitz wrote their first script in a perfectly conventional manner; no trace of literary expressionism can be found in their style.

In a later essay in his book *The Cabinet of Dr. Caligari: Texts, Contexts, Histories,* Michael Budd refuses to recognize the significance of the original *Caligari* film script, which at the time of his writing was preserved by the Stiftung Deutsche Kinemathek in Berlin. He describes it merely as "an early script for the film," saying "we do not know its status in the production process."[50] Without ever questioning that the manuscript was composed by Mayer and Janowitz, he doubts the originality of the script on the basis that there are differences between it and the film. Aside from the status accorded this manuscript, it must be granted that it is an important contemporary document closely linked to the production of the film. Although throughout Budd's discussion of *Caligari* one can perceive a decisive overestimation of the "film script" and the intentions of the authors, he is not prepared to consider this new discovery of the Stiftung Deutsche Kinemathek. It is curious indeed: Kracauer discussed and condemned *Caligari* on the basis of a film script that he did not know. He simply accepted Janowitz's testimony about his so-called intentions, and Kracauer's exegete, Michael Budd, refuses to consider the recently discovered original film script for *Caligari* out of concern that he might have to draw conclusions that would be at variance with Kracauer's thesis. Instead, Budd dwells on Kracauer's practice of problematizing the film's frame. Since the essays in Budd's book add nothing to the understanding of Wiene's contribution to the production of *Caligari,* a more intensive discussion of the book is not necessary at this point.

S. S. Prawer is the first to comment broadly on Mayer and Janowitz's film script. This original scenario leads him, like us, to reject Kracauer's thesis of a revolutionary tendency that was distorted by the addition of a frame. According to Prawer, the frame as it is in the film adds a dimension of ambiguity that deepens the film as a work of art. He sees the ambiguities and uncertainties in the film as reflections of the early Weimar period and not as a projection of future tyranny. In other words, he prefers the frame in the film to the frame in the script. Moreover, his interpretation of the Caligari figure differs from Kracauer's fundamentally:

> Kracauer saw Caligari as a "tyrant" figure – a view that is justified if one looks at the role he plays in controlling his somnambulist and possibly

his role as director of the madhouse. In other respects, however – in his attitude to duly constituted authorities and to the Holstenwall establishment – he is, like Lang's Mabuse, a dangerously subversive force. Nor can he simply be seen as a negative figure. Even if he is taken for the murderous "mad scientist" Francis sees in him, our reaction to him must be complex and ambiguous. He is, after all, the one character who does what his nature leads him to do, regardless of the consequences; who lives to the full, and whose fall – if fall there is – has something of tragic grandeur about it.[51]

This is an example of a fresh and original approach to *Caligari* that was possible only because the author moved beyond Kracauer's seductive thesis. In fact, in his study of the terror film genre, Prawer reveals a whole range of themes and motifs that he is able to trace back to *Caligari*. Thereby he does indeed make a good case for the film as archetypal but certainly not in Kracauer's sense.

Michael Minden is familiar not only with the recently discovered *Caligari* script by Mayer and Janowitz, but also with the text of Janowitz's "*Caligari*: The Story of a Famous Story." He recognizes that both documents problematize Kracauer's thesis and grants that "the screenplay is less susceptible to political interpretation than even Janowitz suggests."[52] For Minden the original frame story is evidence for the conservative frame of mind of the manuscript, which he considers historically regressive: "The whole manuscript reflects the nineteenth century." Strangely enough, these considerations do not lead Minden to a fundamental critique of Kracauer's perspective. In the final form of the *Caligari* film he sees a subsequent psychologizing of an original anti-authoritarian idea. This position is inconsistent and Minden does not justify it methodologically.

John D. Barlow is also familiar with the original *Caligari* script, and he tries to integrate the information from this source into Kracauer's basic perspective, but nevertheless begins to distance himself from him on methodological grounds:

> In the last analysis the arguments about original intentions and attitudes are not going to unlock any secrets. If *Caligari* is reactionary, as Kracauer claims, its ideology will be evident in the movie itself, where the moviegoer who is unaware of production intrigue can perceive it. An ideology not evident in the final version is simply not there at all.[53]

His rejection of Kracauer's methodology allows him to explore a new perspective on *Caligari* by introducing the modernist narrative model that he finds in Kafka's novels; these contain a third-person narration, but everything is reported solely from the main character's perspective. Despite the outer appearance of an objective narration, the reader identifies only with the main character's subjectivity. Similarly, in the closing frame of *Caligari*, according to Barlow:

> It would then be possible to maintain that not only the main story was told from Francis's point of view, but the frame story as well, the difference being that Francis fabricated the main story while the frame story is what he perceives without a conscious attempt at fabrication. This would account for the degree of difference in the distortion: Francis's normal view of the world is already distorted, but his attempt to explain himself is even more distorted.[54]

In his study on the theory of style, *Der expressionistische Film*,[55] Jürgen Kasten examines the history of the reception of *Caligari* without taking sides for or against one-sided interpretations of the film. Only toward the end when he describes the film aesthetically does it become clear that Kasten proceeds completely independently of Kracauer. Here he turns to the finished film and explores Wiene's execution of the plot and his use of the camera. Since Kasten completely dispenses with a political discussion of *Caligari*, his eyes are open to the purely aesthetic product, which can be discussed in the context of romantic and neoromantic horror literature.

The above-cited publications indicate a tendency in recent years to view Kracauer's book merely as a historically conditioned response to Weimar cinema, and to play it down as a social and political explanatory model for the rise of German fascism. This apparently applies to Kracauer scholarship even more than to film historiography. A perusal of the secondary literature on Kracauer published in connection with the one hundredth anniversary of his birth[56] shows even at first sight a noticeable reserve concerning *From Caligari to Hitler* in favor of his other writings, above all the posthumous "Mass Ornament." It is not at all difficult to recognize Kracauer's writings of the 1920s, especially his film criticism, as valuable source material. By contrast, the case of Wiene demonstrates that Kracauer's later attempt at a systematic treatment of Weimar film history served to constrict rather than expand our perspective. Without a doubt, *From Caligari to Hitler* maintained interest in Weimar cinema at a time when Weimar film history could not be studied in any detail. Now, however, when film archives are joining forces to facilitate research on the German silent film, it is time to return Kracauer's book to the shelf.

The academic discussion of *Caligari* has, of course, continued after the publication of the German version of our book. A sensational discovery by the Italian film historian Leonardo Quaresima has fueled controversy over the "real" authorship of *Caligari*. In the Federal Archive in Berlin, Quaresima discovered a contract dated 19

April 1919 and signed by Mayer and Janowitz, which stipulated the conditions of their sale of the *Caligari* screenplay to Decla Films. According to the contract, the authors sold their manuscript for 4,000 Marks "with all the author and ownership rights." Decla reserved the right to make "changes in the manuscript that we might sooner or later find appropriate," and the authors agreed to "assist without honorarium" in these changes. In return, Mayer and Janowitz were assured that "the names of the authors ... be explicitly mentioned in the film itself and wherever possible in all Decla advertisements about the film."[57]

While this contract makes it clear that the authors were aware that their script faced possible dramaturgical revision before being filmed (thus, their screenplay could not have been a "straightjacket" as Janowitz referred to it twenty years later), another document allows for conjectures that they were pleased at least with the commercial success of the finished film and were willing to participate financially. On 14 March 1922, Mayer and Janowitz signed an agreement in which they consented to a novelization of the *Caligari* story (the story of the finished film instead of the screenplay) as a *ciné-roman*, which was eventually published the same year.[58] In return, Mayer and Janowitz received 2,000 francs as royalties. This contract, also discovered by Leonardo Quaresima in Berlin, makes it clear that the screenplay's authors not only agreed to changes in the manuscript prior to the film's production, but that they sold the rights to a novelization of the finished film, leaving no room for their ideological opposition to revisions deemed necessary by the film company. By signing this contract in 1922, they implied acceptance of the finished film with all its changes, including the framing device, which may be the most important factor in the popularity of *Caligari*.[59]

The history of a sound film remake of *Caligari* leads us into the 1930s. Besides the above-mentioned novelization, other media exploits – such as a dramatization or an adaptation for a radioplay – were contemplated by Ufa, which was the legal successor to Decla. As was the case with many popular silent films, *Caligari* was also considered for a sound film remake in the early 1930s. But matters had by then already become complicated. Robert Wiene, who in the early 1930s had founded his own production company, Camera Film Productions, applied to Ufa to obtain the sound film rights. At this point it was not clear whether Ufa was even in a position to grant these rights, since the contract they had negotiated with Mayer and Janowitz in 1919 could not have included stipulations about sound film practices. Thus, the rights to a sound film remake were probably still with the authors. Wiene maintained that he had acquired

these rights from Mayer and Janowitz as early as 1931. He next negotiated with Ufa about the rights to the title, and these negotiations
dragged on until July 1934, when an agreement was reached according to which Wiene was granted the right to produce a sound film
remake. But the agreement stipulated that the remake was not to be
released in the U.S. before November 1934.[60]

Ultimately, Wiene's plans did not materialize. This seems due
partly to the fact that he had not acquired the sound film rights from
Mayer as he had earlier claimed. Ufa must have been well aware of
this, since they were negotiating with Wiene and Mayer at the same
time and acquired from Mayer an option to a sound film remake of
Caligari as part of their activities to press Mayer – at the time a
moneyless émigré in Prague – for the remainder of 2,850 Marks
the author still owed to Ufa for financial advances he had accepted
before being forced to leave the country. Although Ufa eventually
gave up their option, Wiene was still unable to act on the basis of his
rights, apparently failing to find sufficient funding. Meanwhile, he
informed Ufa that he had three different versions of a screenplay
written by "famous writers."[61] For the role of Cesare, he had con-
tracted Jean Cocteau, who publicly agreed to Wiene's offer in a letter published in *Paris-Midi* in December 1934.[62]

In fact, the Cinémathèque Française preserves a French-language
script of a sound film *Caligari*, which does not state the name of the
author or authors but cites London Rex Film as the owner of the
copyrights. Although the silent *Caligari* differs greatly from this
screenplay, it inspires the inner plot of the sound film a great deal. A
framing device even quotes the silent version in the form of a screening of the film during which the protagonist falls asleep and has a
weird dream. Although a number of historical figures – Napoleon,
Hitler, Mussolini, and Lenin – are part of the narrative, the screenplay still cannot be read as a warning against the Nazi dictatorship
east of the Rhine, nor against the rising danger of war. On the contrary, the script has another agenda, aesthetic in nature. While the
silent *Caligari* was widely acknowledged to have added expressionism to the film's aesthetics – though at a time when expressionism in
literature and the arts was no longer avant-garde – the sound script
apparently aimed at introducing surrealism at a time long past its
peak, thus making surrealism acceptable for a wider audience.[63]

Thus, Wiene was apparently prepared to commence shooting,
but he did not have his budget complete. Eventually he must have
abandoned his plans, although as Jürgen Kasten has discovered, at
times the remake must have been the dream of Wiene's life. In a letter of 1934, Wiene admitted, "For years I've been possessed by this

thought (making a new version of *Caligari* with sound)."[64] At this point, already physically ailing, Wiene was apparently no longer in a position to be his own producer. Thus, the sound film remake of *Caligari* was never made. John Kay's 1962 film with the same title has little in common with the original, not even in atmosphere.

Notes

1. Siegfried Kracauer, *From Caligari to Hitler: A Psychological History of the German Film* (Princeton, N.J.: Princeton University Press, 1947), 67.
2. Michael Budd, ed., *The Cabinet of Dr. Caligari: Texts, Contexts, Histories* (New Brunswick, N.J.: Rutgers University Press, 1990), 221–39, contains several excerpts from this manuscript.
3. Kracauer, *From Caligari to Hitler*, 11.
4. Kracauer in a letter to Carl Mayer on 29 May 1944 (Carl Mayer Papers, SDK, Berlin); in the first paragraph of this letter he summarizes the book's thesis.
5. Kracauer, *From Caligari to Hitler*, 8.
6. Ibid., 3.
7. Ibid., 15.
8. Ibid., 22.
9. Prof. Dr. Leidig, "Die Filmindustrie in der Volkswirtschaft," *Illustrierte Zeitung* 153, no. 3975 (1919): 2.
10. Kracauer, *From Caligari to Hitler*, 8.
11. We readily grant Kracauer's contributions to sociology. We also recognize the value of his film criticism as an important primary source for the films of the 1920s and 1930s, documented in Thomas Y. Levin's *Siegfried Kracauer: Eine Bibliographie seiner Schriften* (Marbach a.N.: Deutsche Schillergesellschaft, 1989).
12. Ibid., 61, n1. The same information can be found almost verbatim in Kracauer's letter to Carl Mayer on 29 May 1944: "I would like to add that my studies and experiences have been supplemented by information received in endless conversations with Fritz Lang, Henrik Galeen and Mr. Janowitz. The latter made it possible for me to base my *Caligari* interpretation on his inside story of this crucial film which has remained unknown until now." (Carl Mayer Papers, SDK, Berlin). Kracauer is so convinced of the truth of Janowitz's information that he does not even contact Mayer for confirmation.
13. Hans Janowitz, "*Caligari*: The Story of a Famous Story," unpublished manuscript, New York Public Library, Theater Collection, 32.
14. Carl Vincent, *Histoire de l'art cinématographique* (Brussels: Trident, 1939), 144, n3.
15. Janowitz, "The Story of a Famous Story," 48.
16. For example, Hermann Warm claims that it was the set designers who proposed the expressionist sets for the film and that Wiene, "immediately recognized the possibilities and agreed to the implementation of this style." Beyond that, Warm asserts that the scriptwriters were especially opposed to the expressionist stylization. Cf. Hermann Warm, "Gegen die *Caligari*-Legenden [Against the *Caligari* Legends]," in *Caligari und Caligarismus*, ed. Walter Kaul (Berlin: SDK, 1970), 11–16.
17. Janowitz, "The Story of a Famous Story," 51.

18. Hans Janowitz, SDK, second draft, p. 73. We have reason to question Janowitz's commitment to social criticism during the Weimar period, especially when we consider the film scripts he authored after *Caligari: Der Januskopf (The Janus Head); Marizza, genannt die Schmuggler-Madonna (Marizza, Called the Smuggler Madonna); Die Geliebte Roswolskys (Roswolsky's Mistress); Mutter, dein Kind ruft (Mother, Your Child Is Calling)*. Beyond that, he wrote lyric poetry, a selection of which was recently made available in a small volume, Hans Janowitz, *Asphaltballaden*, ed. Dieter Sudhoff (Siegen: Uni-GHS Siegen, 1994), and a bohemian novel, *Jazz* (1926). In 1924, after his father's death, he took over the family's salad-oil business in Prague, which he ran until his emigration to New York in 1939. In New York, in addition to composing the unpublished "Story of a Famous Story," he established a company that manufactured perfumes, which he headed until one year before his death in 1954.
19. Following a suggestion of Lotte Eisner, Gero Gandert found the film script among the Werner Krauss Papers in 1976. The manuscript is now in the possession of the SDK, Berlin; it has recently been published: Helga Belach and Hans-Michael Bock, eds., *Das Cabinet des Dr. Caligari: Drehbuch von Carl Mayer und Hans Janowitz zu Robert Wienes Film von 1919/1920* (Munich: edition text + kritik, 1995).
20. Belach and Bock, *Das Cabinet des Dr. Caligari*, 51f. Hans Feld, a former editor of *Der Film-Kurier*, already referred to this frame in a letter dated 19 October 1969 and published in *Filmkundliche Mitteilungen* (DIF) 2, no. 4 (1969): 19; Janowitz evidently had not forgotten this fact, as the last line of Feld's letter shows: "Incidentally, this version was confirmed by Hans Janowitz in Prague, where I lived as a refugee from 1933 to 1935." The same information is available in Feld's "Carl Mayer – der erste Filmdichter," in *Caligari und Caligarismus* (Berlin: SDK, 1970), 25f.
21. Barlow's argument that the first-person narrator heightens the credibility of the story does not take into account the subjectivity of the narration, which is maintained throughout the entire script. Cf. John D. Barlow, *German Expressionist Film* (Boston: Twayne, 1982), 32. S. S. Prawer also misunderstands this very point in the same way. Cf. S. S. Prawer, *Caligari's Children: The Film as Tale of Terror* (Oxford: Oxford University Press, 1980), 169.
22. "The story blew that Wiene frame up like an explosive – und [sic] the dramatic nucleus worked as it should, and was felt everywhere." Hans Janowitz, "A Chapter about Carl Mayer and His World without Words," unpublished manuscript, n.d. (after 1947), Janowitz Papers, SDK, Berlin.
23. Kracauer, *From Caligari to Hitler*, 67.
24. Janowitz, "The Story of a Famous Story," 8.
25. Hermann Warm claims that the set designers favored a sharp distinction between the main story and the closing frame and had consequently suggested a realistic décor in the frame. Apparently, they did not understand Wiene's intent. Cf. Warm, "Gegen die *Caligari*-Legenden," 15.
26. Before *Caligari* Carl Mayer wrote a film script for *Frau im Käfig (Woman in the Cage)*, directed by Johannes Guter and Hanns Kobe. Only three months after *Caligari*, Karl Gerhardt's *Johannes Goth* (1920), based on a film script by Mayer, premiered; possibly this film script was also composed before *Caligari*. For Hans Janowitz there is no evidence of any film authorship before *Caligari*.
27. Belach and Bock, *Das Cabinet des Dr. Caligari*, 81.
28. Ibid., 57.
29. Sequences 38–40 and 43–51, in Klaus Peter Hess, *Das Cabinet des Dr. Caligari: Protokoll* (Stuttgart: Focus, 1985). Hess describes sequences 45–51 as having a continuity in which the camera gradually moves from a long shot to a close-up.
30. Belach and Bock, *Das Cabinet des Dr. Caligari*, 65.
31. Ibid., 83f.

32. Ibid., 110.
33. Prawer sees in the plaque only a confirmation of the scriptwriters' intent to present the inner plot as real and not as subjective. He fails to see that the plaque with its inscription trivializes the traumatic nature of the story. See Prawer, *Caligari's Children*, 169. Janowitz in his "The Story of a Famous Story" also fails to realize that the peaceful conclusion announced by the plaque precludes the revolutionary, anti-authoritarian message he claims for his scenario.
34. Letter from Rudolf Kurtz to Lotte Eisner on 23 March 1958, in Lotte H. Eisner, *Ich hatte einst ein schönes Vaterland: Memoiren* (Heidelberg: Wunderhorn, 1984), 266.
35. C. Dennis Pegge, "*Caligari*: Its Innovations in Editing," *The Quarterly of Film, Radio, and Television* 11, no. 2 (1956): 136–48. In contrast to Pegge's computation, Klaus Peter Hess in his shot analysis, *Dr. Caligari: Protokoll*, counts 272 shots and 74 titles.
36. Belach and Bock, *Das Cabinet des Dr. Caligari*, 77–92.
37. Sequence #246, in Hess, *Dr. Caligari: Protokoll*, 15 f.
38. Sequences #215 and #229, ibid., 70, 73 f.
39. Sequence #14, ibid., 15.
40. Sequences #17 and #19, ibid., 15 f.
41. Sequence #246, ibid., 80.
42. Title 29, ibid., 24.
43. Sequences #75–79, ibid., 32 f.
44. Sequences #141–168, ibid., 51–57.
45. Prawer, in *Caligari's Children*, traces the history of the horror film to *Caligari* as the archetype for the genre.
46. Barry Salt, "From *Caligari* to Who?" *Sight and Sound* 48, no. 2 (1979): 119–23.
47. Thomas Elsaesser, "Social Mobility and the Fantastic: German Silent Film," *Wide Angle* 5, no. 2 (1982): 14–25.
48. Michael Budd, "Contradictions of Expressionism in *The Cabinet of Dr. Caligari*," *Indiana Social Studies Quarterly* 34 (1981): 19–25.
49. Ibid., 21.
50. Michael Budd, "The Moments of *Caligari*," in *The Cabinet of Dr. Caligari: Texts, Contexts, Histories*, 28.
51. Prawer, *Caligari's Children*, 177.
52. Michael Minden, "Politics and the Silent Cinema: *The Cabinet of Dr. Caligari* and *Battleship Potemkin*," in *Visions and Blueprints: Avant-Garde Culture and Radical Politics in Early Twentieth-Century Europe*, ed. Edward Timms and Peter Collier (Manchester: Manchester University Press, 1988), 287–306.
53. Barlow, *German Expressionist Film*, 34.
54. Ibid., 48.
55. Jürgen Kasten, *Der expressionistische Film: Abgefilmtes Theater oder avantgardistisches Erzählkino? Eine stil-, produktions- und rezeptionsgeschichtliche Untersuchung* (Münster: MAkS Publikationen, 1990).
56. Michael Kessler and Thomas Y. Levin, eds., *Siegfried Kracauer: Neue Interpretationen* (Tübingen: Stauffenburg, 1990; *New German Critique*, no. 54 [1991]). Special issue for Siegfried Kracauer, ed. Mark M. Anderson.
57. Cf. Leonardo Quaresima, "L'atto di nascita' del *Caligari*," *Cinema & Cinema* 18, no. 62 (1991): 19–24.
58. Georges Spitzmuller, *Le Cabinet du Docteur Caligari: Ciné-roman fantastique* (Paris: Ciné-Collection, La Renaissance du Livre, 1922).
59. Cf. Leonardo Quaresima, "Wer war Alland: Die Texte des *Caligari*," in *Carl Mayer: Im Spiegelbild des Dr. Caligari – Der Kampf zwischen Licht und Dunkel*, ed. Bernhard Frankfurter (Vienna: Promedia, 1997), 99–118.
60. Cf. Uli Jung and Walter Schatzberg, "Ein Drehbuch gegen die *Caligari*-Legenden," in Belach and Bock, *Das Cabinet des Dr. Caligari*, 113–38. For more details,

see Jürgen Kasten, "Besessene und Geschäftemacher: Zur Rezeptionsgeschichte von *Das Cabinet des Dr. Caligari*," in Frankfurter, *Carl Mayer*, 136–46.

61. These facts are conclusively recounted by Kasten, *Der expressionistische Film*, 139f.
62. Cf. Jean Cocteau, *Kino und Poesie: Notizen* (Munich: C. Hanser, 1979), 104f.
63. For a more detailed account of the sound film script, cf. Jung and Schatzberg, "Ein Drehbuch," 133f.
64. Kasten, *Der expressionistische Film*, 140.

Chapter 4

✦ ✦ ✦

POST-*CALIGARI*-PERIOD FILMS
1920–1921

D uring the immediate post-*Caligari* period, Wiene was extremely
productive, working on ten films. He directed six of these himself
and wrote at least two of the scripts as well. In addition, he prepared
four scripts for other directors. In 1920/21 he had a contract with
Decla-Bioscop, for whom he made five films (he had directed *Caligari*
for Decla before the merger). In this same period he also worked with
Ungo Film, Maxim Film, and Stuart Webbs Film Company.

Of these ten films, only *Genuine* (1920), *Die drei Tänze der Mary
Wilford* (*The Three Dances of Mary Wilford* [1920]),[1] and *Die Rache einer
Frau* (*A Woman's Revenge* [1921]) are still available from various film
archives. We will discuss and analyze *Genuine* and *Die Rache einer
Frau* in some detail. For a description of the remaining films we must
rely on the available documentation from the time.

**DIE DREI TÄNZE DER MARY WILFORD (*The Three Dances of Mary
Wilford*)**   This film was made either just before or at the same time
as *Caligari*[2] and had its premiere late in April 1920, that is, before the
new *Reichslichtspielgesetz* (national censorship law) became effective in
May 1920. Nevertheless, the film was censored by the Censorship
Board in Berlin and two scenes were eliminated: one scene in the
prelude in which two children are trained to become pickpockets,
and a second in the first act in which there is a wild dance sequence.[3]
According to a number of reports, the film was a sequel to Leo
Lasko's 1919 film *Die Sünderin* (*The Sinner*).[4]

Only one review was available with a partial summary of the film's plot. The daughter of the earlier film's central character, hardly grown up herself, becomes involved with a criminal. All of her efforts to break with the past fail because she cannot free herself from this relationship. The stages of her brief adult life are marked by three significant dances: the first saves her lover from the police, the second keeps her out of jail, and the third leads to her death.[5]

An anonymous critic reviews the film positively, though he finds the script burdened with too many events that, according to him, the director does not keep in bounds. His most interesting observation, however, is about something entirely different, namely, the issue of dance and music in silent film. In general, he maintains, silent film dances are filmed in such a way that the rhythmical movements of the dancers are disrupted, and he insists that this be changed, especially in a film that offers as many dances as *The Three Dances of Mary Wilford.* This applies, he continues, especially in dance films, to the musical score, which he characterizes as entirely problematic. He concludes that dance movements and accompanying music must be appropriately synchronized.[6]

GENUINE

> *Genuine* is an expressionistic film because expressionism was a success. But instead of being a method of composition, in a way it became the content of the film. Expressionistic film died from this paradoxical discrepancy. *Genuine* was official proof that these films were not working commercially. Their time was over.[7]

This categorically negative verdict on the film *Genuine* seems to be the source of most second-hand opinions about the film, which have never been revised, primarily because hardly any prints of the film have been available to film scholars. As late as 1982, John D. Barlow in his book *German Expressionist Film*[8] had to rely on secondary sources for his plot summary and his critical judgment of the film. Only Francis Courtade in his book *Cinéma expressioniste*[9] based his discussion of the film on a close shot analysis of two fragmentary prints, one from the Cinémathèque Française in Paris and the other from the Cinémathèque de Toulouse, apparently the only prints available in Europe. The 16mm print from the American Rohauer Collection, which was accessible to us, has never been referred to, much less analyzed. Siegfried Kracauer and Lotte Eisner follow Kurtz's above-quoted judgment. Both maintain that the primary motivation for *Genuine* was to attempt to reproduce the commercial success of *Caligari.* Courtade, to be sure, goes beyond these sparse observations. Since he is limited to the theme of his book, however, he must establish links between this film and an alleged expressionist tradition; in so doing he fails to analyze the film adequately.

Similar to Courtade, Jürgen Kasten, who bases his analysis on the Paris fragment, approaches the film from the perspective of style analysis. After providing a well-documented account of the film's production, he criticizes the stylistic inconsistency of the scenery and reproaches the director, Wiene, for following "the decorator's creative decisions without a convincing stylistic concept."[10] Kasten also sees *Genuine* simply as a failed attempt to repeat the commercial success of *Caligari.* At best he accords Wiene technical skill.

The film criticism following the 1920 premiere is, however, much more varied. Although critiques invariably referred to *Caligari,* there were also those that compared the film to Lubitsch's *Sumurun,* which had its premiere at almost the same time. What interested many of those contemporary critics, both in the plot and in the décor, were the exotic and fantastic fairy tale motifs. This quality, as well as the fame of actress Fern Andra and painter César Klein, whose participation was extensively publicized by the production company Decla-Bioscop, accounts for the warm reception of the film.

The film opens in the living room of Percy, a young painter. Two friends of his come to visit him and find him irritable, even mad about a painting he has completed. As they urge him to get rid of it, an old man who wishes to buy the painting enters. Despite his friends' admonitions, Percy refuses to part with it. After they leave he uncovers the life-size portrait of Genuine, lies down to read, and falls asleep. Genuine's portrait comes alive and she steps out of the frame. Now her story begins.

Many years ago the originally pure and innocent Genuine was abducted by a mysterious oriental sect, who corrupted her and forced her to participate in their primitive, blood-sucking ritualistic practices. Some time later she is kidnapped by slave traders and sold to Lord Milo, an old eccentric, who takes her to his remote, secluded house in a small Irish village. (According to Courtade, Lord Milo is identical with Percy's would-be customer in the frame story.) In order to imprison her, he has subterraneous tropical chambers built, which are enclosed by glass and contain trees and exotic plants from the equatorial regions from which she originated. He gives her the most enchanting garments and lets her drink the blood of birds. Nevertheless, all this does not assuage her savage lust for blood.

In the village there lives a harmless barber who shaves Lord Milo daily. He knows nothing about the mysteries of the lord's house, which is guarded by a huge black man who is in Milo's service. One day the barber's nephew, Florian, his apprentice, fills in for him. That same day, Genuine manages to escape from her golden cage; she seduces Florian, and manipulates him into murdering Milo. Florian remains in the house, intoxicated with his love for Genuine; and, in possession of Milo's magic ring, he gains control over the mysterious black servant. Genuine, however, cannot live without blood and demands that Florian kill himself as proof of his love for her. He refuses to accede to her demand; she takes the magic ring and orders the servant to kill Florian and bring her his blood. Instead, the servant frees Florian, forces him to leave the house, and brings her his own blood. However, at this point Genuine's blood lust has abated; her rejection of the blood offering amounts to a first awakening of her true, original self. Now, Percy, Lord Milo's grandson, arrives. (He is identical with the young painter in the frame story.) He had announced his visit in a letter that Milo had received with ill will. Milo, who apparently had observed and recorded Genuine's behavior carefully, wondered how Genuine in her blood lust would respond to Percy.

The moment Percy sees Genuine he falls hopelessly in love with her. He writes to a friend and asks him to come and share his happiness. When his friend arrives, Genuine's savage blood lust has again gotten the better of her. She demands Percy's death, but when his friend pretends that Percy has killed himself, Genuine realizes that she has truly fallen in love with him. Through the mediation of the friend, who is the very epitome of self-restraint, and through her love for Percy, Genuine is cured of her obsession.

Meanwhile, however, Florian, at his uncle's house, has fallen into a delirious fever due to his unfulfilled love for Genuine. The uncle, having learned from his nephew that Genuine induced him to commit murder, goes to the police and brings back a mob to search the house for the "witch." The mob invades the house and kills the servant; at this point, however, Genuine has already been murdered by the madly jealous Florian.

The film received mixed responses. There were reports that some viewers of the film were so disappointed that they demanded a refund of their admission fee. For the most part, however, film critics and film journalists explored the film with serious analyses; they cited the script of Carl Mayer, the acting of Fern Andra, the painted sets of César Klein, the photography of Willy Hameister, and the directing of Robert Wiene. The *Film-Kurier*, which had begun to establish a reputation for incisive film criticism at that time, had a lengthy article about *Genuine* on 3 September 1920 in which the flaws and virtues of the film are elucidated. The reviewer, L. K. Fredrick, faults

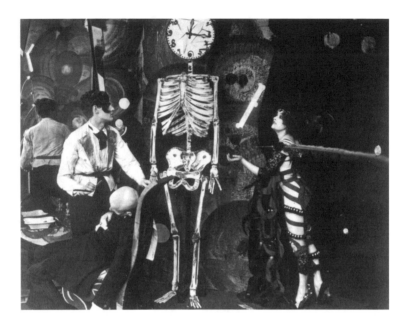

Genuine Director: Robert Wiene (1920) –
Hans Heinrich v. Twardowsky, John Gottowt, Fern Andra

the film for its lack of logical and psychological coherence. Yet he
overrides his own objections by stating that the substance of the film
was to be found "in the magic world of the fantastic."[11]

Eugen Tannenbaum saw in *Genuine* yet more proof that modern
artistic forms can be creatively applied to narrative film:

> With this film, author Carl Mayer and director Robert Wiene continue
> their effort to achieve a pure cinematic style and introduce new ideas into
> image creation, a promising process that began with the expressionistic
> *Caligari* film. This "Tragedy of a Strange House" also deals with a fantas-
> tic story full of dark secrets and mysterious circumstances, mysteries of
> an insane secret sect, the bizarre moods of a mad eccentric. Here also
> modern painting is assigned a significant role, noticeable even in the
> tumbling letters of the inserted titles … .[12]

In *Freie Deutsche Bühne*, the film critic Balthasar (Roland Schacht)
describes *Genuine* as a filmic experiment that even goes beyond *Caligari*. Although he sees some weak points in the plot of *Genuine*, he
finds strength in its stylization:

> This Wiene is a scenic genius. (His choice of César Klein as an aid alone
> shows his clear and purposeful intentions.) It is not the fantastic and con-
> sistent stylization of the decoration alone that will no doubt have its imi-

Genuine Director: Robert Wiene (1920) –
Hans Heinrich von Twardowsky, Fern Andra

tators, but the right feeling for the effect of something on the screen. Illusion is not the goal, but visual effects ... . Wiene creates a forest made of cardboard and canvas. He does without nature because he wants to deliver fairy tale ...[13]

Likewise, the *Berliner Tageblatt* maintained that *Genuine* led the way from Naturalism to the realm of the fantastic.[14]

Despite the film's flaws in plot and character development, the above-cited critics see the film's virtues in its stylized visual components. In this light, the often-heard contention that *Genuine* was nothing more than a failed attempt to imitate the commercial success of *Caligari* merely by copying its style must be rejected. What the two films have in common is not only the sets with painted décor, but also their shared interest in the reflection of the psychological and fantastic dimensions of the plot. What distinguishes *Genuine* from *Caligari* is its fairy tale, even mythological treatment of the fantastic.

The psychological motifs in this fantastic narrative, such as the Oedipal conflict, the liberation of the libido, madness, and a conscious-subconscious polarity are not developed in depth as in *Caligari*, *Raskolnikow*, and *Orlacs Hände (Orlac's Hands)*, but are suggested visually and symbolically. *Genuine*'s exoticism links the film more back to *Furcht (Fear)* rather than to *Caligari*. At the time, it is this

Genuine Director: Robert Wiene (1920) – working photo

visual style, this exoticism, which makes *Genuine* a companion piece
of mainstream films such as Lubitsch's *Sumurum* (1920), Joe May's
Die Herrin der Welt (*Mistress of the World* [1919]), and Fritz Lang's *Die
Spinnen* (*The Spiders* [1919/20]), to name only a few.

The basic visual motif of the film is the division of Lord Milo's
house into surface and subterranean areas. The subterranean area in
which Genuine is held is a tropical grotto with exotic plants. Her
master has recreated here what seems to be her natural element – an
unbridled, uninhibited eroticism that he can observe and control at a
distance. Even after she has freed herself and caused the death of her
master, she still brings her lovers to her underground abode. This is
the realm of her savage lusts, where she consumes her male victims.
To be delivered from these primitive instincts, Genuine must leave
the grotto for good. Her love for Percy induces her to do that but trag-
ically puts her at the mercy of the crazed Florian, who kills her.

As long as Lord Milo was alive and she was contained in her subterraneous grotto, her blood lust was held in check, and her eroticism remained harmless. Once these restraints are lifted, her lusts
emerge in full flower and we see Genuine as a dangerous female
beast preying on her male victims. Her return to civilized humanity
is achieved only in the upper realm. There, through the mediation of
the rationality of Percy's friend, her perverted destructive lust is

transformed into a human love that can reciprocate Percy's. Here we have familiar fairy tale motifs: a fall from innocence, followed by many travails, a beneficent intervention, and a return to true humanity. There is even a moral: Genuine must die because her previous destructive sexuality must be punished. What is unique about the film is that this simplistic fairy tale psychology is transformed into lavish visual images.

The antipode to Genuine is more the old Lord Milo than his grandson Percy. The available American fragment of the film provides little information about Milo. He is a bald, thin, old man, always dressed in black, who moves with staggering, jerky motions. He is an eccentric who travels much but in odd, out-of-the-way places. His strange house is not located in a major metropolitan area, but in a remote, small Irish village where he has it set apart by a huge forbidding wall.

The film shows Milo and Genuine together only once in the subterraneous grotto that he has built especially for her. Beyond that, his study seems to be his favorite room, and it is here that he also receives his daily shave. What stands out most in the study is the large mirror in front of which he is shaven, a skeleton with a clock in place of the skull, and an old-fashioned standing-desk where he

Genuine Director:
Robert Wiene
(1920) – Fern Andra

keeps a large ledger into which he presumably enters observations about Genuine. Apparently, the room adjacent to the study is a laboratory, judging from the stylized décor, which seems to consist of odd experimental equipment. Probably Milo is an eccentric scientist with a predilection for unusual, morally questionable experiments. Even his grandson's visit is for him only another opportunity for his strange research: "My grandson, Percy, tells me he is coming; he may come … How will Genuine react when she sees him? How much of her cruel instincts will she show?" At this point he is standing at his desk, excitedly writing in his ledger and gesticulating wildly. It appears that he plans the encounter between the two as an experimental situation.

A number of constellations now become apparent. The opposition between Milo and Genuine works on various levels: old/young, male/female, above/below, master/slave. In the constellation of Milo and Percy, there are the contrasts old/young and father/son. The same goes for Milo's relationship with Florian, who is Percy's alter-ego. Milo had planned to manipulate Percy in one of his experiments. However, Florian, manipulated by Genuine, executes an Oedipal rebellion and murders the old man. Florian, weak and inexperienced (his first appearance in the house is introduced by the title "Florian's first experience with life!"), easily falls prey to Genuine and loses all control. Percy, on the other hand, is more experienced and resourceful when he becomes the object of Genuine's love. Only through the intervention of Percy's friend, Henry, however, is Genuine's blood lust finally transformed into normal human love and socially acceptable sexuality. At the climax of the film, Henry takes over the ordering function that Milo had at the beginning. He restores an order that was lost with Milo's murder, but this one is a more rational and human order. His function as Milo's alter-ego is visually symbolized by his gaunt physiognomy and his dark clothing, which are reminiscent of the old count.

As a representative of normal, bourgeois society, Guyard, the old barber, is an antipode to Milo. He is Milo's only link to the outside world, but he remains totally outside of Milo's plans and manipulations. Nevertheless, Guyard is the one who sends Florian into the house – precipitating the tragic action – and he is the one who brings the mob into the house to put an end to the mystery and reestablish bourgeois order. At the end, Guyard is the only one who weeps over the tragic resolution.

DIE JAGD NACH DEM TODE (The Hunt for Death) Robert Wiene, in collaboration with Johannes Brandt, prepared the scenario for the

first two parts of this monumental serial film. The third and fourth parts were written by Robert Liebmann.[15] The sensational plot revolves around Allan (Nils Chrisander), an engineer who is distracted from his duty – the building of a railway line from Calcutta to Peking – by his passion for the Indian dancer Malatti (Lil Dagover). He is fired, and in his despair he exhorts his Tibetan servant Lubzang (Bernhard Goetzke) to kill him. For Lubzang's protection he provides both a suicide note and his life insurance policy. However, Malatti's unexpected reappearance inspires him with a renewed yearning for life. In their ensuing quest to find Lubzang to nullify the dreadful command, they undergo numerous adventures throughout the Orient. In the course of the most exotic exploits, Malatti loses her life and the sought-after documents threatening Allan's life fall into the hands of sinister forces. Lubzang, himself, never had the intention of fulfilling his master's desperate wish; but now with the documents in alien hands, Allan's life is truly at risk. To preserve himself he becomes involved in a series of new adventures, which are related in the remaining parts of the film series.[16]

The reviewers of the time received the film with mixed responses. Karl Gerhardt's direction was generally praised, as was the photography by Paul Holzky and the art direction by Hermann Warm. Some of the critics found the involved plot a bit too unbelievable, while others observed that the Grunewald landscape was not especially persuasive in representing Tibet. By contrast, Hans Wollenberg described the film in the most positive terms and accentuated its originality and authenticity, thereby giving Wiene and Brandt their due. Beyond that, he singled out Hermann Warm for special praise, contrasting the expressionism of Warm's work in *Caligari* with the realism and even naturalism of the present film.[17]

Thematically this film stands in close proximity to *Furcht* (*Fear* [1918]) and *Genuine* (1920), in that modern Western culture is confronted with an exotic Oriental culture with disquieting consequences. Allan in *Die Jagd nach dem Tode* (*The Hunt for Death*) violates a sacred prohibition by entering the "forbidden city" and almost becomes a victim of avenging forces, just as Count Greven in *Furcht* desecrates the Hindu temple by stealing the sacred statue and thereby falls victim to the priest's revenge. Malatti, like Genuine before, is enslaved by a primitive tribe practicing blood rituals, just as was the case with Genuine. In all three films the exoticism of the Orient represents a nether world that threatens the foundations of rational existence. In *Caligari* there is also the threat to rationality, but it is represented psychologically through the ambiguity of the borderline between sanity and insanity. This is a purely modern dilemma. Thematically speaking, and not from the perspective of film methodology, *Caligari* is thus no isolated exception in Wiene's oeuvre. Rather, a screening of *Furcht, Genuine,* and *Die Jagd nach dem Tode* makes clear that Wiene had dealt with the problem of threatened rationality several times in and around 1920.

DAS BLUT DER AHNEN (The Blood of the Ancestors)   From the few contemporary reviews available, we cannot gather a conclusive plot summary. It is clear that the topic is the reestablishment of the monarchy in an unspecified country. The pretender to the throne is found, but unknown to the people, this dynasty is afflicted with a mysterious blood disease that causes insanity to all its members every seven years. Though the exact conclusion of this five-act tragedy is unknown, it is clear that the dynasty's fatal flaw reappears and disables the aspirant to the throne.

The reviewer in *Der Film* highlighted the script by Wiene and Johannes Brandt for its logical construction and captivating plot sequences,[18] whereas the *Deutsche Lichtspiel-Zeitung* and *Der Kinematograph* questioned its contemporaneity.[19] Aros (Alfred Rosenthal) was an even less sympathetic critic; he maintained that Wiene and Brandt drew on a story by the popular author Gaston Malmaison without giving credit to their source.[20]

DIE NACHT DER KÖNIGIN ISABEAU (The Night of Queen Isabeau)   The historical background for this film is the reign of the mad king Charles VI of France and his Queen Isabeau in medieval Paris around 1400. The script develops a fictitious plot in which the mad king governs over dwarfs and other mad folk while the constable, Rauol de Clisson, assumes the king's powers and tyrannizes his subjects – most specifically the queen, whose clandestine affairs he observes with envious interest. He tries in vain to force her to reveal the identity of her latest paramour. Isabeau attempts to use her formidable seductive powers to gain her freedom from him and finally in desperation stabs the constable to death. Dashing off to her lover, the queen finds him in the arms of another. Crushed by her disappointment, she returns to the palace, where she gradually loses her mind and joins her husband in his kingdom of madmen.[21]

The critics agreed that Wiene had an outstanding cast at his disposal; only Fern Andra was occasionally criticized. Primarily they comment on Wiene's "masterful" directorial style, which had "every effect worked out to the minutest detail, the reins always firmly joined in one hand."[22] By contrast, *Der Film-Kurier* notes that in its realization of a "very difficult, more experimental task" there remained a "certain

*Die Nacht der Königin
Isabeau (The Night of
Queen Isabeau)*
Director: Robert
Wiene (1920) – Fern
Andra, Fritz Kortner

feeling of cool distance."[23] Unfortunately, no print of *Die Nacht der Königin Isabeau* has survived. The plot summaries, the critiques, and the stills lead one to believe that it might have been a significant film revolving around one of Wiene's central themes, insanity.

BRILLANTEN *(Diamonds)* This film belongs to the genre of the detective film. The customs officer Taylor, a shady character, coerces Ethel Wilkens to spy on Dick Nielson, whom he suspects of smuggling valuable jewelry into the country. After a number of involved incidents set within a high-society milieu, it turns out that Dick Nielson himself is an undercover detective who has been trying to establish evidence for his suspicions that Taylor is a corrupt officer. The plot concludes with the triumphant Nielson bringing Taylor to justice.

Only one review of this film was available to us. It consists mostly of a plot summary but adds a rather severe criticism of director Friedrich Féher's tendency to introduce grotesque scenes within an otherwise serious and well-structured storyline. Secondly, the reviewer finds fault with Féher's all-too-loose direction of the cast, saying he apparently gave them too little instruction in the characterization of their roles.[24]

DIE RACHE EINER FRAU *(A Woman's Revenge)*

This film, based on a novella by d'Aurevilly ... is a disappointment. Through five acts a commonplace idea is rolled out that even Robert Wiene's directorship could not enlighten. On the contrary: This piece of work from Wiene was the greatest disappointment of the evening. Nothing new, in particular no pacing anywhere, no movement – and temperament alone could have helped over the long passages and bleak spots. Where is the spirit of Wiene that once gripped us with a *Caligari*, that let us look forward to new paths of film taste, even without expressionistic excess?[25]

This review of the film is characteristic of the negative criticism with which *Die Rache einer Frau* was received. The objections to the film apply to the nature of the subject matter, the casting, and the quality of the acting. The novella by Barbey d'Aurevilly was considered too weak and unconvincing in its plot to be appropriate for a contemporary film script. Vera Corally, formerly of the Imperial Theater in Moscow and playing the lead role, was regarded as too theatrical for a film actress, and the rest of the cast was seen as too undistinguished to compensate for her inadequacies. It is, however, difficult thoroughly to evaluate this negative criticism of the film because only a sixty-minute fragment of the film has survived; the entire fourth reel is missing.[26] We must, therefore, rely on the reviews in the trade press for plot summary.

The film begins with a frame story in which a gentleman, Henri de Tressignies, meets a mysterious lady in a shady nightclub, who apparently solicits the attentions of gentlemen for the purpose of prostitution. He becomes curious about her story and accompanies her to her quarters, where he learns her sad and tragic story. As a vivacious young woman no more than eighteen years of age, Sanzia-Florinda (the mysterious lady in the frame) was married off by her parents to the distinguished, but middle-aged Duke of Sierra Leone, even though she was in love with her impoverished cousin Esteban. The duke, cold, distant, and busy with his state affairs, neglects his young wife, but at the same time confines her jealously to his castle, suspecting her of liaisons with her lover. One day her lover flees from her bedroom just in time to avoid being caught with her. Sanzia-Florinda swears she was alone, and the vindictive duke, knowing the truth, releases his bloodhounds. She pleads for her lover's life but the duke is not satisfied until the hounds have torn him to pieces. With her story told, Sanzia-Florinda now explains to her sympathetic listener that she has left her husband to become a prostitute to shame him, to break his pride, and to take her revenge.

Henri de Tressignies is moved by Sanzia-Florinda's story and wants to be of service to her. However, after their first meeting he cannot find her anymore. One day he receives a letter from her in which she reminds him of his wish to inform her husband, the duke, about her circumstances. Now is the time to do so, she tells him, and she can be found in the hospital for fallen women. Henri tries to see her in the hospital but learns that, by order of Sanzia-Florinda, only the duke can be admitted. The duke finally comes to see his wife, who by that time is on her deathbed. With her last breath she summons him to look at her shame, which is her revenge against him for having broken her heart. Triumphant in the belief that she has broken his pride, she dies. In the last scenes of the film, we see her lying in state, as she had instructed, with a plaque on her bier that states, "Here lies the Duchess of Sierra Leone, she died as a penitent fallen woman." A meddling priest had inserted the word "penitent," undermining the triumph of her revenge.

The narrative structure of *Die Rache einer Frau* is defined by a threefold division of Sanzia-Florinda's life: her free and lively youth in her parents' home, her suffocating, constrained life in her husband's castle, and her libertine existence as a woman of the streets. The social hierarchy, as determined by her parents and her husband, determines her life in the first half of her life. That hierarchy denies her freedom of choice and violates her sense of self to an extreme degree. Her extreme response – the life of a prostitute to shame her husband – is driven by her lust for revenge. In that response she gains a degree of self-determination that had been denied her. Her triumphant revenge is the only fulfillment she can attain, but at the terrible cost of becoming a social outcast. The alternative, subordination to her husband, would have meant sacrificing all feeling, all self. Her triumph, however, is short lived. By adding the word "penitent" to the plaque she had designed, the priest restores her to the social order but only, once more, by violating her self-determination.

Another perspective on Sanzia-Florinda's tragedy is found in a number of dance sequences in which she is either an active participant or a passive onlooker. In the frame story at the nightclub, she is compelled irresistibly to dance wildly to the music of some gypsy fiddlers. She had been a bored observer of some traditional ballroom dancing at the club, but once the gypsies were fetched she was transformed into a passionate dancer. Later in the flashback, she is like this once more when, as a young woman, she had danced spontaneously, wildly with some gypsies in front of her parents' home. At this very point the parents announce the arranged marriage to the duke and they do so with the words, "Is this appropriate for a lady who will soon be the bride of the most distinguished gentleman of the country?" – as if to drive home the point that she must sacrifice what she has been. At her husband's castle, she is an uninvolved onlooker of a highly formal ball. At the same time, a lively folk dance is taking place outside in front of the castle. Sanzia-Florinda observes the folk dancers at a distance, from the balcony, with a melancholy that reveals the desperation of her life. These dance sequences show that the vigor of her spontaneous, natural self makes her adaptation to a life lived according to strict social conventions impossible. It is part of her tragedy that she rediscovers her natural self only in her self-destructive lust for revenge.

The relationship of the film's male characters to Sanzia-Florinda reveals clearly the inevitability of her tragic end. Each of the men has his own sphere of interest, but in each instance that sphere does not correspond to her needs. The father's very appearance signals the benevolent patriarch whose kindness toward his daughter in no way precludes an arranged marriage that will heighten the social standing of the family. The decision was made by the father without any prior consultation with her. In this he acted, of course, within the tradition of arranged marriages among aristocratic families. The Duke, in turn, by having a lawyer represent his marital interests, likewise was operating within that tradition. For him it is desirable to have a young, attractive wife from an established family who will support his social life and professional career; he seeks and expects no more. His cold-bloodedness emerges only when he perceives a threat to the honor of his name. His urgent need to defend his honor is, of course, what makes him so vulnerable to his wife's strategy for revenge.

Young Esteban, however, who lives in the same house with Sanzia-Florinda, as his uncle's guest, and is her frequent companion, has career expectations that place him within the framework of his elders' tradition. When he sees her dance with the gypsies his desire for her is evident. However, he does not allow an open conflict between love and ambition to arise. When the marriage is announced, he swallows his disappointment and leaves. Later he becomes her secret lover, with fateful consequences.

Henri de Tressignies plays a special role in the story since he is not among the men who manipulate Sanzia-Florinda. As a gentleman of means, he frequents a disreputable nightclub where he seeks the company of women. He is attracted to Sanzia-Florinda but also curious about her since she is evidently a lady of his class. With this duality of interest, he accompanies her to her quarters, apparently as a customer. While she is in his arms she makes sure that he notices her husband's portrait, and in response to his question, narrates her story. The fragmentary nature of our print does not reveal how he reacts to her tale. It is clear that he takes no immediate action to help her, but he cannot forget her either. After she disappears from the scene, he tries unsuccessfully to find her. When she writes him from her deathbed in a "hospital for fallen women" asking him to inform her husband of her circumstances, he becomes her mediator. After her death he witnesses the final scene at the hospital. He places flowers on her bier and looks at her for a long time. As a detached observer he fulfills his role as a stand-in for the spectators.

Even after her death Sanzia-Florinda is not granted satisfaction. The priest, in whom she had placed her last trust, dilutes her inscription to make her into a penitent sinner and reconcile her with official Christian morality. He thereby denies her her only means of revenge against a man who was shielded from retribution for his sins by that same official Christian morality. The three traditional social institutions – the family, marriage, and the church – simply in being what they are, deny her a self-determined, humane existence.

The only other main female character in the film is Sanzia-Florinda's mother, who evidently has internalized and accepted the entire traditional framework of her caste. When Sanzia-Florinda meets the duke for the first time, her reaction to her future husband is highlighted by an iris frame closing in around her head. In that iris, shot in deep focus, the worried mother looks first at the duke and then at her visibly disturbed daughter. She understands but, of course, knowing a woman's duty in that tradition, does nothing.

Robert Wiene organized the unity of the film around the representation of Sanzia-Florinda's subjectivity. He achieved this by using a framing device that allows most parts of her story to be told in flashbacks, that is, from her point of view. Moreover, a large number and a great variety of close-ups demonstrate that the entire film revolves around Sanzia-Florinda's inner world. Henri, however, who stands explicitly outside the plot, assumes a narrative function as a mediator between the tragic heroine and the audience. He is present but more as a pretext for the story to be told; he does not influence her action. Thus, the subjectivity of Sanzia-Florinda's story is not affected by him.

DAS SPIEL MIT DEM FEUER (Playing with Fire) Diana Karenne, apparently in her first screen role in Germany, plays an actress who has the predilection of trying out in real life any role she is to play on the stage. A young playwright composes a play designed for her in the lead role. Following her practice, the actress enters the criminal milieu indicated in the play to prepare herself. She thereby becomes involved in a burglary that takes place, unknown to her, in the house of the duke who is her devoted admirer. Guilt-ridden, she turns to the playwright for understanding in her dilemma but discovers that her admirer divorces art from life in such a way that he cannot condone her actions. The noble duke, however, surmising the truth and fully recognizing her fine qualities offers her his hand in marriage.[27] The reviewers were delighted with the film's play within a play. While the young playwright reads his manuscript to a select audience in the actress's salon, the action is acted out on the screen. This scene, which presents a parody of a typical sentimental drama, was seen by the reviewers as the highlight of Wiene's and Kroll's direction. Beyond that there were reservations about the mixture of farce and tragedy in the film.[28]

DER SCHRECKEN IM HAUSE ARDON (Panic in the House of Ardon)
This film of the Stuart Webbs Film Company must have been finished prior to 4 August 1920. For reasons beyond the grasp of even a reviewer of the time, it did not receive its premiere before late in July 1921. Apparently, the film was originally known under the name of *Die Welteroberer* (*The World Conquerors*).

In the storyline, an international syndicate attempts to obtain the scientific secrets of the chemist Ardon. They use hypnosis on his wife to achieve their ends. Ardon discovers the truth, kills the gang's leader and, recognizing that his wife did not act according to her own will, forgives her complicity. In the only review accessible to us, the author does not venture an evaluation of the film.[29]

DAS ABENTEUER DES DR. KIRCHEISEN (The Adventure of Dr. Kircheisen)
Hermann Thimig plays the young chemist, Dr. Kircheisen, who discovered a serum that restores people on the verge of death to their full physical and mental faculties for one hour. While waiting for his fiancée, he is called to the elderly Baron Vogh, who has a desperate request. The baron's Indian servant lies on his deathbed after being bitten by a poisonous snake. The baron pleads with the chemist to restore the Indian to consciousness for one more hour with his serum. Dr. Kircheisen, enchanted by the baron's daughter and hoping to obtain her hand in marriage, consents and indeed brings the Indian back to health. Only then do we learn that with his own esoteric potion, the Indian had aged both the baron and his daughter in order to fulfill the baron's wish to see his young daughter as a grown-up woman and himself in his old age. However, when the Indian lay dying from the snake's poison the baron realized with horror that his servant's magic would no longer be available to return them to their normal state. During his brief period of restored health, the Indian concocts the antidote and saves the baron and his child. Just at that moment Dr. Kircheisen's fiancée, Marga, appears and wakes the chemist from his bizarre dream.[30]

The reviewers criticized the film quite severely since it did not work as an adaptation of a popular novel. According to one review, the director, Rudolf Biebrach, had not given coherence to the narrative and the actors, and had failed to make their characters credible.[31] Thematically, however, there are a number of aspects to this film that are relevant to Wiene's oeuvre as a scriptwriter. The clash of Oriental exoticism and Western rationalism is satirized in the film. The Indian's mysterious potion and the chemist's serum, though arrived at by entirely different procedures, exemplify the same human aspiration to subordinate reality to human will. It is also noteworthy that the potion representing an Eastern culture brings maturity and age, whereas the serum – proud product of Western science – brings youth, though only briefly. Both the potion and the serum constitute transgressions against nature; but the potion appears only in the scientist's dream, suggesting a scientist's fantasy wish to justify the scientific quest.

Notes

1. Although this film is extant and preserved by the Bundesfilmarchiv in Koblenz, we were not able to view it because the print is still nitrate and in poor condition. It is not clear when the archive will restore the film.
2. In *Die LichtBildBühne* 13, no. 4 (1920): 20, we find a note reporting that *Caligari* is near completion, and on the same page another note indicates that *Mary Wilford* has already been completed.
3. See Herbert Birett, *Verzeichnis in Deutschland gelaufener Filme: Entscheidungen der Filmzensur 1911–1920* (Munich: Saur, 1980), 299.
4. *Die LichtBildBühne* 13, no. 4 (1920): 20.
5. *Der Film* 5, no. 18 (1920): 47.
6. *Der Film-Kurier* 2, no. 86 (1920).
7. Rudolf Kurtz, *Expressionismus und Film* (Berlin: Verlag der LichtBildBühne, 1926), 73.
8. John D. Barlow, *German Expressionist Film* (Boston: Twayne, 1982).
9. Francis Courtade, *Cinéma expressioniste* (Paris: Henri Veyrier, 1984), 69–76.
10. Jürgen Kasten, *Der expressionistische Film: Abgefilmtes Theater oder avantgardistisches Erzählkino? Eine stil-, produktions- und rezeptionsgeschichtliche Untersuchung* (Münster: MAkS Publikationen, 1990), 65.
11. *Der Film-Kurier* (3 September 1920).
12. Eugen Tannenbaum, *B.Z. am Mittag*, 3 September 1920.
13. Balthasar, *Freie Deutsche Bühne*, 12 September 1920, p. 59f.
14. *Berliner Tageblatt*, 9 September 1920; cited according to a clip from Adolf Schustermann Zeitungsnachrichten Bureau, held by DIF.

15. The series as a whole, as well as the first part, appeared under the title *Die Jagd nach dem Tode;* the subsequent parts were entitled: *Die verbotene Stadt (The Forbidden City), Der Mann im Dunkel (The Man in the Dark),* and *Die Goldmine von Sar-Khin (The Gold Mine of Sar-Khin).*
16. Cf. *Der Film-Kurier* 2, no. 239 (1920), and *Der Kinematograph* 14, no. 720 (1920).
17. *Die LichtBildBühne* 13, no. 43 (1920): 34.
18. *Der Film* 5, no. 46 (1920): 33.
19. *Deutsche Lichtspiel-Zeitung* 8, no. 30 (1920): 3; *Der Kinematograph* 14, no. 722 (1920).
20. *Deutsche Lichtspiel-Zeitung* 8, no. 46 (1920): 3.
21. Cf. *Illustrierter Film-Kurier,* no. 39 (1920), (program brochure) and *Der Kinematograph* 14, no. 723 (1920).
22. *Der Film* 5, no. 47 (1920): 37.
23. *Der Film-Kurier* 2, no. 256 (1920).
24. *Der Film-Kurier* 2, no. 275 (1920); this is also the source for our plot summary.
25. *Der Film-Kurier* 3, no. 88 (1921).
26. This print has been preserved at Gosfilmofond in Moscow; we owe thanks to the late Mark Strochkow and his staff for making a safety print of the film available for our study.
27. Cf. the official program brochure of the Decla-Bioscop.
28. *Der Film-Kurier* 3, no. 117 (1920); *Der Film* 6, no. 22 (1921): 35; *Der Kinematograph* 15, no. 745 (1921).
29. *Der Film* 6, no. 31 (1921): 67; we thank Herbert Birett for passing his information about this film on to us.
30. Cf. the official program brochure of the Maxim Film Company.
31. *Der Film-Kurier* 3, no. 223 (1921); *Der Film* 6, no. 40 (1921): 43; *Der Kinematograph* 15, no. 763 (1921).

Raskolnikow Director: Robert Wiene (1923) – Grigori Chmara

Chapter 5

✦ ✦ ✦

FILMS FOR THE LIONARDO AND NEUMANN PRODUCTION COMPANIES 1922–1924

The period between 1922 and 1924 marked yet another turning point in Wiene's career. He formed his own company, Lionardo, and started a close cooperation with the newly founded Neumann Productions. The establishment of Lionardo most likely indicates Wiene's intention for greater control over the production of his films such as *Die höllische Macht (The Infernal Power)* and *Der Puppenmacher von Kiang-Ning (The Doll Maker of Kiang-Ning)*. His association with Neumann Productions clearly signified a greater orientation toward quality films with subject matter from world literature.

It is an indication of Robert Wiene's versatility that he frequently shifted from one genre to another. As a screenwriter he had previously adapted several novels and plays to film, not all of which were necessarily works of highbrow culture. In 1923, however, he adapted two major works of classical Russian literature, Dostoyevsky's *Crime and Punishment* (which he directed himself) and Tolstoy's *The Power of Darkness* (which his brother Conrad put on the screen).

These two films were part of the 1923 program of Neumann Productions and were designed to gain this young company a wide reputation for art films. Later in the year Wiene directed a monumental religious film, *I.N.R.I.*, and at the same time, he was apparently working on a screenplay based on Shakespeare's *A Midsummer Night's*

Dream.[1] Thus, in this period Wiene directed four films – for two of which *(Raskolnikow* and *I.N.R.I.)* he wrote the scripts – and he provided his brother, Conrad Wiene, with the script for *Die Macht der Finsternis (The Power of Darkness)*. Of the films in this group, only *Raskolnikow* and *I.N.R.I.* are still available, and we have analyzed these in some detail.

DIE HÖLLISCHE MACHT *(The Infernal Power)* Die höllische Macht is the first film Robert Wiene made for his own Lionardo Company. Although a number of Wiene filmographies include the film, providing some filmographic data, we were not able to obtain any reviews in the major film journals of the time. According to the Censorship Board, the film must have been completed by 21 December 1922.[2] Beyond the names of the actors and the art director, no further significant information is available. Unfortunately, we cannot say whether *Die höllische Macht* was released at all.

RASKOLNIKOW The following passage from *Reclams deutsches Filmlexikon* of 1984 is representative of the conventional wisdom about Wiene's *Raskolnikow* in the post-World War II period:

> In spite of several more films in an expressionistic manner, Wiene's style did not gain in depth or development. *Raskolnikow* (1923; based on Fyodor Dostoyevsky's *Crime and Punishment*) did have the formal creative qualities of the *Caligari* film, but not its complexity of performance.[3]

This simplistic generalization about the film is surprising, since it reveals no progress whatsoever in the film criticism of *Raskolnikow* beyond the works of Siegfried Kracauer and Lotte Eisner in the 1940s and 1950s. In his *From Caligari to Hitler*, Kracauer simply refers to sets reminiscent of *Caligari*,[4] whereas Eisner credits the achievement of the film only to set designer Andrei Andreyev.[5] Richard B. Byrne in his 1962 doctoral dissertation, *German Cinematic Expressionism: 1919–1924*, does not analyze the film because he claims the film is "extant only in preservation negative form."[6]

A more thorough evaluation of the film is found in John D. Barlow's *German Expressionist Film* (1982). He recognizes the development of the sets beyond those found in *Caligari* due to the spatial depth that they provide:

> Space in *Raskolnikow* also has a more concrete reality. For example, in a scene at a restaurant we look past a table in the foreground, where the action is concentrated, into another room on a different level, at the back of which is a balcony – yet another level. The depth achieved in this shot

is striking, a surprising early example of deep focus, and it is made dynamic by the beams and angles of the walls and by the railing on the balcony, whose balusters are all leaning to the right.[7]

Barlow's evaluation of the deep focus is quite revealing. He fails to take note, however, of how Wiene's *mise-en-scène* makes use of it: After his conversation with Zamyotov, the police secretary, in which he taunts the officer, Raskolnikov leaves the restaurant, walks through the length of the room, goes up the stairs at the very back, and then looks back at the officer, whom we see in the foreground sitting with a puzzled look. Wiene films the scene with a long shot that allows the audience an objective and comparative view of the subjective states of both men.

Barlow is the first to recognize Wiene's filmic representation of Raskolnikov's psychological states: "Wiene uses dreams and subjective shots to put the viewer inside Raskolnikov's consciousness."[8] Moreover, in a number of examples he describes a harmony between the design of the sets and the psychological states that Wiene seeks to articulate.

By contrast, Ilona Brennicke and Joe Hembus's *Klassiker des deutschen Stummfilms* (1983) avoids any significant analysis. They content themselves with a plot summary, a lengthy quotation from Rudolf Kurtz, and the assertion that the film is expressionist.[9] Francis Courtade expresses dissatisfaction with the simplistic accounts of the film given by Kracauer and Eisner, but he himself discusses *Raskolnikow* only in terms of filmic expressionism by focusing primarily on Andreyev's stylized sets. He does not, however, analyze Wiene's interpretation of Dostoyevsky's novel both as scriptwriter and director.

Jürgen Kasten's *Der expressionistische Film* provides the most thorough analysis of *Raskolnikow.* In examining Wiene's adaptation of Dostoyevsky's material, he points out that in its narration the film deviates significantly from its source. For Wiene, he maintains, what is at issue is less the problem of the superior individual but more the psychological conflict between the deed and the penance that follows. Kasten concludes that, "In Wiene's staging concept that wants to do justice both to the literary content and the audience's expectations, there is an obvious aesthetic discrepancy between the psychologizing, almost realistically underplayed attitudes of the actors and, in the expressionist sense, the newly constructing architectural stylizations."[10]

Already before the release of the film the press called attention to the remarkable circumstances under which the film was being made. Peter Scharow, a member of Stanislawsky's Moscow Art Theater and himself in the cast, wrote an article more than a year prior to the

premiere, in which he described how the Russian ensemble cooperated to transform a classic Russian novel into film. For Scharow it
was a special challenge to apply the specific acting method of the
Stanislawsky troupe to the alienating work process of the film. The
ensemble considered this film an experiment that could succeed
only under the direction of an experienced and sensitive director:

> It was also important to assign the realization to artists who, without
> neglecting the milieu, would carry the content of the piece beyond the
> narrow concept of time. Therefore, we are happy to have found a direc-
> tor in Robert Wiene who not only joins us in his respect for the author,
> but whose art holds the prerequisites for achieving a production that will
> transcend dry reality, based on his previous creations and their break
> with naturalism.[11]

The film reviews that appeared after the film's premiere on 3
November 1923[12] in the Berlin Mozartsaal received *Raskolnikow* as a
masterpiece, and specifically cite Wiene's visual representation, the
sets of Andreyev, and the film debut of the Stanislawsky group. Similarly, the reviews applaud the visualization of Dostoyevsky's novel:

> Robert Wiene has fully exploited the tremendously powerful material in
> Dostoyevsky's fiction and emphasized the film effects … . As far as
> Wiene did the directing, he has also succeeded in finding a common
> course with the actors and in bringing out performances they fulfill with
> the strength inherent in the Moscow Art Theater.[13]

The review in the *LichtBildBühne* specifically cites Wiene's
ingenious visual representation of the investigating commissioner,
Porfiry Petrovich: "The most powerful, cleverly constructed and self-
contained performance was without doubt the portrayal of the investigating judge by Pawel Pawloff, in his study laid out like the web of
a spider, an extraordinarily ingenious idea, one that is typical of
Wiene's style."[14] *Der Kinematograph* also credits the screenplay with
"finding external expression for emotional frames of mind without
violating the author's intention by introducing alien elements … ."[15]

Although Kurt Pinthus, in his essay on *Raskolnikow* in *Das Tage-
Buch*, raises questions about the filming of Dostoyevsky novels altogether and urges directors to invent their own film stories rather than
adapt literary plots, he does grant that in this particular film Wiene
succeeded in capturing Dostoyevsky's spirit:

> Of all previous Dostoyevsky screen adaptations, this one written and
> directed by Wiene is the most successful … The whole thing is very excit-
> ing, it devours you; one can imagine Dostoyevsky's greatness and depth;
> one is shaken, exhausted, chastened. And that proves that more is

retained here than the criminal case and, on the other hand, that more cinematic effort went into this than mere expanded psychology; it proves that this mixture is possible in film.[16]

Béla Balázs, in his review in *Der Tag* of 28 December 1923, has a more general view on the film both as an example of expressionist cinema and as an adaptation of Dostoyevsky. He clearly sees the differences between *Caligari* and *Raskolnikow*: "On the cautious pretext of 'How an insane person sees the world,' Robert Wiene showed this in the *Caligari* film. In his *Raskolnikow* he has no pretext and, therefore, his expressionism is more cautious and restrained."[17] In his opinion, however, the expressionist stylization in the film is not consistent enough. As for the problem of the filmic adaptation of Dostoyevsky, Balázs doubts that the film medium as yet has the maturity and depth to convey the Dostoyevskian psychological universe. In this respect, *Raskolnikow*, despite the "sensitive directing of Robert Wiene, despite the excellent actors, despite individual scenes which belong to the best of the best" had to fail.[18]

Raskolnikow had an original length of 3,168 meters and hence a running time of more than two-and-one-half hours. However, as it seems, all prints that exist now are fragmentary. A restoration of the film was recently completed at the Netherlands Film Museum in Amsterdam. This print apparently approximates the length of the original very closely. Unfortunately, the restored print was not available to us for our study. We therefore base our analysis on four prints from Western and Eastern Europe, and the United States, two of which we could observe very closely. The one print stored in the Münchener Filmmuseum has a running time of seventy minutes at twenty-four frames-per-second and has part Russian, part Italian titles. The other print, which belongs to a private collector in the United States, has a running time of seventy-six minutes at twenty-four frames-per-second and has English titles. The two prints vary in the sequencing of events and in the contents. We calculate that both prints, put together, might amount to 85 to 90 minutes.

Moreover, a closer comparison of the two reveals that many of the medium and long shots differ slightly in camera angle, thus indicating that the film must have been shot with more than one camera. This procedure was not unusual in the silent film era and served the purpose of having more than one negative print in order to speed up the distribution process. In the case of *Raskolnikow*, however, the different camera angles sometimes affect the meaning of the images. For example, before and after the murder we see Raskolnikov enter and leave Aliona's house several times. Usually, he hesitates in front of the door for a second. The camera angle in the Amsterdam print shows Raskolnikov standing next to a lamppost near the door. However, this very same shot in the American print was taken by a camera placed further to the left, and Raskolnikov is thus put right behind the diagonal lamppost and is, so to speak, crossed out by it.

Wiene followed Dostoyevsky's novel very closely. For the novelist, the psychological condition of Raskolnikov was of central importance. For Wiene, that theme becomes the major motif of his film. With his title, *Crime and Punishment*, Dostoyevsky may have wanted to accentuate the significance of the moral dilemma raised by the circumstances associated with Raskolnikov's crime. By replacing that title with the name of the main character, Wiene seems to have shifted attention even more to Raskolnikov and his haunted psyche. Crucial to that haunted psyche is the old pawnbroker, Aliona Ivanovna, and her relationship to Raskolnikov's subjectivity before and after the murder.

Before the crime we see him thinking of her, and Wiene represents his thoughts with the following image: To the right is Aliona, very large, sitting on what seems to be heavy bags of money; to the left of her and below her we see a large crowd of people with their hands extended toward her with pleading gestures. She apparently responds by laughing uproariously and vindictively. In the Munich print this scene appears a second time, most likely as a dream.

After Raskolnikov faints at the police station, he falls into a delirious fever in which his torment is represented by a montage sequence with a huge head of Aliona in the center and a number of much smaller images of Aliona revolving about her in wild confusion. After his first meeting with the commissioner, Raskolnikov's psychological condition worsens and he relives the murder in a nightmare: The old man who had accused him of murder leads him up the stairs to the pawnbroker's apartment. There Raskolnikov finds an armchair covered by a blanket under which he discovers Aliona, who laughs at him maliciously. While he strikes her with the ax several times, she continues her wild laughter and with every blow new heads appear. Finally, a gigantic head of the old woman appears and fills the screen. As he attempts to flee, a mass of people confronts him at the stairway with everyone pointing accusing fingers at him. What these three visions have in common is the visual dominance of Aliona, which strikingly contrasts with her real-life situation where she appears small, repulsive, and unworthy. With these three sequences Wiene succeeds in demonstrating the overwhelming presence in Raskolnikov's consciousness of Aliona and his crime against her.

In the novel as well as in the film there are two further central characters, Porfiry Petrovich and Sonya Marmeladov. In the film there are three encounters between each of these two and Raskolnikov. Wiene creates visual leitmotifs for each of them: Petrovich, the hunter, who vigorously pursues Raskolnikov, is visually linked with a spider, which lurks in its web and waits for its prey, an image to which contemporary reviewers have often referred; Sonya's leitmotif is more subtle – the burning candle, with which she is associated, points to the illumination she will eventually bring Raskolnikov.

In the duel between Raskolnikov and Petrovich, the psychological vulnerability of the one and the psychological mastery of the other become apparent. In the film we know that the commissioner has reason to suspect Raskolnikov. Even before their first encounter, we see Petrovich in his office perusing Raskolnikov's treatise and examining his pawned pocket watch, which had been confiscated after the murder. Consequently, we are aware of his suspicions and can observe and understand his psychological manipulation of the student. Short, stocky, and extroverted, he radiates confidence in contrast to the tall, thin, brooding Raskolnikov, who becomes more and more unbalanced. Petrovich's last ploy to destabilize Raskolnikov by surprising him in his room succeeds but not according to his intellectual scheme. In his despair Raskolnikov turns to Sonya and takes refuge in her religiosity.

At the same time that Raskolnikov becomes entangled in Petrovich's machinations, he begins to be drawn into Sonya's sphere by feelings of an entirely different sort. Already in his first encounter with Sonya at her father's death, there is an immediate rapport based on a recognition of each other's suffering. After his first encounter with Petrovich and the ensuing nightmare, he visits Sonya in his distress. Visually, the most striking scene in this meeting is when the two sit side-by-side reading the biblical story of Lazarus by the light of Sonya's candle. From this point on, the unifying image of the film becomes Raskolnikov's growing religiosity inspired by Sonya's example.

A striking illustration of Sonya's association with Christianity is the image of her head bent slightly to the side surrounded by a bright aura reminiscent of Renaissance portraits of the Madonna. (This image appears in the Munich print and seems to represent Raskolnikov's point of view.) Another example of Wiene's strategy of identifying Raskolnikov with Christianity takes place in his room when he is startled by the stranger who had accused him of murder. He shrinks away and, with his back against a beam on the wall, his arms raised, he takes on the pose of the crucified Christ. This scene prefigures the final image of the film, which shows a Raskolnikov, ecstatic in his religious transfiguration. His face is illumined by an unreal light, and he crosses himself slowly, deliberately, turns his eyes upwards, and breathes a deep sigh that brings a look of calmness and release to his face. This image is not in the novel and marks a shift of emphasis in Wiene's interpretation of Dostoyevsky.

Wiene does not focus as much as the novelist on Raskolnikov's Nietzschean ideas, but stresses instead his distorted and anguished subjectivity. The sets by Andreyev contribute much to this interpretation of the novel. Moreover, the many close-ups of Raskolnikov's tormented face heighten the link between the sets and his subjectivity.

The Stanislawsky troupe likewise contributed much to an authentic conversion of this novel to film. Besides the language barrier – which was solved by Assistant Director Mark Sorkin who served as an interpreter – the main problem was, of course, adapting the Stanislawsky method for stage actors to the completely different demands a film actor has to fulfill. The contemporary reviews lauded the result. From today's point of view, the authenticity of the entire enterprise is due mostly to the endeavors of the Russian actors.

DER PUPPENMACHER VON KIANG–NING (The Doll Maker of Kiang-Ning) This Lionardo production had its premiere in Berlin in November 1923. Once again Carl Mayer was the scriptwriter and Willy Hameister was the cameraman. César Klein, who had built the sets for *Genuine*, was the art director together with Walter Reger. The lead role was played by Werner Krauss.

Somewhere in China an artist tries to fulfill his creative urge by making life-size dolls. He creates them and is enchanted and captivated by them. In the grip of his obsession, he brings his favorite doll to a high-society gala celebration to exhibit it proudly. As a prank, a living mannequin more beautiful than the artist's favorite doll is placed in competition with it. Shattered by what seems to him to be his artistic failure, the artist destroys his work and attempts to seize the living doll for himself. The crowd rescues the woman and the deranged artist plunges to his death.[19]

From a team of film people as experienced as the one enumerated above, a successful and exciting film could have been expected. Indeed, the available stills support such an expectation. However, the reviewers took the film apart with rare unanimity. Apparently, what was unforgivable about the film was that it tried to represent Chinese culture with German actors in Berlin and failed. What seemed to complicate the process even further was that the actors, in trying to represent the gestures of mannequins – and Chinese mannequins at that – became confused and conveyed neither filmic language coherently.[20]

Thematically, the exotic milieu, the blending of Western and Eastern cultures, and the dichotomy between art and life suggest a fascinating filmic discourse, a judgment that unfortunately can be corroborated only by an examination of the stills. It is puzzling that the reviewers repeatedly cite the alleged unfilmic elements in this film. This dilemma, however, cannot be resolved until the film is found.

I.N.R.I. In post-World War II film criticism there are only few and scanty comments about *I.N.R.I.* Kracauer briefly alludes to the film's religious content, which is reason enough for him to reject it with contempt: "The political significance of many a religious conversion could not have been exhibited more directly."[21] Charles Ford, in his *Der Film und der Glaube,* cites the film as the first aesthetically valuable film version of the story of Christ, but strangely enough numbers it among the expressionist films.[22] Ilona Brennicke and Joe Hembus, in their *Klassiker des Deutschen Stummfilms,* critique *I.N.R.I.* for its political tendency but for all their comments rely on a single film review of 1923 in which the highlights of the film are discussed.[23]

Indeed, early on the contemporary film press had attracted a public interest in *I.N.R.I.* Already on 27 January 1923 the *LichtBildBühne* announced that the rights to Peter Rosegger's novel of the same title

I.N.R.I. Director: Robert Wiene (1923)
working photo – Grigori Chmara (left) Robert Wiene (last on the right)

(1905) had been purchased by Neumann Productions for filming. A week earlier the same journal had reported that *I.N.R.I.* would have its premiere on Christmas Day in "all major cities of the world." On 19 April 1923 (even before the shooting of the film had started) Neumann Productions had purchased full-page advertisements in the film journals in which a summary of the contents of *I.N.R.I.: Ein Film der Menschheit (A Film of Humanity)* was given.[24]

From this point on, there are frequent, detailed reports concerning the shooting of the film. The *Film-Kurier* covered the mass scenes twice, on 23 July and 28 September 1923. Wiene is described as the master of 600 extras, whom he had photographed with three different cameras. The reporter especially referred to Wiene's strategy of having "the magic of the Jesus figure" become manifest in the reactions of the masses that surround him. On 19 December 1923 advertisements in the *Film-Kurier* refer to the film's premiere on Christmas Day. Of course, *I.N.R.I.* did not have premieres in all the major cities of the world but at least in "thirty-four of the major metropolitan areas of Europe."

In an interview with the film journalist Paul Ickes, the producer of the film, Hans Neumann, relates the film to Germany's status as a defeated nation:

> We are a people defeated in war, many foreign countries are accusing us of barbarism and quarrelsomeness, we are slandered! So I hope that the film *I.N.R.I.* will open the world's eyes to the fact that we have grasped the true sense of Christian humanity: The irreconcilability among nations must disappear; we have common human goals before us, all of us! And that is why I have called my film a film of humaneness.[25]

In the same interview, Neumann summarizes the controversial frame story of the film that provides the link between the life of Christ and the European situation after World War I. The significance of that frame, which is unfortunately not available in the extant fragments of the film, will be discussed later.

The press campaign for *I.N.R.I.* had set the stage for the film's reception. After its premiere, the film was reviewed in film journals and newspapers throughout Germany. Neumann Productions published a brochure in which quotations from fifty-seven of those reviews appeared. Naturally, the tone in these statements is positive and laudatory. Nevertheless, it is striking that the appreciation of Wiene's direction, the acting of the eminent cast, and the spectacular sets and mass scenes are frequently cited.

In the *LichtBildBühne* the reviewer Hildebrandt stresses Wiene's contributions to the film's success:

The strong, enduring impression the film made on the audience on Christ-mas Day proved that Wiene found the right way. Without lapsing into the mystical, he succeeded in casting the majesty of the Christ figure in a memorable form. He consciously devoted his admirable art of directing, which we already know from the *Caligari* film, to his quite realistic con-cept of the suffering and death of the Savior. With very unobtrusive and, thus, all the more effective means, he succeeds in projecting the person of Christ as the dominating figure in all of the mass scenes. Whether he is walking through the excited masses after the sermon on the mount or whether Pilate is showing him to the crowd beside Barrabas, he is always at the center of events, draws all eyes to himself. On the whole, the mass scenes are brilliantly directed: differently than Lubitsch, but equally well, Wiene knows how to demonstrate the force of large crowds.[26]

The reviewer of *Der Film* calls attention to the political and social significance of the film:

Robert Wiene and Hans Neumann are both the fathers of this film, and Robert Wiene as the director plays the main part if the grand scheme of what he wanted was actually realized. Starting from the basic story, he took care to integrate the faithful narration, the allegory of the Jesus fig-ure, into the film events, so it projects itself as a memento, an appeal to brotherly love, including in areas of global political and economic con-cern. The director had a difficult task to accomplish, and only with the absolute restraint of the performances for the sake of the overall purpose was it possible to succeed.[27]

Our examination of the film is based on two prints: one from Det Danske Filmmuseum in Copenhagen, a fragment of about fifty-five minutes with Czech titles,[28] and one from the Österreiches Film-archiv in Vienna with the original German jump titles.[29] This print runs approximately seventy minutes and is probably the most exten-sive version of the film currently available. The all-important frame story gives the biblical story its explicitly contemporary impact; it is missing in this and all known archival copies. With its monumental dimensions, *I.N.R.I.* stands out in Wiene's oeuvre. It is his longest film (3,444 meters), with thousands of extras and a cast of star actors that was never even approximated in any of his other films.

In his visual presentations of the major characters – the two Marys, the disciples, and Jesus – Wiene largely follows traditional Renaissance pictorial conventions, but he subverts this popular imagery by his representation of the Judas character, which radi-cally breaks with the biblical account. In this account Wiene relies on Rosegger's novel and the contemporary German political situa-tion more than on the biblical story. The treacherous Judas, who betrays his master for thirty pieces of silver, becomes a passionate

I.N.R.I. Director: Robert Wiene (1923)
working photo: The sets in the Staaken Studio

political activist in the film, an underground rebel, who is devoted to
Jesus because he expects him to lead the Jewish uprising against the
Roman army of occupation. His betrayal of Jesus is not an act of
greed but rather a political strategy calculated to force Jesus into a
role as a revolutionary leader. Judas sees only political value in
Jesus's charisma; the money that is pressed into his hands takes him
completely by surprise. All that remains of the biblical account of
Judas is the kiss.

In the first half of the film, Judas very soon becomes the film's
dominant figure along with Jesus. Wiene makes it very clear in the
beginning of the film that Judea is under a cruel Roman occupation,
that the people of Judea are suffering, and that Judas is a leader in an
underground movement to overthrow Roman rule. When he hears
reports of Jesus, he immediately perceives in him the future charismatic leader of the Jewish people and without hesitation joins him as
a devoted follower.

Visually, Wiene privileges Judas over all other disciples. He is
never seen as an integral part of the faithful but is usually seen standing aside, alone, watchful, passionately following his master's words,
which sets him apart from all the others. A number of times he is
seen standing across from Jesus as if he were his antagonist. In contrast to the other disciples, who are shown primarily in group por-

traits around Jesus, Wiene highlights Judas's prominence by giving only him a scene where he is alone with Jesus and by presenting only him outside the direct vicinity of Jesus. Moreover, Judas is shown in a number of close-ups, more often, in fact, than any of the other disciples. In this way, Judas is perceived both in the plot and through his visual presentation as a devoted follower and at the same time as the most independent disciple, who pursues his own political agenda.

In contrast to the New Testament account where Judas is at best a peripheral figure, in the film he acquires a central role, second only to Jesus. Moreover, though he fails, he never loses our sympathy. Jesus fulfills his mission and Judas does not; but he never becomes the story's villain. We understand his idealistic motivation and can sympathize with his misguided expectations for a savior in the political rather than the spiritual arena. For Wiene, then, Judas becomes the central discourse for the film. *I.N.R.I.* was made primarily to tell Judas's story and only secondarily to retell the biblical narrative.

The explanation for the centrality of Judas in the film can be found in the frame story, which though inspired by the Rosegger novel of 1905, relates to the contemporary political situation in Germany in 1923. Since the film version of the frame is apparently lost, it must be reconstructed from reliable sources. The producer Hans Neumann gave the following summary: The carpenter Ferleitner, an anarchist and nihilist, wishes to serve mankind by assassinating a high government official. He is arrested, put on trial, and condemned to death. Ferleitner considers himself a modern Christ who must sacrifice his life for his mission. The night before his execution he attempts to attain clarity about his idealism, which he feels is misunderstood by society, by writing out the life of Jesus. In so doing he recognizes his error and realizes that salvation cannot come through acts of violence but only through self-sacrifice and love of one's neighbor. With this new clarity about his own deed and the meaning of the Christian gospel, he accepts the death sentence with composure.[30]

Judas parallels Ferleitner in the frame story. Like Judas, Ferleitner is seen as a sympathetic but misguided idealist or fanatic. Wiene created the Judas figure to portray the dilemma of a political activist in Germany in the year 1923. There was no shortage of self-acclaimed idealists and no shortage of assassinations then. Wiene saw no solution in their fanaticism, no matter how well intentioned it was. For that reason, he turned to the Christian gospel as a possible solution for Germany in that year of crisis, 1923.

The frame story, which was the primary reason for the elaboration of the Judas role far beyond what is found in the New Testament accounts, was the source of some controversy before the

Censorship Board.[31] Although representatives from the Christian churches raised no objection, the spokesman for the Commission on the Supervision of Public Law and Order (Reichskommissariat für die Überwachung der öffentlichen Ordnung und Sicherheit) opposed the frame on the grounds that political radicals of both the left and the right might find support in a sympathetic portrayal of a political assassin:

> I have to say that the film could influence a not inconsequential number of our people in such a way that it would encourage them to intervene, like this man, in the political circumstances. Therefore, from the standpoint of public order and security, I would like to propose not to show the film in this form, since certain people's ideas would be reinforced through such a film.[32]

The Commission accordingly recommended fundamental changes in the frame story and for that reason the author and director of the film was summoned. Wiene categorically rejected the recommended changes: "he could not make changes that would eliminate the political murder from the film, since the sense of the whole film would thus be distorted and destroyed."[33] Wiene's objection to changes in his work was not solely on aesthetic grounds; he quite deliberately wanted to relate the film to the contemporary political situation in Germany in 1923. After all, the assassinations of Matthias Erzberger, Walther Rathenau, and many others had contributed so much to the chaos of Weimar Germany.

Although the film in its final form was approved four days after the hearing, we have reason to believe that the film was shown in Germany and especially abroad primarily without the frame, especially at Christmas time, to highlight the story of Jesus. This may account for the fact that in film histories the political significance of *I.N.R.I.* is not recognized and that the film, when it is acknowledged at all, is perceived as a conventional treatment of the New Testament.

DIE MACHT DER FINSTERNIS (The Power of Darkness) Apparently both the director Conrad Wiene and the scriptwriter Robert Wiene stayed with the original literary source as much as possible, given that they were working with an authentic Russian theater ensemble whose players knew the text intimately. As in the plot of *Raskolnikow*, we have here a story of guilt and penance:

> The story centers around the character of Nikita, a dissolute self-harassed young man of the village, veering from sexual excesses to drunken despondency as his erotic nature drives him. He is loved by Akulina, the wife of the villager, Peter. Their passion is a wrecking one to both since

Nikita's nature urges him to other girls of the village, particularly Akulina's younger sister, and this spectacle of infidelity tears at Akulina's heart. Finally, in order to get Nikita to herself, she is involved in the poisoning of her husband. Then she discovers that her sister is to bear a child and that Nikita is the father. She forces him to kill the new born infant and bury it with his own hands. After this deed, when the villagers are gathered to celebrate his nuptials with Akulina, remorse strikes Nikita down, and ... he makes full confession of his sins. It is on this note of the ecstasy of repentance and expiation that the film closes.[34]

The film received universal acclaim as a contribution to film art, though some reviewers doubted that it would appeal to the broad populace. The Russian actors of the ensemble were lauded for their skill and their authentic representation of the Russian mentality, and the set designers were given credit for their effective reproduction of the milieu of a Russian village.[35] The reviewers were unanimous in their view that the film had done justice to Tolstoy's play.

Notes

1. *Die LichtBildBühne* 17, no. 14 (1924): 23. This project did not materialize for Robert Wiene. Hans Neumann directed the film in 1925 based on a script written by Neumann himself and Hans Behrendt. See *Kino-Journal*, no. 761 (1925): 18.
2. According to Gerhard Lamprecht in *Deutsche Stummfilme* (Berlin: SDK, 1970), *Die höllische Macht* was evaluated by the Berlin Censorship Board on this date.
3. Herbert Holba, Günter Knorr, and Peter Spiegel, *Reclams deutsches Filmlexikon* (Stuttgart: Reclam, 1984), 408.
4. Siegfried Kracauer, *From Caligari to Hitler: A Psychological History of the German Film* (Princeton, N.J.: Princeton University Press, 1947), 109.
5. Lotte H. Eisner, *The Haunted Screen: Expressionism in the German Cinema and the Influence of Max Reinhardt* (Berkeley and Los Angeles: University of California Press, 1973), 27.
6. Richard B. Byrne, "German Cinematic Expressionsim, 1919–1924" (Ph.D. State University of Iowa, 1962), 7.
7. John D. Barlow, *German Expressionist Film* (Boston: Twayne, 1982), 56.
8. Ibid., 57.
9. Ilona Brennicke and Joe Hembus, *Klassiker des deutsche Stummfilms, 1910–1930* (Munich: Goldmann, 1983), 212f.
10. Jürgen Kasten, *Der expressionistische Film: Abgefilmtes Theater oder avantgardistisches Erzählkino? Eine stil-, produktions- und rezeptionsgeschichtliche Untersuchung* (Münster: MAkS Publikationen, 1990), 86.
11. *Filmschau*, 1 August 1922.
12. The film must have been completed by the end of 1922. It passed the Censorship Board on 9 March 1923. We do not know why it was held back for more than six months.

13. *Der Film* 8, nos. 43–44 (1923): 24.
14. *Die LichtBildBühne* 16, no. 4 (1923): 13.
15. *Der Kinematograph* 17, no. 872 (1923): 7.
16. *Das Tagebuch* 4, no. 46 (1923).
17. According to Béla Balázs, *Schriften zum Film. Erster Band: Der sichtbare Mensch. Kritiken und Aufsätze 1922–1926* (Berlin: Henschel, 1982), 262.
18. Ibid., 297f.
19. *Reichsfilmblatt*, nos. 45–47 (1923).
20. Ibid.; *Die LichtBildBühne* 16, no. 44 (1923): 20; *Der Film-Kurier* 5, no. 248 (1923).
21. Kracauer, *From Caligari to Hitler*, 109.
22. Charles Ford, *Der Film und der Glaube* (Nürnberg: Glock und Lutz, 1955), 76.
23. Brennicke and Hembus, *Klassiker des deutsche Stummfilms*, 196; they cite Friedrich Sternthal's review in *Das Tagebuch*, 29 December 1923.
24. According to an advertisement in *Die LichtBildBühne*, 23 June 1923, the subtitle of the film was changed to *A Film of Humaneness* "to eliminate any propagandistic presumptuousness."
25. *Die Filmwoche*, 2 December 1923.
26. *Die LichtBildBühne*, 29 December 1923.
27. *Der Film*, 6 January 1924.
28. This version is undoubtedly based on one of the prints in the possession of the Czech film archive in Prague; they also possess three reels of unmounted *I.N.R.I.* material.
29. This print, a negative on nitrate material, was delivered to the Austrian Filmarchive in 1983 by a Mr. Dörfler of the Viennese Haydn Cinema. Our gratitude is due to Mr. Josef Navratil of the Austrian Filmarchive, who made the film available for this study.
30. *Die Filmwoche*, 2 December 1923. According to another source, Ferleitner is not executed but dies in his cell, suggesting a divine forgiveness for his crime; *Die LichtBildBühne*, 29 December 1923, p. 15.
31. In fact, in Ireland *I.N.R.I.* was banned precisely for the radically different portrayal of Judas; cf. *Der Film* 10, no. 34 (1925): 21.
32. Minutes of the Proceedings of the Censorship Board, Berlin, 15 November 1923. We are grateful to Eberhard Spiess for making this unpublished manuscript of the DIF available to us.
33. Ibid.
34. *National Board of Reviews Magazine* (September 1927).
35. *Die LichtBildBühne* 17, no. 71 (1924): 16.

Chapter 6

✦ ✦ ✦

THE VIENNESE FILMS 1924–1926

After his successes with Neumann Productions, Wiene was called to Vienna by one of the leading Austrian film companies, Pan Film. At the time, the Austrian film industry was in a severe crisis, and Pan Film evidently hoped to improve its fortunes by attracting one of Germany's most successful directors.[1] During this crisis, Pan Film remained one of the few internationally active film companies, with its seat in Vienna and branches in Berlin, Prague, Budapest, Warsaw, Bucharest, Zagreb, and Cracow.[2] At Pan Film Wiene was appointed as *Oberregisseur* and apparently was granted the right to co-produce his films as Robert Wiene Productions.[3]

At this point Wiene was at the peak of his film career, with a number of artistic and commercial successes to his credit. A number of film journalists interviewed Wiene and observed his work on the set. The American theater review *The Billboard* devoted two issues to an in-depth interview with him. Both issues announced on their front covers the story entitled, "Courage in the Movies," by Barnet Braverman.[4]

Of the five films Wiene made in Vienna from 1924 to 1926, three have survived, *Orlacs Hände (Orlac's Hands)*, *Der Rosenkavalier*, and *Die Königin vom Moulin Rouge (The Queen of Moulin Rouge)*. We shall discuss them in some detail.

PENSION GROONEN (Boarding House Groonen)   In Wiene's first film in Vienna he returned to the light-comedy genre. The film script was prepared by Pan Film Company's Ludwig Nerz, who also wrote the scripts for three other of Wiene's Viennese films. Although the film was completed in 1924, the Viennese premiere did not take place

Notes for this section begin on page 135.

Robert Wiene, time
and place unknown

until 9 January 1925. Whether *Pension Groonen* was distributed in
Germany is doubtful.

In the film, the destitute count Nikolaus Groonen marries the
daughter of an American multimillionaire businessman. His wife's
generous dowry allows him to continue his elegant lifestyle, which,
among other things, includes a number of flirtations. However, once
the money runs out and the father-in-law – whom in his arrogance
the count has not deigned to meet – declines any further payments,
the count is confronted with the crisis of his life. His practical American wife finds a unique solution by turning their castle into a boarding house, which she makes into a success by taking charge of the
entire operation. In the meantime, the count's continued flirtations
make her feel neglected, a complaint she conveys to her father back
home. Her brother Tom is sent to Vienna to scout out the situation.
He takes a room in Pension Groonen under an assumed name and
promptly falls in love with his sister-in-law, the beautiful countess
Hedwig. Since neither the count nor his sister know Tom's identity,
a number of misunderstandings and confusions develop. The count
sees in him a competitor for his wife's affections and in his jealousy

discovers once again his love for his wife. A duel is supposed to set-
tle the competition between Groonen and Tom, but it does not take
place once Hedwig confesses her love for Tom. At the end there are
two happy pairs, and the newly arrived father's aggravations immediately melt upon seeing his grandchildren.[5]
The reviewers unanimously liked *Pension Groonen* for its effective
portrayal of light-comedy action. *Das Kino-Journal* described the film
as, "A really original film that holds a tasteful middle course between
comedy and drama and conveys a tinge of parody through subtle
burlesque highlights."[6]

ORLACS HÄNDE (Orlac's Hands)   *Orlacs Hände* was based on Maurice
Renard's novel *Les Mains d'orlac*, which had been translated into German by Norbert Jacques in 1922. The scriptwriter Ludwig Nerz and
the director deviated from the novel in significant respects to make an
effective psychological film plot out of a trivial and fairly confused
novel.[7] Contemporary film critics considered *Orlacs Hände* to be one
of the major German-language film releases of the year 1925. They
hailed Wiene's *mise-en-scène*, Nerz's script, and the acting of Conrad
Veidt, Fritz Kortner, and Alexandra Sorina. Apparently, the reviewer
for *Die Filmwelt* had visited Wiene on the set during the shooting of
Orlacs Hände and gives the following portrait of Wiene at work:

> Director Robert Wiene has created a unique atmosphere in this film. He
> has succeeded in uniting two film principles: suspense-packed action
> and subtle psychology. The train disaster is just as brilliant an achieve-
> ment as, for instance, the scenes of Orlac's delusion. Incidentally, those
> who have ever seen this director at work – concentrated, highly tense,
> extracting from every actor everything he can give, and supervising the
> scene to the minutest detail – know that every Wiene film has to become
> a masterpiece.[8]

The *LichtBildBühne* concentrated more on the adaptation aspect of
the film and highlighted the representation of the fantastic in an otherwise realistic environment,[9] while the *Film-Kurier* noted "that one
has found the right director for the rendering of the mysterious psychology and the suspense-laden story of this film. The enigma of
man's fate is a subject that Robert Wiene knows how to deal with."[10]
The *Deutsche Allgemeine Zeitung* uses *Orlacs Hände* to reflect on Wiene's
position within the German film industry in general: "Wiene matches
Lubitsch, Murnau, Lange [sic], and Grune, surpasses them in consistent scene sequencing, and forces Veidt, Sorina, and Fritz Kortner to
play together in a way that seems to have been last achieved with
Jannings and Bergner in *Nju*."[11]

These quotations from the contemporary film press demonstrate most clearly that *Orlacs Hände* was not simply considered a failed attempt at imitating *Caligari*, as later commentators unanimously assert, but quite the contrary: it was seen as an original work of art by a skillful director whose oeuvre could be compared with the best. Only post-World War II criticism attempted to describe *Orlacs Hände* as no more than an imitation of *Caligari*'s expressionism. Siegfried Kracauer affords the film only a brief mention in a footnote,[12] and Lotte Eisner examines a few selected scenes that serve to substantiate her thesis about expressionist elements in the German silent film.[13] Walter Fritz in his 1969 history of the Austrian film makes only a passing reference to the film.[14]

Orlacs Hände (Orlac's Hands) Director: Robert Wiene (1924) –
in the foreground: Conrad Veidt, Robert Wiene, Alexandra Sorina

John D. Barlow discusses the film only briefly and feels obliged, in support of his overall thesis, to find and describe expressionist elements: "This film contains a potpourri of typically expressionistic gestures – superimpositions, dark streets, shadows, the supernatural, exaggerated acting, actors in trances, a mysterious mansion with threatening corridors – but most of it is filmed in a basically naturalistic style."[15] This comment, however, is characteristic of the ambivalence of Barlow's treatment of *Orlacs Hände* as an expressionist film. The film's motifs seem to fit his thesis, whereas the representation of those motifs does not. Consequently, he exaggerates the significance of the expressionist motifs and neglects the many nonexpressionist elements of the film, such as the naturalist camera style:

> The train wreck, although staged entirely with a naturalistic set, is shot to highlight its disorder. As in the set of *Raskolnikow*, there are no parallel lines. We find instead an emphasis on crisscrossings and oblique angles, all shot in a shadowy atmosphere, with steam from the rescue train floating through the transecting searchlight beams.[16]

Contemporary critics praised this very scene for its realism.[17] With his bias in favor of expressionism, Barlow devalues the naturalist elements; that the psychological motifs unify the film even more than the stylization of the décors does not seem to occur to him.

Francis Courtade has analyzed *Orlacs Hände* a little more exhaustively. He maintains that though the film has expressionist elements, that alone does not suffice to describe it. In contrast to Barlow, Courtade grants that the film is only partially expressionist, with many realist motifs. Hence, in the train wreck he rightly sees an example of realist cinematography. Nevertheless, once again, the theme of his book forces him to limit himself to examining the film's expressionist elements. Consequently, he also is misled about Wiene's artistic design. It is interesting to note that at this point Courtade, though necessarily limited in his view of Wiene's oeuvre, pays homage to his originality as a filmmaker. He hails Wiene's ingenuity in these four "expressionist" films (*Caligari, Genuine, Raskolnikov, Orlac's Hands*), but is, of course, not able to appreciate their role within his total career as a director.[18]

There is a discernible tendency in modern German film historiography to reevaluate the canon of German expressionist films with the result that expressionism in the film medium is receiving a more precise definition. The critique of *Orlacs Hände* is a case in point. While Barlow felt obligated to look for expressionism in the film where there was none, and while Courtade had already become more cautious about the film's expressionism, Jürgen Kasten in his study on expressionist film[19] does not even mention *Orlacs Hände* at all, and rightly so. Consequently, the tendency of post-World War II film criticism to take *Caligari* as a standard by which to measure all of Wiene's later films is no longer valid and surely does not apply to *Orlacs Hände*. Indeed, it is high time to discuss the thematic, formal, and plot-related differences from *Caligari*.

The plot revolves around the famous piano virtuoso, Paul Orlac, who loses both of his hands in a train wreck. Urged by Orlac's wife, the skilled surgeon Dr. Serral transplants the hands of Vasseur, a recently decapitated murderer. Orlac recovers physically very soon, but becomes vulnerable to fantasies about his hands, which lead him to become estranged from his wife and from himself. A mysterious stranger pursues him and reinforces his imagined fear that his hands could drive him to commit murder. Orlac can no longer play the piano, the main source of his livelihood. His wife's attempt to secure material support from Orlac's father fails. Orlac then visits his father, but it is too late; he finds his father murdered, stabbed with the very knife that he had previously found stuck in his door. Convinced that he is responsible for his father's death, Orlac grows hysterical, almost to the point of insanity. In this condition Nera, the real murderer, approaches him and attempts to blackmail him. With the help of the police and his wife's maid, Regine, Orlac's innocence and Nera's complicity are established, and Orlac is reconciled with himself and his wife.

We have had two fragmentary versions of the film available to us for our examination: a 16mm print provided by the Österreiches Filmarchiv and a different 16mm print obtained from the Rohauer Collection. The latter is even more incomplete than the former; still, it contains scenes that are vital for the understanding of the plot. *Orlacs Hände* would be a simple crime story were it not for Paul Orlac's growing derangement, which is worsened by Nera's claim that occult phenomena are involved. Each one by itself permits the viewer to gain an overall grasp of the plot. However, only when both are taken in unison do we gain an insight into the rapidly moving events that lead the conflict to clear resolution. All is obscured through Orlac's growing derangement, as reinforced by Nera's reference to occult phenomena. However, normal police work and the unraveling of ordinary human motivation yield rational explanations and a resolution of the plot within a realistic framework. Nera can develop his conspiracy against Orlac only with the help of an accomplice, Regine, who is under his spell, but who betrays him to the police at the very end. Only the Rohauer print reveals the motivation behind this turn of events. Regine, who lives in slavish fear of Nera, is at the same time devotedly in love with Paul Orlac. In the end her love wins out over her fear.

What distinguishes *Orlacs Hände* is the complex psychological motivation of all its major characters. Paul Orlac, the introverted artist stunned by the trauma of his accident, becomes unusually vulnerable to his own fears and anxieties as well as to the diabolical manipulations of the unscrupulous Nera. Once enmeshed in Nera's network, his artistic sensibilities do the rest and he becomes helpless and uncommunicative. His counterpart, Nera, is his opposite in every respect. Cool, calculating, cunning, he is the classical villain. With astonishing intelligence and resourcefulness, he establishes a strategy for driving Orlac out of his mind and into dependence on him. He is in complete control of events until Regine betrays him. Focusing entirely on his victim, Orlac, Nera fails to notice that Regine has ceased to be totally subservient to him. Regina's betrayal so surprises him that he too loses control and bursts into rage, but only briefly. As soon as he recognizes that there is no way out, he regains his composure and playfully places himself at the disposal of the police.

Orlac's wife, Yvonne – accustomed to playing the loving, submissive wife – is transformed by her husband's adversity into a strong, resourceful, active woman. It is she who rescues him from the train wreck; she who persuades the surgeon to undertake the operation; she who goes to the father; she who takes her husband to the police; and, finally, she who comes with the contrite maid to unmask Nera. Once Orlac is restored to normalcy, she resumes her traditional role. Regine, with her small yet significant role, also reveals an interesting psychological constellation. Whereas Yvonne's submissiveness follows social conventions and thus can be suspended temporarily, Regine is entirely characterized by her submissiveness. Nera, recognizing Regine's vulnerability, dominates and manipulates her to the core. Most of the prints of *Orlacs Hände* available in Europe do not reveal that Regine also cares for Orlac. Only in the Rohauer print does the conflict between her fear of Nera and her love for Orlac become apparent. Thus, only in this version does the resolution of the plot, which otherwise appears as a *deus ex machina* ending, become psychologically plausible.

Only the father remains a psychological mystery in the film as we know it. His strange appearance, his peculiar domicile, his odd servant, his rejection of his son and daughter-in-law are not adequately rooted in the exposition of the narrative. On the one hand, this may be due to the incompleteness of the available prints of the film; on the other hand, neither the contemporary reviews nor the film programs hint at an explanation of the father. Only the novel gives at least a clue. There he is revealed as an eccentric spiritist who disapproves of his son's profession and marriage.

Although the father's spiritist dabblings are not revealed in the film, the gothic, mysterious architecture of his house creates a fitting background for his musings. The father's sphere, thus defined, is decisively in contrast to the son's sphere as represented in the latter's modernist home. The contrast between the two is further accentuated by the fact that although both homes are shown from the outside several times, the father's is seen only by night and Orlac's only by day. What is perceived externally only as a visual contrast between father and son, is intensified internally, that is to say, psychologically, in the father-son conflict. That conflict clearly emerges in the conversation between the father and Orlac's wife. His blunt rejection of pleas for financial help is evidence of a long-standing feud between father and son. When Orlac finds his father murdered with the dagger he had discovered in his own home, he feels himself guilty of the crime. At this point two conflicts merge: the psychological conflict between father and son and the criminological duel between Orlac and Nera. From the fragments we have examined, the Orlac/Nera conflict emerges only toward the end of the film. However, from the titles listed on the censorship card,[20] it can be gathered that the conflict breaks out much earlier. Consequently, the rational resolution of the plot at the end does not have the appearance of a *deus ex machina* strategy but has a logic that is deduced from the course of the action. The complicity between Nera and the maid, Regina, is indicated in the Rohauer print, but becomes much clearer when we draw on the titles from the censorship card. Moreover, the criminological work of the police then becomes consistent with the final rational elucidation of the plot.[21]

The underlying unity of the film does lie in the duel between Nera and Orlac. It is Nera's manipulations that provide an impetus for the unfolding of the plot beyond Orlac's accident and recovery. Nera is revealed as a highly intelligent arch-villain who is a master of psychological techniques in the tradition of Dr. Mabuse. In the film he expertly and diabolically exploits the weaknesses and dependencies of the maid, Regine, and of the traumatized Orlac. In the final exposition it becomes clear that Nera had also ruthlessly exploited his friend Vasseur by faking evidence that led to the latter's conviction and execution.

Although the aesthetic unity of *Orlacs Hände* is apparent to a contemporary viewer of the film, the plot's consistency and continuity is not self-evident from a screening of one of the fragmentary prints alone. It can be observed, though, in a reconstruction of the film undertaken in 1996 by Matthias Knop of the Deutsches Institut für Filmkunde. While this print is still not entirely complete, it brings to life a surprising example of an early psychothriller.

DER LEIBGARDIST (The Bodyguard) The film's plot revolves around a jealous actor who suspects his new wife, an actress herself, of being unfaithful. To put her to the test, he disguises himself as an officer in the king's guard and begins to court her vigorously. Soon he is invited to her box in the very theater where he must portray Hamlet on the stage. What ensues are a number of quick changes of clothes so that he can alternately play both roles. Before long she favors him with a kiss, which is all the proof he needs to confirm his suspicions of her infidelity. Fortunately, a mutual friend discovers the truth about the actor's strategy and helps the wife persuade her husband that she had already known of his subterfuge before the kiss. The crisis is averted and a reconciliation takes place with good humor.[22]

Most reviewers were delighted with Wiene's film version of Ferenc Molnár's highly successful comedy. The *Reichsfilmblatt* noted, "'There are no dead spots, there is always contact, an electrical spark, between the actors. Polished, brilliant directing that has achieved its goal: It has become a witty feuilleton in pictures."[23] Friedrich Porges's magazine *Mein Film* saw in *Der Leibgardist* evidence that the Austrian film could well compete with foreign imports:

> Robert Wiene, who is among the film directors with the most artistic, refined feeling and whose real strength is the minute creation of the psychological scene, made a film from Molnár's *Guard Officer*, here in Vienna with a cast that counts as the best of film and stage. This Austrian film of the *Guard Officer* by Pan Productions is of a refinement that does credit to the director, but beyond the excellence of the director and his cast reveals technical perfection in film production, which proves that in Austria, too, films can be produced that are not just equal to foreign productions but even surpass them in artistic and technical quality.[24]

All the more surprising is the dissenting opinion in the *LichtBild-Bühne* where the reviewer faults the film for doing justice neither to the original play nor to the film medium in the adaptation.[25]

DER ROSENKAVALIER Of the five films Wiene made for the Pan Film Company in Vienna, *Der Rosenkavalier* (1925/26) was undoubtedly the most outstanding. The film version of the well-known opera by Richard Strauss was made by Wiene after consultation with the composer and the librettist, Hugo von Hofmannsthal. According to the initial agreement, Hofmannsthal was to write a film script and Strauss was to compose a musical score appropriate to the film. Apparently, the Pan Film Company tried from the very beginning to link the film with the opera in a number of ways: besides Strauss and Hofmannsthal, the set designer, Alfred Roller, who had already designed the opera for the stage, participated in the film, as did Michael Bohnen, who was cast in the role of Ochs von Lerchenau, which he had already played in numerous stage productions. More-

Friedrich Féher, Michael Bohnen, Robert Wiene, Richard Strauss, and
Carmen Castellieri during the shooting of *Der Rosenkavalier*
Director: Robert Wiene (1926)

over, the premiere of the film was scheduled to take place in the
Dresden opera house on 10 January 1926, the very place where the
opera had premiered nearly fifteen years earlier on 26 January 1911.

Hofmannsthal was working on a *Rosenkavalier* film script as early
as 1923.[26] According to his letter to Strauss dated 1 January 1925,
there had been negotiations with Wiene and Pan Film Company for
some time and both had accepted his terms. Hofmannsthal cites a
number of reasons to persuade Strauss to join him in this enterprise.
He describes Wiene as the only German film director, besides
Lubitsch, who has an international reputation and whose films are
well received in the United States. He explains that the film would
do the opera's reputation no harm; quite the contrary, he argues, the
film would create a new interest in the opera. With a specific reference to the anticipated honoraria, Hofmannsthal asked for Strauss's
participation.[27] Four days later Strauss cabled, "Film agreed. Arrive
in Vienna presumably January."[28]

At this point Hofmannsthal's confidence in Wiene seemed to be
boundless. On 6 January 1925 he wrote to Strauss's agent, Otto
Fürstner: "Mr. Wiene is one of the few directors (besides Lubitsch,
the only one) who has achieved world renown. When it comes to a

feeling for the quality of execution, he must be the foremost continental director."[29] On 1 February 1925 he wrote to Strauss: "The director Dr. Wiene, with whom I have had several extended meetings, gives the impression (as his reputation would lead one to expect) of a very sharp, secure and decisive human being, capable of great artistic energy."[30] Also after the completion of the film, but before the premiere, Hofmannsthal in a letter to Wiene expressed his highest appreciation for the film director:

> Dear Dr. Wiene, I witnessed the level of untiring – for the amateur almost frightening – effort with which you and Roller with your score of artistic and technical helpers produced the *Rosenkavalier* film in the course of many months. Now I have seen the film myself and – as I am happy to tell you – with genuine pleasure. The world created for and familiar to the stage was transposed into a strange kind of artistic reality, a world of houses and streets, with gardens and rivers, a world in which the reality of the Austrian landscape combined with an almost unprecedented, correct reproduction of the historical reality to form an eighteenth century of rare liveliness. The musical comedy was transformed into something new, a form of sentimental novel from the Theresian world, but a novel in images. May the curious combination of this screen work with the lively sounding stage play become a source of dual pleasure for many people.[31]

About two years later, however, in a letter to Willy Haas, Hofmannsthal expressed his frustrations and disappointments with his involvements in the film industry as a scriptwriter. His perception seemed to be that he had been granted honoraria primarily for the use of his name and not for his artistic creations. In this connection he referred once more to the *Rosenkavalier* project and to his work with Wiene:

> In those years [1922–23], to explore all imaginable artistic means, I produced several film treatments, among them one *Rosenkavalier* in which, really quite nicely and novel-like, I showed the life of all the figures before the story of the opera begins. (This story would only have filled the last thirty images.) Mr. Wiene, to whom I made this draft available, ignored it completely and made the story of the opera into the most dilettante and clumsy film imaginable.[32]

Keeping Hofmannsthal's earlier satisfaction with the film in mind, this later invective makes no sense, unless the two had had a falling out. According to an article in *Der Film* of 17 January 1926, this had apparently happened[33] and was an open secret already at that time. Pan Film, of course, had bought Hofmannsthal's script to use his name in the marketing of the film but replaced it with a more appropriate one composed by Wiene and Nerz. Hofmannsthal, an esteemed man of letters, must have realized that the film industry had no appreciation for his artistic talents. Although Pan Film had publicized Hofmannsthal's participation in the making of the film in its marketing campaign, only one day after the shooting began, *Der Film-Kurier* reported: "As is well known, Hugo von Hofmannsthal has also taken on the task of writing the script for the film, the scenario of which, however, was really created by Robert Wiene and Ludwig Nerz."[34] And on 27 July 1925 the same journal printed excerpts from the shooting script[35] that were consistent with the beginning of the film but not with Hofmannsthal's screenplay as it was posthumously published.[36]

A comparison between the available script fragment and the film makes it clear that in contrast to Hofmannsthal's text, the film is essentially based on the plot of the *Rosenkavalier* opera and expanded with a few highly effective cinematic situations. While Marshall von Werdenberg is on a military campaign, his wife is having an affair with the young Count Octavian. Because of rumors, the High Commission for the Preservation of Morals spies on the couple. In the meantime, the marshallin recommends to her cousin Baron Ochs von Lerchenau – an aging, impoverished aristocrat – a union with young Sophie von Faninal, the only daughter of a rich businessman recently raised to the aristocracy. Ochs immediately travels to Vienna and visits his cousin at the very same time that she is together with Octavian. To avoid a scandal, Octavian disguises himself as a chambermaid. In this disguise he attracts the attention of the lecherous Ochs. In making his exit, Octavian leaves behind a lace cuff, which is recovered by Valzacchi and Anina who are agents for the High Commission. Sometime later at an outdoor festival, Octavian encounters Sophie and is smitten by her, which arouses the jealousy of the marshallin. At her request, Octavian agrees to present to Sophie a silver rose on behalf of the baron. It is only during this traditional ceremonial act that he recognizes his Sophie as the future bride of Ochs. A controversy between Ochs and Octavian ensues and, after a brief duel in which Ochs is slightly wounded, Octavian must depart. The wedding contract is signed and Ochs and the elder Faninal are delighted.

Meanwhile, the High Commission has informed the marshall of its suspicions concerning his wife's infidelity, and the marshall, after a glorious military campaign, abruptly leaves the field to return to Vienna. There Octavian designs to bring ridicule on Ochs in order to persuade Faninal to renounce the marriage. He induces some actors to perform a play in which the happenings of the silver rose ceremony are satirized. All are upset by the play's true-to-life portrayal but not with the effect Octavian had intended. Furthermore, with youthful exuberance Octavian swears loyalty and love to the marshallin. In the final elaborate scene, a masked ball, all complications are eventually resolved. Ochs is finally exposed as an inveterate lecher and is forced to make his departure, leaving Octavian and Sophie as a happy pair. The marshall and his spouse become reconciled, making a second happy pair, and to everyone's surprise the two spies, Valzacchi and Anina, walk off arm-in-arm as a third happy pair.[37]

Hofmannsthal's film script is essentially different from the above plot outline in that it attempts to tell the pre-history of the opera. The two scripts have the same major protagonists in common but differ in every other respect. In Hofmannsthal's film script, Ochs von Lerchenau is advised to seek the hand of the young and rich Sophie Faninal, but never gets around to it because of his assiduous womanizing. While Sophie is still in the convent she falls in love with Octavian merely after she catches a brief glimpse of him. Moreover, the marshallin is indeed pursued by Octavian and, although she appreciates his admiration, as a married woman she rejects him.

Hofmannsthal's script is not entirely without merit, but there are good reasons for rejecting it. The complex mixture of high drama and comedy with convoluted secondary plots is much too extravagant for either film or opera. For example, the deaths of two children are narrated elaborately without contributing anything to the development of the plot. Moreover, Hofmannsthal suggests filmic devices such as flashbacks, dreams, and subjective visualizations, but with such frequency that it becomes an imposition. Finally, it may be asked, why relinquish the opera's popular and well-known plot in favor of this muddled and obscure innovation? It is, therefore, understandable that the Pan Film Company, at a critical time for the Austrian film industry, would prefer to select an already reputable opera plot over a script with an unfamiliar story and marred by the above flaws. Nevertheless, to do justice to Hofmannsthal, Wiene did adapt several motifs from the poet's script: For the marshall's military campaign at the head of his troops, Wiene apparently drew on Hofmannsthal's idea. The melancholy encounter between the marshallin and Octavian on a bench in a remote part of the grounds with flashbacks to earlier events in her life is also suggested in Hofmannsthal's script.

Hofmannsthal scholarship has responded with only a few and not well-founded comments about his *Rosenkavalier* film script and the film associated with it. Walter Fritz in his essay "Hofmannsthal und der Film"[38] gives the impression that the poet was an experienced film scriptwriter. Yet the evidence is lacking. Of the five scripts Hofmannsthal wrote, only one was filmed, namely, *Das fremde Mädchen* (*The Strange Girl* [1913]), directed by Mauritz Stiller. Since the film is not available, it is hardly possible to judge the value of the script for the filming. As for *Der Rosenkavalier*, Fritz seems not to know that the screenplay was not by Hofmannsthal.

The most authoritative publication about the script, *Der Rosenkavalier: Fassungen Filmscenarium Briefe*,[39] contains the extant twenty-page fragment of Hofmannsthal's screenplay version, correspondence about the making of the film, and a short introduction by Rudolf Hirsch. Hirsch, as Fritz above, makes unfounded claims for Hofmannsthal's experience as a screenwriter. It is on the basis of these claims that he feels justified in reproaching Wiene for having rejected that script. What is not at all clear to Hirsch is that Wiene was a professional and experienced scriptwriter and director by the time he made *Der Rosenkavalier*, and Hofmannsthal was merely an amateur. Hirsch, an apologist for the revered poet, but apparently himself inexperienced with silent films, sees in the script the product of an extraordinary visual imagination. Wiene apparently saw it otherwise. Ernest Prodolliet, in his recent publication on Hofmannsthal's relation to film[40] adds nothing to the discussion, since he had apparently not done any original research on the subject.

It is revealing to look at the reception of *Der Rosenkavalier* in the film journals of the time. Reports on the making of the film were already circulating before the shooting even began on 18 June 1925. Besides the cooperation of Richard Strauss, Hugo von Hofmannsthal, and Robert Wiene, which was elaborately described in film journals, it was Alfred Roller's contribution to the lavish indoor and outdoor sets that was at the core of the reporters' attention. During December 1925 the interest in the film was heightened by reports of previews in several cities. In Prague there was a preview without musical accompaniment,[41] and in Vienna a preview with a small, eight-man orchestra.[42]

There were two spectacular premieres – the first in Dresden on 11 January 1926 and the second on 16 January in Berlin – which were discussed in the press at great length. In Dresden Strauss himself directed the musical arrangement he had prepared for the film; as a consequence the film was subordinated to the music. According to the reviews, Strauss had the film stopped twenty times because his ornamental conducting kept falling behind the film's pace.[43] Nevertheless, at the conclusion of the film, Strauss was met with an ovation. A large music and film audience was attracted to

Robert Wiene, Ludwig
Nerz, Richard Strauss
(2nd, 3rd, 4th from
left) and two
unidentified persons
on the way to the
premiere of *Der
Rosenkavalier* –
Dresden, January 1927

this extravaganza, which was treated as such by the press. Although
the response to the film was uniformly positive, the reviewers were
clearly divided. For the Strauss admirers, he could do no wrong and
was fully justified in highlighting his music. One reviewer, evidently
a Strauss devotee, goes so far as to speak of a Straussian method in
defending his constant interference with the continuity of the film.[44]
Another reviewer was deeply offended by Strauss's "method" of dealing with the film: "He tore the film to shreds, just so he could complete his musical motifs, unconcerned about the length of the
individual scenes."[45] To be sure, the reviewer does approve of the
music but does not want to review the film until it is screened as a film
rather than merely as an accompaniment to a musical composition.

The film received its due at its Berlin premiere at the Capitol
Theater on 16 January. This time Richard Strauss was in the audience and his music was conducted by an experienced film composer and conductor, Willy Schmidt-Gentner, who rearranged the
music to achieve a desirable synchronization between film and
music. Strauss, who had received an ovation in Dresden, now
observed with a grim face yet another ovation that clearly belonged

more to Wiene than to him and, accordingly, he gestured toward Wiene when he appeared on the stage. The reviewer who describes this scene comments further:

> We have to judge here as film people, not musicians. And we have to say that we liked the film a whole lot better than that opera in Dresden ... . [Wiene] has created a masterpiece that does not have to exist merely as an "illustration" of Strauss's music, as an appendage with no independent life of its own, but should be successful everywhere just as a film alone.[46]

Although the two representatives of traditional art, Strauss and Hofmannsthal, were discussed with much fascination in the press, film reviewers also commented on Robert Wiene's contribution, which "combines subtle artistic processing with stage effectiveness."[47] Wiene is acknowledged to have delivered "a highly refined and balanced piece of work in which dramaturgy and direction are so strong that it ... really does not draw a very significant part of its vitality from the spirit of Strauss' music."[48] Another highlights Wiene's sensibilities in representing the rococo milieu, "the likes of which we have never seen before. Old Meissener porcelain figurines, old paintings by Watteau and Boucher have come alive again, breathing the lightness of being and the innocent high spirits of the 'galant' period."[49] In the same context, Wiene is lauded for capturing the tone and mood of Vienna: "He presents us with all these pretty and charming porcelain figurines, he assembles the story into such a graceful minuet that one can only say: delicious. He shows structures ... that delightfully capture the Vienna of that time."[50]

A Viennese film critic, fully aware of the above, goes yet a step further by associating the film with the current crisis in the Austrian film industry:

> Pan Film, at a time of severe crisis, has delivered proof that it is possible to create an excellent film, that the Austrian film industry is viable if it is capable of creating quality and that not the film industry itself but competence has broken down. Performances like *Der Rosen Kavalier* have to prompt the serious film industry to get back to work without relying on coercive measures.[51]

There is a similar commentary in a Berlin film journal: "It was a great and complete victory and, incidentally, the first really overwhelming Viennese film achievement."[52] It is clear from these comments that there were high expectations that quality films and this film in particular would contribute to overcoming the crisis in the Austrian film industry.

An analysis of *Der Rosenkavalier* is hampered by the fact that only seventy-five minutes of the original two-hour running time are still extant; this is large enough, though, to allow an insight into Wiene's directorial concept. Rather than following Hofmannsthal's script, Wiene adheres to the opera's storyline but with a filmic opening-up. He departs from a static stage representation and takes advantage of the flexibility that the film medium suggests. At decisive points, Wiene introduces visually attractive outdoor scenes: the marshall's military campaign, which also distances him from his wife's rococo social milieu; Baron Ochs von Lerchenau's run-down mansion, which at the same time characterizes him; a garden party outside of Vienna where Octavian sees Sophie for the first time; the open-air play within the play at the Mehlmarkt where the silver rose ceremony is satirized; and, finally, the masquerade ball, which ultimately brings comic resolution to the drama.

Beyond these there are numerous brief outdoor incidents, such as the opening scene in which Octavian climbs up the balcony to visit the marshallin, the flashback where she is seen in the garden of a convent summoned to meet her future husband, and the encounter in the park in which Octavian swears his loyalty to the marshallin. With these scenes Wiene adds a light-handedly realistic ambience to the film, which stands in sharp contrast to the opera's playful, imaginary unreality. It seems as if Wiene had tried to replace what is essential for an opera – namely, the arias – with what is outstanding in a silent film – namely, the opulence of the images. He had realized that the musical score, even if written by Richard Strauss, could not possibly be as central to the film as it was to the opera. In his film, visual sensations thus took the place of the musical sensations of the opera.

The opera and the film have the love affair between Sophie and Octavian in common, which unfolds at the very same time that her father and Baron von Ochs negotiate over her dowry. Wiene's cross-cutting allows the audience to participate in both actions at the same time, contrasting the seriousness of young love with the farce of a nouveau-riche father trying to sell his daughter to a greedy, lecherous aristocrat. The sequence with the father and his lawyer at one end of a long table and the Baron with his lawyer at the other end – both trading insults and throwing legal documents at each other – is a scene of high comedy. A similar comic scene is when the High Commission for the Preservation of Morals convenes to consider the charges against the marshallin. There are no dialogue titles; instead, there is a group of arbitrators dressed alike, wearing identical wigs, putting their heads together to form what appears to be an image of conformity rather than critical judgment.

The masquerade ball, of which only a short fragment remains, opens up a stage for many comic situations. The masks cause numerous confusions of identities, in turn adding to the complications, which can be resolved only at the end.

In addition to the premieres in Dresden and Berlin, there were also glamorous opening nights in Vienna on 30 March 1926 with Carl Alwin conducting, and one year later in London with Richard Strauss himself once again on the podium. After that, the Pan Film Company had expected to take the film on a tour of major American cities, a project that did not materialize because of the emergence of sound film.[53] From this point the film is not mentioned until many years later.

It was not until the late 1950s that Joseph Gregor, then the head of the Austrian Film Archive, initiated a search for *Der Rosenkavalier*. Indeed, an incomplete print with Czech titles was found in the Prague Film Archive and, at the same time, Otto Wladika discovered Richard Strauss's score in the state library in Vienna. In 1958 the first screening of the film took place in Vienna, accompanied by a piano arrangement of the score. Thereafter, the Austrian Film Archive made a 16mm copy in sound film speed with German titles and the piano arrangement.[54] The premiere of this print took place at the Mannheim Film Week on 20 October 1961. As far as we know, no additional restorative work was done on this film, and apparently this is the version that has been used at various screenings at film festivals since then.

A lively controversy has developed around the film since the 1970s but primarily about which music should be used with the film rather than about the film itself. On 29 March 1974 *Der Rosenkavalier* was screened at Yale University, with John Mauceri conducting the Yale Symphony Orchestra. For this American premiere, the conductor used the original Strauss score, which he had found in 1972 at the Library of Congress. The film was screened once again on 17 January 1987 in Osnabrück, this time accompanied with music that conductor Armin Brunner had compiled, basically from various Richard Strauss compositions. This version was also performed by David Shallon on the occasion of the festival "Stummfilm und Musik" in the Frankfurt Alten Oper on 8 April 1988.

The three different musical arrangements have since fueled the controversy over the appropriate music for the film, with only passing comments about the film itself. The controversy is reminiscent of the arguments heard after the Dresden and Berlin premieres in 1926. In the former, the music received priority, and in the latter, the film was given its proper due. Until *Der Rosenkavalier* can be properly restored, all reflections about an appropriate musical accompaniment are of secondary significance. The highest priority should be given to a search for a complete print of the film; only with the best possible print at hand does the debate over the musical score make any sense.

DIE KÖNIGIN VOM MOULIN ROUGE (*The Queen of Moulin Rouge*)

Wiene's last motion picture for the Pan Film Company, *Die Königin vom Moulin Rouge*, was made during the summer of 1926 and received its premiere at the Marmorhaus in Berlin on 4 October 1926 and only one month later in Vienna on 5 November. In an advertisement in *Das Kino-Journal*, the Pan Film Company announced that this was to be the first Pan film of the Robert Wiene Production Company in 1926/27.[55] In addition to this, the trade journal *Die Bühne* reported in July 1926 that the Pan Film Company had negotiated a contract with the French Pathé frères Film Company (Société des Cinéromans) for the purpose of producing a series of films. The first of these was *Die Königin vom Moulin Rouge*, directed by Robert Wiene.[56] Although the film must be considered Austrian, the Viennese *Das Kino-Journal* reported that the Robert Wiene Production Company had con-

Die Königin vom Moulin Rouge (The Queen of Moulin Rouge) Director: Robert Wiene (1926) – Livio Pavanelli, Mady Christians

tracted with the Berlin Filmhaus Bruckmann to make three films, the first of which, *Die Königin vom Moulin Rouge*, was already being shot in Vienna and was to be completed in Paris and Berlin.[57]

A most revealing review of the making of the film appeared in *Die Bühne* in an essay entitled, "Paris in Vienna: With Robert Wiene in the Vita Studio."[58] The writer, who signed with the pseudonym "Leonard," gives a rare picture of Robert Wiene at work on the set. Wiene could be seen rushing with great intensity all over the set arranging, ordering, and instructing until he was at the point of exhaustion. The journalist expresses his frustration over the fact that Wiene was so intensely occupied that he never stood still for a moment to answer his questions. Nevertheless, the article describes the work of the French actors and actresses to whose presence in Vienna the title of the report refers. Apparently, the contract between Pan and Pathé provided for the participation of French film stars in Robert Wiene productions. The article is aptly illustrated by caricatures of the stars as well as one of the director Wiene in the center.

Die Königin vom Moulin Rouge is a light situation comedy in a Lubitsch style. Alexander Ferenczy, in accord with the aristocratic setting, provided appropriate high-society interiors in private homes, in bars, and in nightclubs. Exterior location shots of Paris heighten the authenticity of the plot's background.

In the film, Sergius, the young prince of Illyrium, is rather bored with his life at a Paris preparatory school, which he wishes to exchange for Paris night life. His father's unexpected abdication imposes new responsibilities on Sergius, which he promptly shuns in favor of his youthful desire for amusement. Duke Pitschenieff and his young wife, charged with breaking the news to him, arrive too late. Sergius has already run off to the nightclubs. Since the new king must be sworn in by noon of the following day to avoid forfeiting his throne, the duke and the school's director go off in a desperate search to find him. In the meantime, sinister conspirators scheme to delay his arrival. The young duchess who had concealed from her aristocratic husband that she was once the famous nightclub star, Floramye, now has the desire to return to the place of her former glory, the famous Moulin Rouge. There she is recognized by the public and successfully competes for attention with the new star, Liliane.[59] In the meantime, Sergius has discovered Floramye and the two fall in love instantaneously without knowing each other's true identities.

The conspirators intervene by persuading Liliane to lure Sergius to her home. The duke and the schoolmaster appear inebriated at the Moulin Rouge still in search of the king, adding to the confusion. By a series of unforeseeable complications, Sergius ends up a prisoner in Liliane's home, and Floramye finds herself involved in the machinations of Arnold, the valet at the embassy of Illyrium. The sudden return of the ambassador from his honeymoon with his young wife puts an end to Arnold's masquerade as a gentleman. Floramye notices that the ambassador belongs to the conspirators and threatens to reveal their former amorous liaison unless he helps her rescue Sergius, whose true identity is now known to her. On the following day, the court gathers anxiously to await the appearance of the king before the appointed deadline. After a few more comical complications, Sergius does arrive but assumes the crown only when he realizes that with it he has the power to divorce Floramye from her husband and take her for his queen. The duke is rewarded for his services to the crown with a medal and all problems are resolved.

Die Königin vom Moulin Rouge (The Queen of Moulin Rouge)
Director: Robert Wiene (1926)

The comedy of *Die Königin vom Moulin Rouge* relies on a narrative strategy that accords the audience an advantage of information over the protagonists of the film. This calls for split-second timing and a fast pacing of the sequence of events on the part of the film, and full alertness on the part of the viewers in order to keep up with the fast-moving events and enjoy the humor. An example of the dynamics of the comedy is the gradual unveiling of the identity of Floramye/duchess: the audience learns it first; then her former lover, the ambassador, who is now her antagonist; and thirdly the prince. Her husband, the duke, is never let in on the secret. The motif of mistaken identity is at the core of both Georges Feydeau's sparkling stage play and Wiene's delightful visual narrative. And this play with identities does not stop with the plot: in a street scene, Robert Wiene is seen in a cameo appearance, reading a newspaper, looking briefly at the camera with a sly grin.

The central scene takes place in the grand ballroom of the Moulin Rouge, where for the first time all the major characters gradually appear. The structure of the cinematic space is shown by a frequently occurring establishing shot in which we see the length of the dance floor, divided into a vertical and a horizontal axis. The vertical axis is dominated by a broad stairway down which the main players make their entrance – first Floramye, then her competitor Liliane, then the prince and his two ministers, and finally the tipsy duke and school director. The horizontal axis is established by Floramye and Liliane situated at opposite sides of the hall. This juxtaposition is heightened dynamically by dramatic cross-cutting and point-of-view and shot/reverse shots. The foreground of the space is underscored by the perpetual motion of the mass of frolicking dancers.

Die Königin vom Moulin Rouge is certainly one of the significant Austrian film comedies to come out at a time when the Austrian film industry was in a crisis. The decision of the Pan Film Company to invite Robert Wiene to Vienna to make films was intended to return stability to the industry. Indeed, the style and structure of his last Austrian film reveal a most competent filmmaker who is able to lead an ensemble of experienced actors and technicians to highly entertaining achievement.

Notes

1. Ludwig Gesek, *Filmzauber aus Wien: Notizblätter zu einer Geschichte des österrreichischen Films* (Vienna, 1965), p. 51.
2. Friedrich Porges, ed., *Mein Film-Buch: Vom Film, von Filmstars und von Kinematographie* (Berlin: Mein Film-Verlag, 1928), 254, 302.
3. See Anonymous, "Meister der Filmszene, III: Robert Wiene – Oberregisseur der Pan-Film A.G.," *Mein Film*, no. 15 (1926): 2.
4. Barnet Braverman, "Courage in the Movies: Concerning Dr. Robert Wiene, Creator of the Famous Film, *Dr. Caligari's Cabinet*," *The Billboard*, 14 November and 21 November 1925.
5. For this plot summary we draw on *Die Filmwoche*, no. 46 (1924): 1080, and almost verbatim the same text in *Die Filmwelt*, no. 4 (1925): 5f.
6. *Das Kino-Journal*, no. 722 (1924): 15.
7. It is amusing to note that Renard himself was most favorably impressed with the film version of his novel: "The cinematographic adaptation of *Orlac's Hands* gratifies all my wishes. I was never understood so passionately nor interpreted with such power." (*Le Courier Cinématographique*, as quoted by Francis Courtade, *Cinéma expressioniste* [Paris: Henri Veyrier, 1984], 180.)
8. *Die Filmwelt*, no. 5 (1925): 9.
9. *Die LichtBildBühne* 18, no. 6 (1925): 35.
10. *Der Film-Kurier* 6, no. 204 (1924).
11. *Deutsche Allgemeine Zeitung*, 7 February, as quoted in an advertisement of Berolina-Film G.m.b.H. in *Der Film* 10, no. 8 (1925).
12. Siegfried Kracauer, *From Caligari to Hitler: A Psychological History of the German Film* (Princeton, N.J.: Princeton University Press, 1947), 154, n2.
13. Lotte H. Eisner, *The Haunted Screen: Expressionism in the German Cinema and the Influence of Max Reinhardt* (Berkeley and Los Angeles: University of California Press, 1973), 106, 144f.
14. Walter Fritz, *Geschichte des österreichischen Films* (Vienna: Bergland, 1969), 94, 231. His later, more elaborate volume *Im Kino erlebe ich die Welt: 100 Jahre Kino und Film Österreich* (Vienna: Brandstätter, 1997) does not illuminate the reader any further.
15. John D. Barlow, *German Expressionist Film* (Boston: Twayne, 1982), 58.
16. Ibid., 59.
17. "Orlac in Wien," *Die Filmwoche*, no. 41 (1924), 942.
18. Courtade, *Cinéma expressioniste*, 105–09.
19. Jürgen Kasten, *Der expressionistische Film: Abgefilmtes Theater oder avantgardisches Erzählkino? Eine stil-, produktions- und rezeptionsgeschichtliche Untersuchung* (Münster: MAkS Publikationen, 1990).
20. B. 9074, 25 September 1924.
21. The Department of the Interior of the State of Saxony had charged before the Censorship Board that the film revealed methods by which criminals could circumvent police investigations. Although the board rejected this charge, we can perceive from the proceedings how seriously the film was taken for its realism. (Minutes of the Censorship Board, no. 21, Berlin, 5 February 1925; available DIF, Frankfurt).
22. *Illustrierter Film-Kurier* 7, no. 201 (1925).
23. *Reichsfilmblatt*, no. 44 (1925).
24. *Mein Film*, no. 3 (1926): 2.
25. *Die LichtBildBühne* 18 (1925).
26. On 11 July 1923 Hofmannsthal wrote the following in a letter to Carl Jakob Burckhardt: "For the moment I am burdened with a task I had to take on for the money: I am writing a film script for the *Rosenkavalier*." Hugo von Hofmannsthal and Carl J. Burckhardt, *Briefwechsel* (Frankfurt a.M.: S. Fischer, 1956), 124.

27. Richard Strauss and Hugo von Hofmannsthal, *Briefwechsel*, ed. Willi Schuh (Zürich: Atlantis Verlag, 1952), 532f.
28. Ibid.
29. Hugo von Hofmannsthal and Richard Strauss, *Der Rosenkavalier: Fassungen Film-scenarium Briefe*, ed. Willi Schuh (Frankfurt a.M: S. Fischer, 1972), 339.
30. Ibid., 535f.
31. Ibid., 343.
32. Hugo von Hofmannsthal and Willy Haas, *Ein Briefwechsel*, ed. Rolf Italiaander (Berlin: Propyläen, 1968), 82f.
33. *Der Film* 11, no. 3 (1926): 16.
34. *Der Film-Kurier* 7, no. 145 (1925). Not everyone was aware of this because many reviewers of the film continued to refer to the film's script as having been authored by Hofmannsthal. To the best of our knowledge, neither Wiene nor Pan Film made any public efforts to dispute this.
35. *Der Film-Kurier* 7, no. 201 (1925).
36. Printed as a fragment in Hofmannsthal and Strauss, *Der Rosenkavalier.*
37. For this summary we have drawn on the film's extant fragment as well as the original program booklet issued by the distribution company, Filmhaus Bruck-mann, Berlin; we owe thanks to Klaus Jaeger, the late director of the Düsseldorf Film Archive for making this document available to us.
38. Walter Fritz, "Hofmannsthal und der Film," in *Hofmannsthal und das Theater: Die Vorträge des Hofmannsthal-Symposiums, Wien, 1979*, ed. Wolfram Mauser (Vienna: Halosar, 1981), 3–12.
39. Hofmannsthal and Strauss, *Der Rosenkavalier.*
40. Ernest Prodolliet, *Das Abenteuer Kino: Der Film im Schaffen von Hugo von Hof-mannsthal, Thomas Mann und Alfred Döblin* (Freiburg, CH: Universitätsverlag, 1991), 9–38.
41. *Das Kino-Journal*, no. 801 (1925): 8–11.
42. *Reichsfilmblatt*, no. 2 (1926): 29.
43. *Der Film-Kurier* 8, no. 9 (1926).
44. *Reichsfilmblatt*, no. 3 (1926): 55.
45. "Richard Strauss dirigiert den *Rosenkavalier*," *Die LichtBildBühne* 19, no. 8 (1926): 1–3.
46. *Die LichtBildBühne* 19, no. 14 (1926): 3f.
47. Ibid.
48. "*Der Rosenkavalier* in der Dresdner Staatsoper: Richard Strauss als Filmdirigent," *Reichsfilmblatt*, no. 3 (1926): 39.
49. *Die LichtBildBühne* 19, no. 14 (1926): 3.
50. "*Der Rosenkavalier* in Dresden," *Der Film* 11, no. 3 (1926): 16.
51. "*Der Rosenkavalier* vor dem Publikum," *Das Kino-Journal*, no. 818 (1926): 19f.
52. *Die LichtBildBühne* 19, no. 14 (1926): 4.
53. Cf. Fritz, "Hofmannsthal und der Film," 10.
54. For the above we draw on ibid., 10.
55. *Das Kino-Journal*, no. 843 (1926): 16; this advertisement announced a preview of the film on 27 September 1926 at the Vienna Haydn-Kino.
56. *Die Bühne* 3, no. 89 (1926): 36. In France this film was distributed under the title *La Duchesse des Folies Bergere.* The only extant print, an original processed by Pathé frères, is a fifty-seven-minute fragment owned by the Cinémathèque de Toulouse. It is an early acetate print on 35mm, which has retained much of the original tinting.
57. *Das Kino-Journal*, no. 835 (1926): 7f.
58. *Die Bühne* 3, no. 92 (1926): 37f.
59. In the French print, the duchess is called Floramye, whereas in the German pro-grams she is called Crevette and her rival's name is Floramye instead of Liliane.

Chapter 7

✦ ✦ ✦

The Last Silent Films
Berlin 1927–1929

D uring the last silent film period in Berlin, Wiene was the director of six films, all of which were screened from 1927 to 1928.
These films, completed in quick succession, were all comedies or
melodramas revolving around strong female characters. Already his
last Viennese film, *Die Königin vom Moulin Rouge (The Queen of Moulin
Rouge),* had had just such a strong woman at the center of the plot.
Lily Damita was his favorite actress for these roles, starring in *Die
berühmte Frau (The Famous Woman), Die Frau auf der Folter (The Woman
on the Rack),* and *Die grosse Abenteuerin (The Great Adventuress).*

From 1927 to 1928, Wiene wrote only one film script, namely,
Heut' spielt der Strauss (Strauss Is Playing Today), which his brother
Conrad directed in 1928. In 1929, the year of the first German sound
films, Wiene made no films at all. To be sure, in 1929 he was at work
on a significant film project, which was to be named, "Selfridge or
Chambre Nr. 3." It was intended to be a German, French, and
American co-production; but it did not materialize.[1] Whereas in
Vienna Wiene was under contract to a single film company, now
with his last silent films he negotiated contracts with several different
production companies.

We were fortunate in obtaining prints of *Die Geliebte (The Mistress)*
from the Italian National Film Archive in Rome, *Die berühmte Frau
(The Famous Woman)* from the Czechoslovakian Film Archive in
Prague, and *Unfug der Liebe (Folly of Love)* from the Federal Film

Archive of Germany, which had obtained the film from the National Center for Cinematography in Bois d'Arcy, France.

Die Geliebte (The Mistress) Director: Robert Wiene (1927) –
Edda Croy, Harry Liedtke

DIE GELIEBTE (The Mistress)　　After two years in Vienna with Pan Film, Wiene returned to Berlin to make *Die Geliebte* for Paneuropa Film. The exterior shots were made in Vienna, where the plot is supposed to take place. All interiors were shot in Berlin.

According to the reviews, the film was extraordinarily well received at its premiere. *Der Kinematograph* even reports that the police had to be called to manage the crowds for a Sunday screening in the Tauentzien-Palast film theater.[2] In its review of the premiere screening, *Der Kinematograph* describes the film as most pleasing to the audience because of its melodramatic appeal. Moreover, the presence of film star Harry Liedtke in the lead role was seen as assuring the film's success throughout Germany.[3] *Die LichtBildBühne* calls *Die Geliebte* "a work of high cultural quality" that deserves its popular success because it fulfills the public's expectations with delicacy and good taste. Similarly Wiene's work is praised: "The directing of Robert Wiene is remarkably subtle. The charming comedic tone at the beginning is maintained with much wit and sensitivity and gives the film its class … With this film *Caligari* director Wiene has recaptured his original elegance and spirit."[4]

The film's plot, which is based on a play by Alexander Brody, takes place in Vienna toward the end of World War I. Anna von Ziska (Edda Croy in her first film role) is the beautiful daughter of an upper-class family that has lost its wealth. Prince Augusto (Harry Liedtke) notices her in a chance encounter and immediately falls in love with her. Anna, however, is unapproachable and would have remained so, had it not been for her parents' plight. She at first suspects that the prince sees in her simply another one of his many affairs. Though she will have none of this, she does see in him an opportunity to help her parents. Consequently, she proposes to play the role of the prince's lover in public for his esteem, but in private to remain Platonic. The prince, delighted to get this far with her, consents to the arrangement. The family's fortune improves, indeed, and all is well until Anna's mother sees the young couple in public one day. In Anna's ensuing conversation with her mother, her deep feelings for the prince are revealed for the first time. The prince, in turn, more deeply in love with her than ever, gives her a written and signed proposal of marriage.

In the meantime, however, the prince's grandmother, the formidable old duchess (Adele Sandrock) who rules over the family affairs with an iron hand according to the dictates of tradition, has made other plans for the prince. Anticipating grave changes in the social order, she seeks to arrange a wedding between her grandson and a young woman from an old worthy aristocratic family. She summons all concerned to her palace to announce Augusto's engagement. When Anna arrives, the duchess, thinking that she can be bought, asks her price in exchange for the prince's written declaration of marriage. Anna resolutely tears the paper to pieces and confronts Augusto with an ultimatum. Without hesitation, the prince turns his back on family tradition and follows his love.

The revolution breaks out and the monarchy is threatened. Under these circumstances the duchess tries once more to establish contact with the prince. She visits him in the villa to which he has withdrawn with Anna. To her shock she finds the two married and apparently totally removed from her sphere of influence. Believing to have lost what is most dear to her, the old woman sinks into an armchair with the words, "Everything is crumbling and I am alone." The prince responds by having his grandmother join hands with Anna, who says reassuringly to her, "Not everything crumbles. One thing remains eternal – Love. Love, the sublime law which guides the universe."[5]

The only print of this film is preserved by the Cineteca Nazionale in Rome. It has Italian rather than German intertitles. Although the plot itself is rather complete, the entire background of the revolutionary political activity in Austria toward the end of the war is missing here. German reviews of the time reveal that the political element was there but functioned only on the periphery of this melodramatic comedy. What is central to the exposition is not revolution but the change taking place in the social structure that was gradually enveloping the aristocracy and the bourgeoisie.

The pillars of strength in this film are the two women, young Anna von Ziska and the old duchess. Each has strength of character and abides uncompromisingly by her principles. The duchess is a product and defender of the traditions that have molded her and many generations of her family. She sees it as her sacred duty to pass these traditions on. With her imposing cane and old fashioned horse-drawn carriage, she comes and goes as the family's matriarch. Her own son – though he does not dare to contradict her in anything – seems not to be a too worthy representative of the heritage she wishes to maintain. Therefore, all her hopes rest on Augusto, her grandson. Anna, who feels obligated to restore her parents' fortune without compromising herself, also rests her hopes on Augusto.

Anna has the more difficult task. She does not fight for traditions, but for respectability and love. She is sure of her own feelings toward the prince, but she cannot be sure of his since she knows his reputation as a lady's man. In this situation, she forces the prince to demonstrate character, and she does so at some risk to herself. By playing the role of his lover in public but remaining chaste in private she risks yielding her virtue – after all, she does love him – and losing the prince. By restraining her feelings and remaining steadfast, she forces the prince, who originally does not know what he really wants, to want her on her terms. By remaining firm in her commitment to the bourgeois moral code, she triumphs over the fickleness of the aristocratic leisure class. She has no quarrel with an aristocratic hierarchy as such. She simply demands that aristocrats take bourgeois moral standards seriously and, even better, subscribe to them. Here the thematic orientation of the classical bourgeois tragedy is reversed into its opposite.

Most likely the film's commercial success was due to the immense popularity of film stars Adele Sandrock and Harry Liedtke. Nevertheless, from today's point of view and compared to his other leading roles of the time, Liedtke disappoints in his colorless portrayal of the prince, which becomes all the more noticeable with the appearance of Adele Sandrock, whose commanding presence enlivens the last half of the film. Today it is difficult to grasp the reviewers' enthu-

Die berühmte Frau (The Famous Woman)
Director: Robert Wiene (1928) – Lily Damita

siasm for *Die Geliebte* not only because of the unfortunate cuts of at least twenty minutes of the original running time, but also because in its plot development it hovers somewhere between comedy and melodrama. The lack of a clear genre definition and the elimination of the political background make it difficult to contextualize the film.

DIE BERÜHMTE FRAU (The Famous Woman)   This is the first of three films that Robert Wiene made with Lily Damita, a French actress who at that time was a celebrated star on the German screen. And it was Lily Damita's vibrant contribution that earned universal accolades for *Die berühmte Frau.* The reviews invariably praised Otto Kanturek for his marvelous photography, which involved numerous location shots in Barcelona, Spain. Although Melchior Lengyel's script, based on his popular play *Die Tänzerin (The Dancer),* was disparaged for its lack of originality, the film's story was a crowd pleaser.[6] Wiene was blamed for inadequately guiding the actors[7] but commended for his cultivated *mise-en-scène.*[8]

Lily Damita plays Sonja Litowskaja, the star of the famous dance ensemble Gerald. Gerald (Warwick Ward) himself has raised Sonja from childhood to be a great dance star. Although he is in love with her, he hesitates to declare his true feelings because of their difference in age. During an engagement in Barcelona, Duke Olivarez

---

(Arnold Korff) visits the group and, noticing Gerald's affection for Sonja, advises him to act before a younger man steals her from him. The young nobleman, Alfredo de Cavalcante (Fred Solm), is that younger man and it is love at first sight when he sees Sonja dancing "The Dying Lyly." Sonya reciprocates his love and leaves the ensemble to live with him. Alfredo loves her dearly but demands that she never dance again because he does not want to be reminded of her background. Sonja complies, although she is passionately devoted to her art.

For a period of time the two lovers live in happiness. Then one day the Gerald dance ensemble returns to Barcelona for another engagement. Just then Alfredo visits his parents to prepare them for his forthcoming marriage. Meanwhile, in Barcelona, as chance would have it, the dance group's prima ballerina has taken ill. Duke Olivarez reminds Gerald that Sonja lives not far from the city. She is asked to dance just once more, but she remains steadfast in her love to Alfredo and her promise to him never to dance again. As she struggles with her difficult decision, she hears street music that gradually begins to possess her until her passion to dance breaks through. She does dance and relishes her triumphant success but has every intention of returning to Alfredo.

In the meantime, Alfredo having returned home early encounters Duke Olivarez, whose intention it is to explain that Sonja is not for him but is destined for dance. Alfredo, who has witnessed Sonja's devotion to her art on a number of occasions, recognizes the truth of Olivarez's advice. He writes his beloved a letter, setting her free. Accompanied by Gerald, Sonja returns, reads the letter, and collapses. Gerald, with his maestro's eye notices Sonja's exquisite, delicate movements even in her despair as she sinks to the ground. "Never have you played 'The Dying Lyly' so well as now," he calls out to her and exhorts her to repeat it again and again until she has mastered it to perfection. She does so and finally recognizes that her heart and soul belong to her art. Alfredo sees the scene through the window, does not fully understand it, but realizes that Sonja has left him forever.[9]

The dichotomy of art and life – certainly not an original theme – provides the framework for *Die berühmte Frau* and gives ample opportunity to reveal Sonja's psychology, her inner life as it was shaped by the art of dance from childhood. From her earliest years, her relationship to life was to subordinate it to dance and the fame that stardom would bring her. After all, the film's title *Die berühmte Frau* places her fame as a public personality at the center of the film. Thus, Sonya's first appearance in the film is not in person but in a representation on posters pasted on trucks driving through the industrial harbor area of Barcelona. In a way, then, the dichotomy between art and life is both announced and slightly problematized very early in the film when the famous woman's persona is paraded through an area that is the very antithesis of the glamorous world of dance. Then, when she appears in person as a young woman in training, she somewhat peevishly – even childishly – complains about having to renounce life's pleasures for the sake of art: "What do I get from my life; training, rehearsals, performances, catching trains, hardly ever sleeping, hardly ever eating – always working, working to become famous! I'm fed up! Fed up! Fed up!"[10]

The film's main development takes place between this childish tantrum at the beginning and her collapse toward the end when Gerald rescues Sonja from her despair by guiding her in transforming her real-life anguish over the loss of Alfredo into the role she has danced so many times in "The Dying Lyly." In this transformation, Sonja has matured both as a woman and as an artist. Alfredo originally fell in love with her when he saw her dance that very dance in a public performance. Now, at the end, he watches her dance the role, secretly observing a Sonja who has transmuted life into art in a way that is far beyond his comprehension, far beyond his appreciation. The extent to which dance, which brought Sonya and Alfredo together, separates them at the same time is illuminated in an earlier scene: After a bullfight to which he has taken her for innocent amusement, Sonya, captivated by the bullfighters' "dance" with the bull, recreates at home the scene in a dance of her own design, in which her expressiveness and self-oblivion are beyond Alfredo's grasp. He responds by proposing immediate marriage, hoping thereby to remove her from her reckless passion for dance and integrate her into his stable, bourgeois way of life. At the end, both Alfredo and Sonja know that such a resolution is impossible for her.

Sonja's relationship to Gerald is fundamentally different. To begin with, they both belong to the same profession. Dance is central to them both. However, the psychology of the two could not be more different. When Sonja hears music she *must* dance. That compulsion characterizes her expressiveness, her unrestrained temperament, and her drive to create. Gerald has, by contrast, a character that induces him to control, mold, and shape. His guiding force shaped her artistic temper. He provides the controlling limits, which allow her to articulate her creative drive. Unlike Alfredo, Gerald is not offended and disturbed by her wildness; quite the contrary, he knows that with his control he can shape that wildness into art.

When Sonja falls into Gerald's arms at the end, it is not only for protection but also for guidance so that she can fulfill herself as an artist.

The success of *Die berühmte Frau* rests on Wiene's proper direction of the three major actors in their representation of the plot's major dilemma, the dichotomy of art and life. With a refined sense for the psychological nuances of this familiar theme, Wiene creates a number of effective melodramatic sequences that heighten the tension and narrative complexity. Sonja is clearly the central character, but with subtle strokes, Wiene also allows the characters of Gerald and Alfredo to become visible as contrasts to each other and to Sonja. He accomplishes this by carefully guiding the emotional networks of the three main characters.

There is no question that Lengyel's script and Wiene's direction are highly effective and competent in the development of the three main characters both as individuals and in their relationship to each

Die Frau auf der Folter (The Woman on the Rack) Director: Robert Wiene (1928)

other. Contemporary critics chided the scriptwriter and the director for the characterization of the secondary roles, Duke Olivares, Alfredo's parents, and the two servants – and rightly so. Olivares's advice to Gerald and Alfredo, for example, seems unmotivated and can be justified only as a narrative catalyst. It is also puzzling why a charismatic actor like Alexander Granach, who at the time had a considerable reputation among German audiences, should have been cast in the insignificant role of Alfredo's butler. However, these flaws do not damage the core of the film, which is carried by the three major characters.

DIE FRAU AUF DER FOLTER (The Woman on the Rack)[11]   In this film, Lily Damita plays the beautiful and loving wife of the English Lord Admaston, a distinguished member of the parliament. Admaston, totally dedicated to his career, neglects his wife, and this is noticed all too clearly by Sir William Collingwood and Lady Atwill. Collingwood develops a passionate love for the neglected Lady Admaston, and Lady Atwill, who once had designs on Admaston, has not yet given up hope. Through Lady Atwill's machinations, Collingwood draws Lady Admaston into situations that give the appearance of compromising her honor. The proud and honorable Admaston is apprised of the circumstances through the treacherous Atwill. In anger Admaston sues for divorce and the entire matter is brought to court. Ellerdine, a noble and devoted admirer of Lady Admaston, succeeds in unraveling Lady Atwill's intrigues, and Lord and Lady Admaston are happily reconciled.[12]

According to the reviewers, *Die Frau auf der Folter* was not one of Wiene's best achievements. Still, Lily Damita's performance is noted and the director is credited for demonstrating his usual competence:

Leontines Ehemänner (Leontine's Husbands) Director: Robert Wiene (1928) – from the left: Oskar Sima, Claire Rommer, Truus van Alten, Adele Sandrock, Georg Alexander (?)

"Since Robert Wiene directed the film, the overall result has been a very refined piece of work."[13] Yet another reviewer describes the director's work on the basis of his own observations in the studio:

> Robert Wiene attempts to loosen up this script, and he does succeed in part, with the help of his knowledge of the world and human nature, with the help of his star Lily Damita, and with the help of Johannes Riemann. Many scenes again show Wiene's subtle and unerring way with characterization.[14]

Leontines Ehemänner (Leontine's Husbands) Claire Rommer plays the part of Leontine, a young French dancer, who has a tendency to marry whenever she is short of cash. After her marriage to François Dubois, she weds the Marquis Versac, who brings her to his castle in the provinces. There she must play the role of the respectable lady of the manor in the presence of a stern and highly principled aunt (Adele Sandrock). She does so for a while, until at a village dance she loses her composure and dances a wild Charleston, which agitates the entire populace. After this scandal, Leontine finds her freedom, so to speak, but not for long because soon after, following in quick succession, a congressman, a professor, and even for

Die grosse Abenteuerin (The Great Adventuress) Director: Robert Wiene (1928) – Lily Damita, Georg Alexander

a while a former husband fall into her clutches. The farce concludes with Leontine looking forward to her next adventure.[15]

The reviewers did not take this film very seriously. They see the strongest points of the film in the acting of Claire Rommer and Adele Sandrock. The director, from whom more was expected, is faulted for the mediocrity of the film.[16]

DIE GROSSE ABENTEUERIN (The Great Adventuress)   A light society comedy is once again built around the popular female star, Lily Damita. According to the available sources, the film was financed mainly by the English, apparently with some American participation as well.[17]

The reviewers tend to agree that the film's plot lacks in clarity and that its effectiveness is carried primarily by the presence of Lily Damita. The plot is framed by the competition between two large aviation firms, one English, the other French. The French industrialist (Georg Alexander) travels to London to strike the final blow against his competitor. In his hotel he becomes involved with a strikingly beautiful diamond thief (Lily Damita), through whom he becomes implicated in a variety of criminal activities. Later it turns out that she is the daughter of the competing English industrialist; she had plotted against the Frenchman to undermine his business offensive. At the end, they marry and the two firms merge.[18]

The film's effectiveness is enhanced by Otto Kanturek's camera work and by Werner Schmidt-Boelcke's music. Although Wiene's directorial work is described for the most part as uninspired, one reviewer does imply that he made the most of the material he had:

> Robert Wiene is the director. He had to make do with quite an improbable script. With some justification, therefore, he focused on the exterior scenery. He inserted shots of the boat between Dover and Calais, took a few wonderful pictures of London, and from the airplane, a few grand hotel receptions – decorative touches that could only enhance the effect of the film.[19]

HEUT' SPIELT DER STRAUSS (Strauss Is Playing Today)   This plot revolves around a father-son conflict in which the elder Strauss, himself a musician, wants to prevent his son from following in his footsteps. Young Johann Strauss (Imry Raday) becomes a composer nevertheless, and his father finally admits on his deathbed that his son is the greater genius. Intertwined with this episode out of the life of the famous composer is, of course, a heart-rending love story.[20]

The Wiene brothers apparently had no greater ambition than to present a good popular version of the well-known biography of the

Heut' spielt der Strauss (Strauss Is Playing Today) Director: Conrad Wiene (1928) –
Imre Rady, Alfred Abel

famous composer. The film and the manuscript found favor in the
eyes of some reviewers, while others panned them:

> The script was written by Robert Wiene – the *Caligari* Wiene. On the
> whole, he mastered the situation by effectively using anecdotal evidence
> and showing the resistance of Strauss's father, who did not want his son
> to become a musician, too. He deserves credit for avoiding drifting into
> too much kitsch.[21]

Hans Feld, however, severely rejected what he perceived as pan-
dering to public taste:

> Heroes and hero worship. This is what the producer speculates on. The
> audience loves to see its stars in situations of joy and sorrow. The broth-
> ers Wiene meet such inclinations. Both are eagerly at their places when
> nothing more counts but to deliver modest entertainment to an unde-
> manding audience.[22]

UNFUG DER LIEBE ***(Folly of Love)***   After having directed only three
films in 1926 and 1927, Wiene directed four films in 1928 in quick
succession, ending with *Unfug der Liebe*, which was also his last silent
film. While his last films had met with mixed responses, *Unfug der
Liebe* was universally praised. Georg Herzberg, for example, in his
review in *Der Film-Kurier* pointed out:

Director Robert Wiene accepts the light tone of the author. Both their work could be somewhat more lively and sparkling. But one is willing to be satisfied with giving credit to the honest attempt to achieve international standards with a German comedy. Wiene's directing is fortunately without the intrusive arrogance that marked many scenes in his last films. He finds a simple line along which the events unfold. Perhaps this return to simplicity is the only way in which Wiene can deliver balanced, well-rounded films again.[23]

The Italian actress Maria Jacobini plays American millionairess Muriel Althon, who has taken over her father's business activities while he enjoys his life in retirement with unusual vitality. One day Muriel notices a handsome and elegant, but impoverished young nobleman, Roger de Barfeuil (Jack Trevor), and takes an immediate amorous interest in him. Roger rejects the monetary offer with which she hopes to draw him to her with the proud comment that he is not for sale. Count Martinez (Angelo Ferrari), a fishy character and fortune hunter, begins to court Muriel. Martinez induces his girlfriend, the vibrant Lily Loulou, to court Muriel's energetic father, Archibald Appelroth, which she does with much success. In the meantime, Roger tries to support himself first by working as a dance escort at a hotel – which he abandons right away – and later on as a chauffeur. Disappointed over Roger's rejection of her overtures and offended by Martinez's forward courtship, Muriel leaves for Deauville, a high-class resort on the French Atlantic Coast.

Martinez, undaunted, pursues her to the resort to continue his courtship and succeeds in persuading her to agree to their engagement. By chance, Roger, working as a chauffeur, is asked to bring a client to the very same spot. After learning of the engagement, Lily persuades Muriel's father to take her along to the resort. When they are all in Deauville, the comedy's complexity heightens and moves toward a climax. Lily is jealous of Muriel, who is always with Martinez. Martinez persuades Roger to pretend to be interested in Lily to distract her and he does so. One evening they are all grouped around two tables, with Martinez, Muriel, and her father at the one, and Lily and Roger at a table across the aisle. The two women eye each other fiercely. Muriel begins to flirt openly with the bewildered Martinez; Lily in turn makes a play for Roger, who responds eagerly because he too has finally become jealous of Martinez. The two couples dance and, continuing to eye each other, move out on the veranda. There the jealous competition heightens when Muriel grabs the reluctant Martinez to press a kiss to his lips. This has the desired effect on Roger, who seizes Lily and kisses her.

The next day there is a decisive turn in the plot when Lily and Muriel have a heart-to-heart talk. Recognizing that there is nothing between Lily and Roger and that Lily really loves the shifty Martinez, Muriel arranges a gift large enough to induce Martinez to marry Lily. With the competition out of the way, she once more pursues Roger, who has returned to Paris. There she waits for him in his simple apartment, and when he appears the two embrace, at long last.

The print of *Unfug der Liebe* that we were able to study is derived from the National Center of Cinematography, Bois d'Arcy, France, which was acquired in the early 1990s by the German Federal Film Archive. It has French intertitles,[24] and some of the characters' names have been changed accordingly. The print is of very good quality and is almost complete, except for some cuts in the exterior shots.

The essential plot of this film is the stuff of which melodramas are made. An impoverished European aristocrat and a wealthy American businesswoman cannot come together because of his pride, his sense of honor, and his rigid formality. The film is transformed into a comedy by the secondary characters, Martinez, Lily Loulou, Archibald Appelroth, and Forster, Muriel's male secretary. Their liveliness and vivacity are in striking contrast to the reserve maintained by the two main characters, especially by Roger, throughout the film.

The self-assured Muriel, in pursuing a reluctant Roger, reverses traditional roles. Muriel's independence, ease with decision making, and assertiveness distinguish her quite clearly from Roger, who is more morose, indecisive, and self-restrained. She is a wealthy businesswoman, a divorcee, and used to having her own way. However, in her approach to Roger she is tactless, to say the least. After several rebuffs, she apparently realizes that her approach is the wrong one, and she changes into a more sympathetic, accessible person without, however, giving up her assertive qualities. This enables her to continue to take the initiative toward Roger but with different tactics.

Roger is finally conquered by Muriel's persistence and affection for him. As an impoverished scion of an old aristocrat family, he now has nothing but his pride to sustain him. His defensiveness is part of his intention to preserve what he has. His circumstances cause him anguish, but he carries his sadness with grace and dignity. In view of this, it is not at all clear why he finally does yield to Muriel's resolute determination to have him. At no point through all the vicissitudes of the plot can a change in attitude toward her be perceived in him.

But what really makes *Unfug der Liebe* an effective comedy? While Muriel courts Roger, Martinez courts Muriel, thereby generating a number of comic situations and complications. As a strategy for approaching Muriel, Martinez engages Muriel's *bon vivant* father in a lively conversation. As a result, the father introduces Muriel to Martinez and Martinez introduces his flighty but vivacious girlfriend, Lily Loulou to the father. It is clear that Martinez and Lily Loulou are suited for each other, as are Lily Loulou and the father. When either of these couples appears, there are scintillating, lively, and comic scenes. When Martinez and Muriel finally appear as a couple, the comedy is anything but light. He is a fortune hunter pursuing a self-serving strategy. His courtship is no more than a caricature of Muriel's courtship of Roger, and there is relief when it fails.

Martinez and Lily Loulou, by contrast, are a perfect match, actually a perfect team for executing his petty embezzlements and confidence games. They enjoy each other tremendously and are loyal to each other without really trusting each other. Lily Loulou is a game partner in Martinez's schemes but keeps a close watch on his womanizing. At his bidding she charms old Archibald and does so with verve and delight; nor is this very difficult, because the old man has an insatiable zest for life. A wealthy man but without any further responsibilities for his business, which he has turned over to his daughter, he shuns conventions and enjoys life with a remarkable joviality that is a joy to watch. He transforms any situation into an occasion for humor and good fun; indeed, when he appears, he is the center of attention and all action whirls around him. At one point, after a night of carousing with Lily Loulou, he returns to the hotel in the best of spirits with balloons in one arm and stuffed animals in the other. His hilarity, exuberance, and (most likely) inebriation are expressed by a trick montage of Paris night-life scenes, which revolve around each other in rotating spheres with Archibald at the very center.

By contrast, Forster, Muriel's loyal secretary, is a comic figure of an entirely different sort. He takes himself and his role very seriously and is chagrined when Muriel involves him as a go-between in her amorous designs on Roger rather than in her business matters, which he wishes to pursue diligently. A chubby, good-natured man, he dutifully executes his employer's wishes, and this is cause for considerable mirth.

The humor in *Unfug der Liebe* is by no means created by slapstick situations nor by characters who are merely ridiculous. Wiene avoids these hackneyed devices in favor of a comic style that emerges from a brilliantly balanced ensemble of character actors who are given freedom to express their comic talents in any given situation. It is a sophisticated humor that is transmitted to the audience by visual means, so characteristic of late silent film acting.

Notes

1. Unpublished documents, Cinémathèque Française, Paris.
2. *Der Kinematograph* 21, no. 1044 (1927): 26.
3. See *Der Kinematograph* 21, no. 1043 (1927): 19.
4. *Die LichtBildBühne* 20, no. 36 (1927).
5. For this plot summary we draw on *Die Filmwoche*, no. 6 (1927): 137, as well as on our screening of the film.
6. *Die LichtBildBühne* 20, no. 267 (1927).
7. *Reichsfilmblatt*, no. 45 (1927): 28.
8. *Die LichtBildBühne* 20, no. 267 (1927).
9. For this plot summary we draw on *Illustrierter Film-Kurier* 9, no. 726 (1927), and on our screening of a print of the film made available by the late Zdenek Stábla from the Czechoslovakian Film Archive. We owe thanks to him for translating the Czech titles and to Roberto Radicati at the Museo Nazionale Del Cinema in Turin, Italy, for providing us with a list of the original German titles.
10. Translated from the list of German titles for *Die berühmte Frau*, available at Museo Nazionale Del Cinema in Turin, Italy.
11. In the United States the film was distributed with the title *A Scandal in Paris*. The reviewers in *Variety*, 12 June 1929 and in *The New York Times*, 10 June 1929 both claim that Fritz Kortner was part of the cast – clearly an error.
12. For this plot summary we draw on the official program brochure of the *Illustrierter Film-Kurier*.
13. *Der Kinematograph* 22, no. 1156 (1928): 14.
14. *Reichsfilmblatt*, no. 37 (1928): 15.
15. *Die Filmwoche*, no. 40 (1928): 1020.
16. *Der Film-Kurier* 10, no. 230 (1928); *Der Kinematograph* 22, no. 1161 (1928): 3; *Reichsfilmblatt*, no. 39 (1928): 11.
17. *Der Kinematograph* 22, no. 1167 (1928). *Illustrierter Film-Kurier*, no. 959 (1928), specifies the production company, Deutsche Vereins- Film A.G. as the representative for Fox Film Corporation, New York.
18. *Illustrierter Film-Kurier*, no. 959 (1928); *Reichsfilmblatt*, no. 41 (1928): 24.
19. *Der Kinematograph* 22, no. 1167 (1928).
20. *Der Kinematograph* 22, no. 1174 (1928): 17.
21. Ibid.
22. *Der Film-Kurier* 10, no. 257 (1928).
23. *Der Film-Kurier* 10, no. 273 (1928).
24. We owe thanks to Karl Hölz for translating the French intertitles.

Chapter 8

✦　✦　✦

THE SOUND FILMS
1930–1938

After not completing a single film in 1929, Wiene turned to sound
film productions in 1930, just as German theater owners were
adapting their movie houses to the new technology. Until 1934, in a
phase of high productivity, he worked not only in various genres but
also cooperated with a different production company for each of his
projects. Moreover, he once again founded a production company of
his own, Camera Film Productions, for which he made *Taifun*. *Taifun*
was also Wiene's last film in Germany, since he shot his last German-
language film, *Eine Nacht in Venedig*, in Budapest. Thereafter he was
an exile in London and Paris, where he was able to establish business
contacts with the film industries, but still could not find financial
backing for a sound film remake of *Caligari*, which he had been
proposing since 1932. His last project, the French-language film *Ultimatum*, was nearly complete when he died in Paris on 15 July 1938.

DER ANDERE (The Other)　Wiene's first sound film, *Der Andere*, was
an adaptation of Paul Lindau's popular play with the same title written in 1893. As early as 1913, Max Mack had adapted this play as a
silent film with the famous stage actor Albert Bassermann in the lead
role and Paul Lindau himself as the scriptwriter. Up until the present
time, Mack's film has been considered a turning point in German film
history since it helped to bridge the gap between a traditional understanding of film as oriented toward theater and a sense of film as a
modern narrative art form. Much in the same way, Wiene's remake

Der Andere (The Other) Director: Robert Wiene (1930) – Fritz Kortner

aimed at establishing the new sound technology as a dramaturgical enrichment of the silent film and not as a detour, as many of his contemporaries viewed it.[1] This was recognized by critics as follows from a review in *Die LichtBildBühne*: "But also the new film version of the Lindau play, this time with the aid of sound, will become a significant turning point in the new German sound film era."[2]

The reviews celebrated Wiene's *Der Andere* in very positive terms. The *Berliner Börsenzeitung* sees in the film "a promising advance in the new territory of the real 'talking' film."[3] Similarly, the *Kinematograph* praised the film as an example of sound film innovation: "German sound film has proven its ability to control the quality of modulation. *Der Andere* shows that there are many more ways to achieve effects, and that the creative work in the sound film studios can equal the best from the stage."[4]

The *LichtBildBühne*, commenting on Wiene's directorial concept, points out that the dramaturgy of sound films calls for a balanced ensemble rather than a star system:

> For good reason, Robert Wiene approaches the production from the performance perspective. His major concern is for the human side; the outer appearance is of secondary importance, and this creates a gripping overall impression. In this, Kortner's performance is the focal point and plays the pivotal role: in the end, the film had to stand or fall with the problematic task of giving this double life credibility. Kortner solved the problem with captivating creative power. But a simple star film in the old style is no longer thinkable in the art of sound film, where even actors in medium and small roles have to open their mouths and fulfill much greater artistic functions than before. Therefore, Robert Wiene clearly put emphasis on a carefully selected and directed cast.[5]

One of the few critical voices against the film was Kurt Pinthus, who compared Wiene's sound remake with the earlier silent film and favored Mack's version, apparently as part of his defense of silent film art against the new sound technique altogether.[6] By contrast, in Vienna, where the film had already been shown 150 times by the beginning of October 1930,[7] the *Neues Wiener Tagblatt* came to the conclusion that, "Robert Wiene, the master director of silent film, has also conquered the word."[8]

In any plot summary of *Der Andere*, one must keep in mind that there are several versions of this story: Paul Lindau's play of 1893, Max Mack's silent film version of 1912/13, Johannes Brandt's sound film manuscript, and Wiene's film version, all of which differ from each other in essential respects. Wiene's film starts with a court scene in which the district attorney, Hallers (Fritz Kortner), calls for the severest penalty in the case before the court on the grounds that only thus will justice be done. Dr. Köhler (Eduard von Winterstein), a psychiatrist testifying as an expert medical witness, vigorously disagrees. As the two – friends in private – leave the courtroom, a bailiff barely intervenes before Amalie Frieben (Käthe von Nagy), the defendant's girlfriend, who is enraged over Hallers's harshness, approaches him, apparently with the intention of striking him.

At home the busy prosecutor continues to work on the case with such self-sacrificing relentlessness that his sister must remind him that her friend Marion has come to play the piano for him. Hallers does join Marion in his sister's salon but, incapable of expressing his concealed feelings for her and visibly disturbed over his emotional conflict, he leaves suddenly to return to work. Alone in his study, tormented by his inner struggle, he undergoes a physical and psychological transformation that results in the emergence of his other self – an uninhibited, pleasure-loving patron of taverns, bars, and other cheap places of amusement. Upon his metamorphosis, he attacks Marion on the stairway of his own house and steals her necklace without her recognizing him. Then he appears at the Hippodrome, a bar built around a circus ring where the customers can ride the horses. There Amalie waits for him, and not for the first time either. They have a couple of drinks and then leave for a tavern, which is frequented by petty criminals and in which Amalie has a room.

Der Andere (The Other) Director: Robert Wiene (1930) –
Fritz Kortner, Heinrich George

The regular guests there know him already and call him the "baron." He seems to be accepted by the gang, except for Grünspecht (Oskar Sima), who is jealous of him because he likes Amalie. He accuses the "baron" of being a police informer and stirs the others up against him. They pounce on him and would have injured him if the muscular Dickert (Heinrich George), the tavern's owner, had not intervened. He does so because Amalie, his sweetheart, begs him and as an inducement tells him about the necklace that the "baron" had shown her. Suddenly the police burst in on one of their regular raids. Amalie hides the "baron" in a secret space behind a closet in her room, and in appreciation for this he gives her Marion's necklace as a gift. Amalie finally realizes who he reminds her of, namely, the hated prosecutor Hallers. Infuriated, she begins choking him until she comes to her senses. She explains the reasons for her resentment and the "baron," wanting to appease her, promises to kill Hallers.

Amalie tells Dickert of the "baron's" plans and Dickert leaves to accompany him. Grünspecht has overheard all this and, thinking of revenge, goes to the police to inform on them. Once Dickert and the "baron" are in Hallers's home, the "baron" undergoes a gradual transformation back to his former identity. By the time the police arrive, Hallers's change is complete and he has no memory at all of the "baron" episode. Dickert, of course, gets caught. At first puzzled by the behavior of the "baron," he soon concludes that the prosecutor has secretly been living it up with liquor and women; and, shrewd as he is, Dickert confronts Hallers, calmly and even impudently offering him a deal. Hallers cannot fully grasp Dickert's motivation, but by this time his self-assurance is dwindling and thus he orders the police to let the man go.

Amalie, having learned from Dickert that the "baron" positively is the detested prosecutor Hallers, visits him, returns the necklace and confronts him with further evidence of his dual identity. Hallers is beside himself and in his emotional crisis breaks down and loses consciousness. Dr. Köhler arrives and with sympathy and understanding helps Hallers to grasp his illness. To guide him in this unusual case, Dr. Köhler discusses his diagnosis and prognosis with two colleagues in which he defends his psychoanalytic approach against traditional psychiatry. For Köhler, a patient's insight leads to a cure; whereas his colleagues maintain that a mental disease of this sort requires incarceration in an asylum. To test his conviction that Hallers's new awareness of his condition will necessarily lead to his cure, Köhler suggests that they wait until ten o'clock in the evening, the time – as he has been able to verify – when Hallers's transformation always takes place. Indeed, at this time Hallers begins to feel distressed when he senses the emerging identity of the other self. He perceives this alter-ego as a visual apparition and the struggle begins. In the adjacent room, Köhler and the other psychiatrists overhear Hallers's toil; then he opens the door and talks to his sister, clear evidence that he is on the way to recovery. The traditional psychiatrist grants that the experiment supports Köhler's view but contends nevertheless that this man could never again serve as a prosecuting attorney. Köhler, however, consistent with his humanistic understanding of mental illness, disagrees and maintains that perhaps now Hallers can all the more occupy that post: "We physicians and judges are here not only to condemn but to heal."

For his first sound film, Wiene had a first-rate ensemble of actors at his disposal. By far the most difficult role in the film, around which all the others are grouped, is the role of the prosecuting attorney Hallers. Consistent with Wiene's interpretation of the story, Fritz Kortner renders the psychological aspects of Hallers's split personality with subtlety and credibility. He plays Hallers's two personalities as separate characters with equal conviction and makes the transitions from the one to the other visible and psychologically comprehensible. Kortner's attorney is a disciplined, emotionally ice-cold, self-righteous, pitiless, hard-driving professional, who in his private affairs is incapable of expressing his feelings to the woman he loves. As Hallers's other self, Kortner depicts a cheerful, uncomplicated, easy-going, enterprising, amoral "baron" who pursues his girlfriend Amalie without inhibitions.

Not only do the two personalities of the attorney differ in regard to sexuality, it is precisely Hallers's repressed sexuality that leads to his first transformation. He cannot open up to Marion, flees from her and his own feelings into his study, and turns into his alter-ego. To be sure, the reversal of the metamorphosis takes place without sexual connotation. The "baron's" existence becomes ever more trancelike, and his original eagerness to break into the house of the prosecuting attorney and to kill Hallers yields to a strange lethargy. His collapse is due more to exhaustion than to the frustration of instinctual fulfillment. When he awakens from that state, he puts on his house jacket, as is his custom, and is once again the prosecuting attorney who has no memory whatsoever of the "baron" or the preceding events. The developments that follow – Dickert's accusations, the torn coat, Amalie's complaints – disconcert him noticeably, but do not lead him to confront his crisis. He falls into a stupor as if he wants to escape reality and vainly takes refuge in his professional work discipline to attempt to master his frightful helplessness. With so much versatility at his command, Kornter enacts the contrasts between a shaken, hesitant, even frightened Hallers and the self-assured professional of earlier days. In his conversation with Dr. Köhler, to whom Hallers confesses his distress, Kortner ranges over an entire scale of moods, from extreme anxiety to rational analysis. The contemporary reviews justifiably described this role as one of Kortner's outstanding achievements. Heinrich George is likewise praised in the reviews for the role he portrays in this film. His Karl Dickert is the good-natured, musclebound petty criminal, a tough customer who knows how to handle himself in his milieu but never looks for trouble. In the tavern both the criminals who frequent the place as well as the police who raid it see him as the key player. George radiates power, strength, and self-sufficiency as he sits there alone, relaxed, occasionally playing his accordion. Nothing disturbs him, not even questions by a police official, whom he handles nonchalantly and treats to one of his songs.

As played by George, Dickert is characterized by a specific sense of humor and by his comic insolence, which he maintains in all situations, whether it be on his home ground in the tavern or when he is caught red handed at Hallers's home. Not one to lose his presence of mind, he is never at a loss for words. Dickert is one of George's street-smart proletarians with a wisecracking urban dialect, which he displays with confidence. George thus anticipates his portrayal of Franz Biberkopf in Phil Jutzi's *Berlin Alexanderplatz* (1931), for which he is still famous today.

Oskar Sima's Grünspecht supplies *Der Andere* with comedy. The sliminess of his character, largely enhanced by the broad Viennese dialect, often serves as comic relief. Sima's character fluctuates between the grandiose phrases and gestures of a womanizer and the cowardly and despicable behavior of an informer, an unmistakable supporting role so prevalent in early German sound film.

Käthe von Nagy plays her Amalie in very deliberate contrast to Marion. While Marion, a member of the upper class, limits herself to social conventions of strict propriety, Amalie, clearly proletarian, gives free vent to her feelings and desires. Her nickname is "Red Male," which already sets her apart from Marion who is always dressed in white. Amalie's role calls for the expression of a wide range of emotions – anger, sadness, hatred, affection, and joy. In contrast to Marion, Amalie has her own range of emotions, which are not guided by social conventions.

Eduard von Winterstein presents a modern, humane, insightful, sympathetic psychiatrist who defends the still controversial Freudian psychoanalytic teaching convincingly against traditional psychiatry. His Köhler has a calm, reserved manner that offends no one and inspires confidence in the ailing Hallers and his professional colleagues. This unfortunately contributes to the one-dimensionality of the character. By making his Dr. Köhler too perfect, von Winterstein puts him on a pedestal and distances him from audience identification. To make matters worse, before the film even starts von Winterstein steps in front of a curtain, bows in all directions, and reads the credits to the audience. Presumably Wiene wanted to suggest that with the addition of sound, the cinema was now on an equal footing with the already legitimate stage. But this nonfilmic strategy undermined the very realism that was intended for the film. By appearing as an actor and as Köhler, von Winterstein no longer lets the audience forget the fictionality of the action. This was an antirealistic, alienating stylistic device, which Wiene could not have intended.

Robert Wiene's familiarity with Paul Lindau's play *Der Andere* antedates even the silent film version of Max Mack's *Der Andere* of 1913. His father, Carl Wiene, played the role of Hallers in performances at the Raimund Theater in Vienna in 1896[9] while his son was attending the University of Vienna. Apparently it was one of Carl Wiene's most successful roles, and it is likely that Robert saw him in his performances in Vienna as Dr. Hallers. It is also likely that Robert Wiene saw Mack's film, which was one of the most celebrated films of its time and throughout the 1920s was referred to as the first "literary" film.[10]

A comparison between Lindau's play and the silent and sound film versions yields some interesting contrasts. Mack's film offers a purely physiological explanation of the emergence of Hallers's split personality. One day as Hallers is having tea with some friends, the discussion turns to a book by Hippolyte Taine, and a title then quotes a specific passage from the book:

> Due to a fall, a severe illness or overexertion, a split personality can develop in man, a sick personality beside a healthy one. Each does not know of the other. In a kind of semi-conscious state, the sick personality can commit acts that the healthy one does not have the slightest conscious recollection of.[11]

Soon thereafter Hallers falls from his horse and six months later experiences symptoms of the above condition, solely as a consequence of his accident, as another title makes clear. The transformed Hallers is played by Albert Bassermann as a primitive kind of outsider who hangs out in taverns with criminals until one day, accompanied by one of them, he attempts to break into his own home. He finally recognizes that he suffers from a split personality and is eventually cured, but there is no hint of a subjective, psychological relationship between the two selves.

In Lindau's play, Hippolyte Taine is mentioned,[12] to be sure, but in addition to the physiological cause of Hallers's aberration – his fall from his horse – emotional stress as a precipitating factor is also emphasized: Hallers had indicated to his neighbor and colleague Arnoldy that he wanted to marry his sister Agnes. Arnoldy, however, had flatly rejected his wish because of the age difference and Hallers's exclusive commitment to his work. In other words, Lindau, more than Mack, gives the subjective, psychological factors their due, in addition to citing the explanations given by Taine, the scientist whose works were still considered at the end of the nineteenth century authoritative on such illnesses. However, though a psychological causation for Hallers's metamorphosis is given initially in Lindau's play, psychological factors cease to play a role in the further execution of the plot. Hallers is pitiful in his puzzlement and alienation as he inquires about his identity and background. But no subjective link is established between the two selves; no hidden, repressed side emerges to demand its due. Only a confused Hallers struggles with a dilemma beyond his comprehension.

In his remake, Wiene follows up and expands Lindau's greater concern with psychological motivation. The causation and development of Hallers's dual personality are deliberately delineated and embedded in a modern understanding of psychology. References to

Der Andere (The Other) Director: Robert Wiene (1930) –
Ursula van Diemen, Fritz Kortner, Hermine Sterler

Taine are replaced with references to Freud and to psychoanalysis, and the physiological basis of the split personality is dropped altogether. An examination of Johannes Brandt's original screenplay[13] makes it clear that this modern understanding of psychology was part of Wiene's conception of the film.

In Brandt's script, Hallers is more of a Jekyll and Hyde figure than in Wiene's film. As Hallers he is the repressed, vengeful prosecuting attorney who cannot express his feelings to the woman he loves. As the "baron" he is a primitive, vulgar, violent man who manhandles Amalie in an effort to gratify his sexual lust. Both sides of the split personality are represented as extremes, reminiscent of Stevenson's popular conception in his *The Strange Case of Dr. Jekyll and Mr. Hyde* (1886). Wiene's Hallers is portrayed with much more subtlety in an attempt to illustrate a modern conception of mental illness. He is neither violent nor brutal but, rather, in his amorality and with his easy-going way with women, he functions as a complement to the restrained and inhibited Hallers.

In Brandt's script as well as in Wiene's film there is an opening scene in the courtroom where Hallers exhibits his self-righteous severity as prosecuting attorney. In the script, the story concludes with another courtroom scene where the cured Hallers appears and to everyone's surprise admits his error and makes a plea for a humane judicial system. Wiene again rejects this switch from one extreme to the other and replaces the last courtroom scene with a professional consultation between Dr. Köhler and two other psychiatrists who evaluate Hallers's mental condition. Hallers, accustomed to passing judgment on others, is now being judged himself. Just as in the first courtroom scene, here too issues of freedom, justice, and humane understanding are raised. The traditionalist judges him severely and would have him incarcerated for life. The modernist, Dr. Köhler, invoking Freud, is able to persuade the others that Hallers is suffering from a curable disease of the emotions. His optimism is based on the belief that insight and awareness are the precondition for a cure: "Dear Colleague, the basic concept of psychoanalysis is that this knowledge is the beginning of the healing process. Freud showed us the way we have to follow." Whereas in Brandt's concluding scene a "born again" Hallers appears with a plea for humane justice, Wiene demonstrates in his final scene that a modern understanding of the human psyche now makes a more humane justice possible.

In his first sound film – and the changes in Brandt's screenplay make that clear – Wiene deals with a subject matter that is singularly representative of his entire oeuvre as director and scriptwriter. Wiene belonged to the generation of filmmakers who brought the silent film to its peak and managed the transition to sound. But in contrast to many other sound film debuts, he designed *Der Andere* as a sound film proper. His use of music as well as of the two songs presented in it is entirely diegetic. The first song is sung by Marion and conveys the problematic nature of her relationship with Hallers. The second one is sung by Dickert several times throughout the film to console Amalie when she is in a melancholy mood. Wiene also uses dialogue dramaturgically: Dickert and Grünspecht, for example, are characterized by their language. They converse in their thick urban dialects – the one from Berlin, the other from Vienna – which adds to the authenticity and to a good deal of the film's humor. Brandt's screenplay gave no indication of this; it undoubtedly was Wiene's invention.

Yet another example of Wiene's dramaturgical use of sound is a scene at the very end of the film when Hallers's crisis is ultimately resolved. This scene is represented solely with sound and not visually. Hallers's struggle with himself – after all, an inner struggle – is not being played out in front of the camera. Only his anguished shrieks are heard while the psychiatrists' reactions are observed. Wiene relies on sound alone to arouse the imagination of the audience.

Technically, the quality of sound in *Der Andere* is not as highly developed as in some of the other films of the time. However, with the Hippodrome scene, Wiene was one of the first who took the voluminous sound equipment out of the studio to make sound shots on location. This scene was filmed in a Berlin amusement park on 16 June 1930.[14]

Immediately after *Der Andere* was completed, Wiene made a French-language version, *Le Procureur Hallers*, with French actors in the same studio in Berlin. Making multiple-language versions of the same film was a common practice in the early sound film period. The French film was produced by the Berlin Terra Film Company on behalf of the French Albatros Company. The two companies had negotiated a contract according to which Wiene would direct a French version, assisted by a Frenchman who would translate Brandt's film script and prepare the French dialogue. Furthermore, the contract stipulated that the French version should follow the German version as closely as possible but that some of the sets should be enhanced in their furnishings. The contract also specified that the shooting should be done between 14 July and 28 July 1930.[15]

It is quite clear, then, that Wiene made *Le Procureur Hallers* right after *Der Andere*, following the German version closely except for the fact that he has Hallers return to the courtroom still as prosecuting attorney but as a cured and more humane person.[16] Presumably this scene is similar to the final scene from Brandt's film script, which had been dropped for some reason from the German version.

Le Procureur Hallers was shown in Berlin in a special screening. The Berlin reviews preferred the German version, claiming that the acting there was more realistic and true-to-life.[17] Several years later both foreign-language versions were shown in the United States. There too the reviews favored the German version by far.[18] Yet another foreign-language version was made in Italy in 1933 with the title *Il Caso Haller*. This Italian-language version was directed by Alessandro Blasetti and followed Johannes Brandt's script.[19]

DER LIEBESEXPRESS *(The Love Express)* [ACHT TAGE GLÜCK *(Eight Days of Happiness)*]

For his second sound film Wiene turned to an entirely different genre, a musical comedy based on the operetta *Es lebe die Liebe* (*Long Live Love*) by Alexander Engel and Wilhelm Sterk; the film was also known by the name *Acht Tage Glück*. With the assistance of Pierre Billon, Wiene also filmed a French version under the title *Nuits de Venise* with a French cast.[20]

The plot revolves around a young woman's wish fulfillment fantasy that becomes reality. Dina Gralla plays a typist, Annie, who one day enters a typewriting contest and wins 3,000 Marks. She decides to use the money for a trip to Venice. An advertisement in the paper for a secretary to accompany her brings a rich young man, Kurt (Georg Alexander), who takes the job on a lark. At a luxury hotel in Venice, an Italian count Orsino (Angelo Ferrari) becomes enamored of her, which makes Kurt very jealous since he had also fallen for her. The singer Enrico Tonelli (Joseph Schmidt), who entertains her with his arias is yet another love conquest. Annie confides to her secretary Kurt that the count has offered her unbelievable wealth if she will marry him. When Kurt responds coolly that she must decide for herself, she is overjoyed because he is the one she really loves. By chance she discovers that Kurt is not the poor man she had thought he was, but quite the contrary. Indignant that he had toyed with her, she leaves Venice to return to Berlin. Kurt goes to great lengths to find his beloved Annie, first in Venice, then on the train, and finally in Berlin. There he does indeed find her at her old job as a typist at the travel bureau. He approaches her and requests two tickets for a honeymoon trip to Venice. She now recognizes his true intentions and the two lovers are united.[21]

Der Liebesexpress was generally well received both in Germany and in the United States as a light-hearted comedy with good music and attractive exterior shots of Venice. One reviewer praised the many comic scenes but attributed their success more to Georg Alexander's acting than to Wiene's skill with sound film, which he questioned:

There are many funny scenes, less due to the ideas of Robert Wiene, who as a sound film director has not gained confidence yet, than to the charming and amiable performance of Georg Alexander, who enlivens the scene even when its fabric grows thin.[22]

Another reviewer gave Wiene credit for overcoming the handicaps of a script that apparently was too dependent on its source:

Wiene's experienced and clean directing cannot quite replace what the script is lacking in pace and ideas. Without doubt, however, he has succeeded in pleasantly highlighting individual scenes and in giving the unfolding story the lightness and elegance which make even familiar situations appear charming.[23]

Der Liebesexpress was released in the United States under the title *Acht Tage Glück*. The New York premiere was at the Belmont Theater on 23 July 1931. According to the reviews in *Variety* and in the *New York Times*, the film was a popular success, as it had already been in Chicago.[24] The reviewer in *Variety* examined the film in somewhat greater detail. He found the score of the musical and Joseph Schmidt's singing excellent but faulted the technical quality of the sound and some of the photography. In his discussion of Schmidt's singing, he described a scene that is most revealing as an example of Wiene's deliberate use of sound:

One exceptionally good piece of business has a phonograph record of Schmidt singing a Neapolitan number. After the disk is about three quarters through, the train lurches and breaks the record, but the song unexpectedly continues through, the singer being in the next compartment, unknown to the phonograph owners.[25]

As far as we know, no print of *Der Liebesexpress* has survived.

PANIK IN CHICAGO *(Panic in Chicago)* Wiene's gangster film *Panik in Chicago* has been overlooked by all contemporary film historians, with the exception of the late Herbert Holba in his Wiene entry in *Reclams deutsches Filmlexikon*.[26] Holba sees a link between the realistic depiction of the gangster milieu in *Der Andere* and *Panik in Chicago*. However, there are major differences between the two films. In *Der Andere* petty criminals communicate in their pubs in their colorful Berlin dialect. By contrast, the gangsters in *Panik in Chicago* simply follow the European stereotype of American underworld characters. The gang leaders, however, are more interesting. Both play dual roles, as tough bosses of their gangs and at the same time as elegant gentlemen in high society. To be sure, in *Der Andere* there is an element of this double identity in the fact that Hallers carouses in pubs and is a highly respected attorney – but the duality is, of course, psychological.

The 35mm print with German dialogue and French subtitles, which we had at our disposal, is preserved by the Deutsches Institut für Filmkunde; it has numerous breaks and no entire sequences are missing, so that the plot can be followed from beginning to end.

The plot begins with a cold-blooded holdup of a bank belonging to Taglioni, who is in reality the gang leader Al Patou. The rumor spreads that the thieves belong to Al Patou's arch enemy, Morand Billy, who is known in high society as the wealthy diamond dealer Percy Boot. Florence Dingley (Olga Tschechowa) lives alone in an apartment, which her friend and lover Percy Boot provides for her. She knows nothing of Percy's criminal affiliations. On the day of the bank holdup, Percy breaks his opera engagement with her to meet with his arch enemy Al Patou in an abandoned warehouse to discuss their criminal ventures. They quarrel and in the ensuing fight Percy Boot is shot.

Percy calls Florence and asks her and his chauffeur Tom (Gerhard Bienert) to meet him immediately at the warehouse. When they arrive they find him dead; the only clue is a handkerchief on the floor with the initials S. O. As the two quickly leave, they hear a shot from the dead man's room. When the police arrive they find the

Panik in Chicago (Panic in Chicago) Director: Robert Wiene (1931)

corpse, and in its hand, a suicide note signed Morand Billy. Police Inspector Renard immediately suspects a link between Boot/Morand and Taglioni, whom he correctly believes to be Al Patou. Renard finds Taglioni in a nightclub with Suzy Owen and Fay Davis. Renard then tries to trick Taglioni into revealing his criminal identity but without success until the very end.

In the meantime, Florence learns from Tom everything about Percy Boot's criminal background. Percy had left her a letter in which he declared that if he died it would be at the hands of Al Patou. Enraged, she seeks out Percy's gang to call for revenge. At that very moment Patou/Taglioni himself enters and challenges the gang. They do not dare to oppose him but Florence plans his fall. She informs the gang that Al Patou plans to smuggle a large shipment of cocaine hidden in mechanical pianos into America.

At a masquerade ball given by Taglioni, Florence confronts him and tells him that she has thwarted his plans for the cocaine shipment. Taglione goes into action to salvage his scheme but is caught in the crossfire between the two gangs and is seriously wounded. His flight leads him to the very room in which Percy had died and where Florence confronts him once more. He persuades her to believe he is innocent of Percy Boot's death, and in an act of compassion, she helps him to escape from the gang that is on his trail. The gang soon

Panik in Chicago (Panic in Chicago) Director: Robert Wiene (1931) –
Olga Tschechova, Hans Rehmann

enter, and believing that Florence betrayed them, kill her. Then the police arrive and arrest the entire gang.

Inspector Renard, while pursuing his investigation of the case, had learned that Percy Boot had had a criminal record in New York, along with his accomplice Fay Davis. She is now arrested and confesses to the murder of her former husband, Percy Boot, who had abandoned and neglected her. At the end, Renard finally can arrest Taglione, whose true criminal identity is revealed by one of Percy Boot's accomplices.[27]

The film's premiere on 23 June 1931 at the Ufa-Palast am Zoo in Berlin was preceded by a number of announcements dating back to 27 December 1930. On that day it was reported that the production company DLS (Deutsches Lichtspiel-Syndikat) had purchased the rights to Robert Heymann's popular novel *Panik in Chicago*.[28] Three days later it was announced that executive producer Leo Meyer had hired Robert Wiene to direct the film. The script was to be written by Friedrich Raff and Julius Urgiss.[29] These two announcements also claim that *Panik in Chicago* was to be shot in German and French versions; however, the French version was apparently only synchronized.[30] In Austria the film appeared early in August 1931 under the title *Panik in der Unterwelt (Panic in the Underworld)*.[31]

On 4 June 1931 the film was approved by the Censorship Board but for adult viewing only. Beyond that, some aspects of the advertisement for the film were censored. The film company challenged this decision; but at a formal hearing the board rejected the claim on the grounds that several of the photos used in publicizing the film, namely, those that showed the bank holdup and the shootout between the two warring gangs, tended to endanger the morals of minors.[32]

Panik in Chicago was an enormous success in all major cities in Germany, as reported in the press. "The D.L.S. branches in Düsseldorf and Frankfurt a.M. had such record bookings for the film *Panik in Chicago* during the following two weeks that several new copies had to be distributed in these districts because the available subsidiary copies could not fulfill the demand for screenings."[33] Other reports refer to the unusual popular acclaim the film enjoyed in Leipzig, Halle, Munich, and Stuttgart.[34]

In the reviews some criticism was leveled against the quality of several of the dialogues and the relative weakness of the female roles.[35] The film as a whole, however was given a most positive evaluation in *Die LichtBildBühne*:

Robert Wiene made a tremendous effort to extract from the story whatever it would give. So he did succeed in creating scenes that will be remembered for a long time. Eerie and ghostlike, everything connected with the lonely house. The dim stairs, the rushing people, or the fabulous night shots of a big city. The glass reflections of a dance scene. Simply masterful! On the whole, the imagery in this film achieves great triumphs. Willi Goldberger, the camera artist, and Robert Neppach, the refined architect, were Wiene's invaluable collaborators.[36]

It is interesting that the journalist emphasizes the pictorial in *Panik in Chicago*. After all, it is with this film that Robert Wiene's visual style begins to change, as the first scene demonstrates. The very first shot shows a gigantic vault being opened by bank attendants. A split second later, bank robbers burst in with shouts of "hands up." In the next hundred seconds, thirty shots show a gang taking over a major bank in downtown Chicago with a thoroughly professional routine. This rapid sequencing represents a general tendency in Wiene's visual style in *Panik in Chicago*. Consistent with this is a more active use of the mobile camera, which along with frequent travelings, pans, and tilts of the camera creates a spatial dynamic – a fairly new feature in Wiene's directorial technique. In addition to this, he constructs complex framing with a variegated organization of levels within the deep focus. Together with unusual fast cutting at certain dramatic moments, Wiene effectively adopts the visual styles of action films.

In the film's early sequences the four main characters – Taglioni, Percy Boot, Florence Dingly, and Inspector Renard – are introduced, as well as information about the double lives of the first two. Thus, from the very beginning the spectator knows more than the active participants and the police, who are investigating the criminal activity of the two major gangs. Throughout the film Wiene continues this strategy of keeping the spectators more informed than the participants of the film. He reverses this strategy only toward the end by introducing surprises for the audience. Just as the audience begins to identify Susy Owen as the prime suspect for the murder of Percy Boot, through careful criminal investigation, the police discover the true identity of Fay Davis and thereby the real murderer; secondly, Inspector Reynard, working behind the scenes, finds a witness who, because of a personal grudge against Taglioni, is willing to identify him as Al Patou.

Structurally, *Panik in Chicago* revolves around three subplots, in each of which Taglioni is one of the two adversaries. There is an early encounter between Taglioni and his arch enemy Percy Booth, who is murdered soon thereafter. This murder precipitates the conflict between Taglioni and Florence Dingly, who "inherits" the gang of her friend Morand Billy (Percy Boot). At the same time the murder and the bank holdup bring police inspector Renard into the picture as Taglioni's (Al Patou) main antagonist who doggedly pursues him throughout the film.

The duel between Taglioni and Renard is fought on a subtle, intellectual level. Both play a game, the rules of which they know very well, and both are "modern" in that they use modern technology to further their ends. Taglioni, for example, signals messages to his gang by means of an electric piano with which he can manipulate the letters of a large neon sign on the rooftop of his house. Renard, in turn, has access to a high-tech transmitter with which he receives radioed photographs from the New York police. The struggle between Taglioni and Renard takes place in the most sophisticated accommodations. Renard, who suspects Taglioni but has no proof, pursues him relentlessly but always with good manners, dressed as the occasion requires. Taglioni, fully aware of his pursuer's intention, is cool and collected in his tuxedo, with his urbane demeanor, to the very end.

Taglioni's struggle with Florence Dingly is not nearly as clear cut. After Morand Billy's death, she becomes Taglioni's adversary and exhorts the gang to attack his cocaine transport as an act of revenge against the man she suspects of having committed the murder. Indeed, she succeeds in bringing him down primarily because he has underestimated her. During a dramatic poker scene, he intimidates her whole gang with his cool ruthlessness, but by refusing to accept her challenge purely out of vanity ("I don't play against women"), he brings about his own downfall.

Although the structure of the film emerges quite clearly through these three subplots and the duels between the major characters, a deficiency in the characterization of the women in the film – specifically in the all-important case of Florence Dingly – mars an otherwise well-balanced film. Florence's sudden transformation from high-society lady to the leader of a mob is not at all convincing, nor is her readiness to give up her revenge on Taglioni and even help him in his escape well motivated.

In *Panik in Chicago* Wiene concentrates on the conflict between the two main protagonists rather than on an authentic depiction of the criminal milieu as he had in *Der Andere*. The gangs appear, thus, for the most part as anonymous and faceless. Taglioni's men are seen only in the bank holdup and the shootout at the end. Morand Billy's gang emerges a bit more clearly, but even in the poker scene, they remain fairly colorless and are given only a minimum of individual characterization. It may have been the Chicago setting that prevented Wiene from using devices such as slang or dialects (all characters speak standard German). Hence, he did not achieve an authenticity the likes of which made the criminal milieu in *Der Andere* so lively. Nevertheless, with all its flaws, *Panik in Chicago* is an unusual example for the early German sound film, which is still overlooked without good reason. In its mixture of crime drama and gangster film it is, according to Herbert Holba, a rarity among German films of the period.[37]

TAIFUN (Typhoon)   The usual information given in the film lexica about *Taifun* is that the film was forbidden in Germany and released only after numerous alterations and cuts on 27 July 1934 under the title *Polizeiakte 909*.[38] What was never made clear is that the new version received a completely different plot, not only through cuts but through the addition of new sequences with new characters and presumably new dialogues superimposed through synchronization on some of the earlier scenes. This becomes incontrovertible when the plot summaries as they appeared in the material printed at the time are compared.

The plot of *Taifun* revolves around the Japanese Dr. Nitobe Tokeramo (Valeri Inkischinoff) and his intimate love affair with Helene Laroche (Liane Haid), a cabaret singer in the "White Lily." Helen lives with Charles Renard Bninski (Viktor de Kowa), a journalist and blackmailer. He is alleged to earn more from what he does not write than from what he does. Tokeramo is in Paris on a secret mission for Japan, the exact nature of which is never revealed. When the leader of his Japanese group, Yoshikawa, learns of Tokeramo's involvement with Helene, he insists that he give her up for the sake of his duty to the fatherland. Meanwhile, Renard has discovered Helene's infidelity and, incited to jealousy, he attempts to blackmail Tokeramo with an incriminating document he has obtained through Helene. When the two men meet, a struggle ensues in which Tokeramo kills Renard.

Tokeramo informs Yoshikawa of his deed and expresses his willingness to take the consequences for it. The Japanese elder, however, counsels that a friend of Tokeramo, Inose Hironari (Veit Harlan), take the blame so that Tokeramo can complete his mission. The case is brought to trial, and in a long courtroom session, the Japanese succeed in deceiving the court about the real circumstances of the murder. Hironari is condemned for the deed. In the last conversation between Tokeramo and Helene, she explains that she has finally understood the motivations of the Japanese and for that reason she concealed testimony that would have brought out the truth. Tokeramo is content to finish his mission in two months and then free Hironari by confessing his crime.[39]

This is the film that Robert Wiene completed in February 1933. The original version – premiered in Vienna on 25 August 1933 – was never distributed in Germany. The journal *Film-Atelier*[40] reported that in January and February Wiene was still preoccupied with *Taifun* (and a French version of the film as well), and the popular *Filmwoche* published an article describing Wiene's work with his ensemble of actors on 2 February 1933. Finally, a handwritten note on the original shooting script indicates that the film was completed on 16 February 1933.[41]

The attitude of the Censorship Board toward *Taifun* presents an interesting insight into the principles of early Nazi film censorship practices. The film was banned on 21 April 1933; the production company appealed, and the board rendered its final decision on 3 May 1933. The hearing was presided over by Dr. Seeger, who had previously chaired the Censorship Board during the Weimar Republic. Present were also four magistrates, a lawyer representing Camera Film Productions and three expert witnesses representing the ministries of justice, propaganda, and foreign affairs.

The representative of the foreign ministry charged that the film depicts Europeans and Asians to the disadvantage of the Europeans who, although represented as French, were clearly recognizable as Germans. This he felt would undermine Germany's reputation abroad. The justice ministry argued that the court scene misrepresented the true nature of jurisprudence in Germany but granted that the court proceedings according to dress and appearance were French and thus really did not constitute a distortion of the German situation.

As regards the presence of a representative from the propaganda ministry, the presiding officer Seeger pointed out that it was necessary to determine whether and to what extent the film's negative depiction of the white race *vis-á-vis* the Asian would damage the people's national self-esteem. The expert witness from the propaganda ministry was quoted as follows:

> On the whole, the film is characterized by a confrontation between Germans and Asians. The issue of race is a central problem at present. The film does comment negatively on the issue by not considering at all the racial instinct of the German people and not sparing them from feelings of inferiority. The film completely evades the obligation to educate the people systematically about the need for race hygiene. Therefore, the German people would not understand if a film that diminishes the German in this way as compared with Asians were to be admitted for public presentation. In these times especially, the appearance of a film that runs so much counter to the intentions of the national government would be intolerable.[42]

The minutes do not summarize the arguments presented in defense of the film by the film company's lawyer, although it is clear that he had been given the opportunity to make his case.

The final judgment against *Taifun* reflects the opinions voiced by the expert witnesses for the foreign and propaganda ministries. In view of the fact that all Europeans in the film were disreputable characters and the Asians by contrast were loyal, noble, and self-sacrificing the magistrates felt that:

> A film like this constitutes a slap in the face of the racial feelings of German countrymen and, to a high degree, offends the national sensitivity of the white race as compared with the colored race. It, therefore, constitutes the legal offence of compromising German reputation and should be banned.[43]

It was also maintained that even though the ostensible setting for the film was French, an audience would experience it as a German reality. The court scene in particular was considered damaging to the German people's confidence in the judicial system. According to the minutes, these were the main reasons for banning *Taifun* in the German Reich.

A plot summary of *Polizeiakte 909 (Police File 909)* will make it clear how the objections of the Censorship Board were met in the restructuring of the film. What emerged was a fundamentally different film from *Taifun. Polizeiakte 909* begins with a crisis conference at a Parisian police precinct about the theft of a dangerous serum from the Gatton factory. Commissioner Morré (Friedrich Ettel) gives strict orders that no information about the case go public. The famous detective Bninski (Viktor de Kowa) is called into the case. Unfortunately, his work is hampered by the factory detective (Josef Dahmen) who had bungled the initial investigation. Bninski soon establishes that a group of Asians are responsible for the crime. In the guise of a journalist and with the help of the nightclub singer Helene (Liane Haid), he manages to establish contact with the Asians. Helene, who had helped the police before, plays her role very well by inducing one of the Asians, Dr. Tokeramo (Inkischinoff), to fall in love with her.

Since the serum that is so important to the Asians is not yet finished, they are now working day and night to complete the formula. They are unaware, however, that Bninski is hard on their trail. Helene manages to steal this formula from her Asian lover and turns it over to Bninski. In attempting to bring the criminals to justice, Bninski is murdered by Tokeramo himself. The Asians try to place the blame for the murder on one of his friends, Hironari (Veit Harlan), so that Tokeramo can complete his work. However, during the trial, the prosecutor (Bernhard Goetzke) ferrets out the truth with clever questioning, and the real murderer and his whole band are arrested. Moreover, the serum is found and is no longer a threat to humanity.[44]

The divergences between the two stories make it clear that *Taifun* and *Polizeiakte 909* are two different films: two figures have been added in the new version, namely, commissioner Morré and the factory detective; the Europeans are not disreputable characters; Bninski is a famous detective and Helene, though a nightclub singer, frequently works with the police; the Asians are not noble, loyal patriots but common, ruthless criminals; and the courtroom scene reveals a judicial system that cannot be deceived by clever subterfuge. Since no print of *Polizeiakte 909* has survived, it cannot be determined how much of Wiene's material was incorporated into the reedited version.

The few reviews of *Polizeiakte 909* that appeared after its premiere on 27 July 1934 indicate that there was some confusion about the nature of the film. One reviewer gives a brief summary, with the judgment that parts of the film were much too artificially constructed. Some of the actors are mentioned, but no reference is made to either the author or the director of the film.[45] Another reviewer notices that neither the director nor the scriptwriter is mentioned in the credits. He criticizes the acting of Victor de Kowa, which according to the reviewer also evoked laughter from the audience.[46] The reviewer of the journal *Film-Atelier* does not even mention the entire crew; only the cast is listed.[47] The review in the *Film-Kurier* is the most illuminating. The reviewer knows that the film has been announced for the 1932/33 season and has been through what he calls the "purgatory of censorship." He refers to Robert Wiene as the film's director and holds him responsible for the dialogue and the acting. What he believes Wiene has intended to be serious, he perceives to be working comically for the audience. Apparently the reviewer has no knowledge of the *Taifun* version and is in no position to recognize how the film was altered to abide by the requirements of the censors.[48]

It seems that only the Reich Film Archive (Reichsfilmarchiv) knew that *Taifun* and *Polizeiakte 909* were two different films. According to its records, the archive possessed both films, as the respective plot summaries indicate. For both films the records provide an extensive enumeration of the crew and the cast. Robert Wiene is cited as the director of both films.[49] There is no clear and decisive evidence whether or to what extent Wiene was involved in the making of *Polizeiakte 909*. He arrived in Budapest on 26 September 1933 for the shooting of *Eine Nacht in Venedig (A Night in Venice)*.[50] It is not likely that he ever returned to Germany.

Taifun tells first and foremost a love story between a French nightclub singer and a Japanese gentleman who is in Paris on a secret mission. The love story shifts to a criminal case when a murder is committed and the Japanese Tokeramo must stand trial. Although Wiene made the film in late 1932 and early 1933, he seems not to have had any political purpose in mind. The Japanese presence in Paris seems to have had a merely exotic function, something that is found so often in Wiene films. The love between a white woman and an Asian man offers an opportunity for the meeting of two cultures, rather than for racial commentary in terms of Nazi ideology.

Wiene tried to develop two separate and fairly distinct milieus that impinge on each other solely through the unexpected affair between Helene and Tokeramo. Bninski, the unscrupulous scoundrel and lady's man, and Helene, the nightclub performer with easy morals, are part of a nightclub milieu. Tokeramo and his friends, dedicated to duty and honor in the fulfillment of their sacred patriotic mission, represent an antithetical pole providing the plot with structure and tension. The clash between the two milieus is the dramatic peak of the film as it leads to a crime and conviction in a dramatic court sequence. Though consistent in its methodology, Western jurisprudence fails to grasp the cultural context of the testimony of the Japanese witnesses and consequently fails to comprehend the crime and the criminal. What the court sequence makes clear is that this institution, with its procedures for giving testimony and cross-examination, is culture bound. An individual, however – in this instance the uncomplicated Helene Laroche – succeeds in crossing over to the other culture and, learning to understand Tokeramo's true motivation, conceals her testimony for the sake of justice as understood by the Japanese.

Wiene based his screenplay for *Taifun* on the play of the same name by the Hungarian playwright Melchior Lengyel, written in 1911. The play was immensely popular and repeatedly produced on German and other European stages. In our contrastive study of Lengyel's play and Wiene's script and film, we observed a number of fundamental differences. To begin with, Wiene tones down the blunt, aggressive nationalism of the play's Japanese. In the film their commitment to duty and devotion to Japanese culture are never questioned, but their vindictive anti-European attitudes, so apparent in Lengyel, are clearly absent. Wiene's Japanese are human, noble, and loyal.

In the play Tokeramo kills Helene and not Bninski. Moreover, in the final act there is a not-too-credible sympathy emerging between Tokeramo and Bninski, both of whom have suddenly discovered their common humanity. Nevertheless, Tokeramo remains Japanese to such a degree that he commits hara-kiri to atone for his disloyalty to Japanese traditions. By contrast, in the film it is Helene's love for Tokeramo that enables her to transcend her cultural limitations and learn to appreciate his culture. Tokeramo, for his part, never rejects her love but also remains loyal to his friends.

The dramatic focus for Wiene's film is the courtroom drama. What is merely a hearing in the judge's office in Lengyel's play is transformed by Wiene into a dramaturgically effective courtroom scene in which the truth emerges in a double sense. An ambiguity surfaces due to the clash between the traditions of Western jurisprudence and the cultural values and practices that bind the Japanese. Subtly, Wiene designs the film so that only Helene and, of course, the audience become aware of this duality.

Taifun was Wiene's fourth sound film. The film's original film script makes it clear that he had fully integrated sound into his filming strategy. Transitions from one scene to the next are frequently conveyed by sound as well as by image. Music also plays a crucial role in the development of the drama. Helene's romantic song about the cherry blossoms of Yokahama draws Tokeramo into her sphere. It is this very song that is played on the radio while Tokeramo kills Bninski and by which the exact time of the crime can later be established.

The camera movement, as was already observed in *Panik in Chicago*, has become more flexible. A number of shots are given an extended duration, during which time the camera explores a given space with pans and/or trackings. Once again as in *Panik in Chicago* Wiene frequently uses deliberately organized framing to structure space. Apparently, in the new medium of the sound film, space acquires for Wiene a different aesthetic problematic. Since sound must be three dimensional, it influences Wiene's visual styles in the sense that he is prompted to provide more instances of space structured three dimensionally.

EINE NACHT IN VENEDIG *(A Night in Venice)*   We do not know how the Nazi rise to power in 1933 affected Wiene's film career immediately. According to the sources we have been able to obtain, the Nazis considered him to be a Jew. However, in the complicated censorship case over *Taifun* there was no reference to that issue; the case was decided on purely ideological grounds. Nevertheless, *Taifun* was the last film Wiene made in Germany.

Robert Wiene and Géza von Cziffra during the shooting of
Eine Nacht in Venedig (A Night in Venice) Director: Robert Wiene (1933) –
in the Hunnia Studios in Budapest

According to Alfred Bauer's filmography of German sound films, *Eine Nacht in Venedig* "was produced in the Hunnia film studio in Budapest as the German version of the original Hungarian film."[51] Practically every film history that has a notation for this film uses that statement by Bauer as its source. However, Hungarian documents from the time do not support this information. In *Filmkultura*, the most significant Hungarian film journal of the time, we learn that Wiene was expected in Budapest in September 1933 for the casting, with the shooting to start before the end of the month.[52] On 26 September Wiene arrived in Budapest and two days later the work began on *"both a Hungarian and a German version."*[53] In a subsequent issue of the journal, we furthermore learn that the interior shooting for both versions was completed by the middle of October and then Wiene, Géza von Cziffra (the co-director of the Hungarian version), Szántó Rezsö (the head of production), and the entire crew traveled to Venice for the location shots.[54]

Three participants in the film – Géza von Cziffra and two of the Hungarian actors, Zsuzsa Simon and György Tarján – confirmed this information. According to them, the whole group, including the German and the Hungarian casts, were in Venice for as long as three weeks due to the bad weather.[55] Cziffra explained that each sequence was filmed twice, first with the German actors and then with the Hungarian actors. Moreover, he claimed that he, together with

Wiene, directed the Hungarian version, and in his volume of memoirs there is a production still showing Wiene and himself at work in the studio.[56] Indeed, the program for the Hungarian version *Egy Éj Velencében* lists both Robert Wiene and Géza von Cziffra as the film's directors.[57] Tarján, in addition, pointed out that the Hungarian screenplay that he had used in preparing his role was a translation of a German script that was written by Wiene.

Egy Éj Velencében (A Night in Venice) Director: Robert Wiene (1933) – working photo: Werner Bohne and Ernö Verebes

From all this it can be concluded that *Eine Nacht in Venedig* was the original film and that *Egy Éj Velencében* was dependent on it. This was consistent with the customary practice of the Hunnia studios in Budapest in the early sound period of renting its facilities to foreign companies. Cziffra explained that the German film production under Goebbels kept the German studios so busy that Hunnia saw an opportunity to offer their facilities. Agota Ivanics, a researcher at the Magyar Filmintézet in Budapest, maintained that the Hunnia management doubted the financial viability of Hungarian-language films. Consequently, they looked for partners for dual-language productions, offering costs thirty percent to forty percent less expensive than in Germany and even fifty percent less expensive than in England. The primary condition was, of course, that the foreign partner produce the Hungarian version as well.[58]

Eine Nacht in Venedig (A Night in Venice) Director: Robert Wiene (1933) – Fritz Fischer, Lizzi von Balla

The plot of *Eine Nacht in Venedig* was based on an operetta of the same name by Johann Strauss. Ellen Hariman (Tina Eilers), the daughter of a New York multimillionaire, is engaged to marry the successful businessman Norden (Fritz Fischer) from Berlin. On the evening before the wedding, Ellen yearns to dance at the hotel where they are staying. Her fiancé, however, is already in bed resting up for the big event. She goes to the dance alone and meets Count Antonio Crivelli (Tino Pattiera) from Venice, who falls in love with her immediately. She too is attracted to him, but the next day he leaves early for Venice. Ellen in her exuberance does not think twice and follows him. Unexpectedly, Ellen's father, John Hariman, (Ludwig Stössel) arrives from America. To protect her mistress, Gina (Lizzi von Balla), Ellen's personal maid, invents the story that Norden and Ellen have already married and are on their honeymoon in Venice.

Now quite a few people are racing to Venice: Ellen's father, who naturally wants to congratulate the happy couple; Gina, who must inform Ellen of the story she has fabricated; and, of course, Ellen's supposed fiancé, Norden. During the trip Norden and Gina discover a mutual attraction. They all arrive in Venice, but Ellen is nowhere to be found. She has lost her handbag with all her money, cannot pay her hotel bill, and wanders through the city in despair, believing herself to be pursued by the police. Late at night, exhausted, she falls asleep on a park bench. There Count Crivelli finds her and brings her, still asleep, to his palace.

The count in actuality is impoverished and has been desperately seeking a buyer for his villa. That buyer presents himself unexpectedly in the person of John Hariman who, believing that Ellen and Norden are already married, buys the castle as a wedding gift for them. After a number of zany escapades, the father must face the truth: his daughter is in love with the count and Norden has fallen for Gina. All's well that ends well, and the operetta concludes with a double marriage.

Eine Nacht in Venedig was designed to be a crowd pleaser. The cast consisted of some extremely popular comic actors of the time, specifically Ludwig Stössel, and Oscar Sima as a Viennese bailiff who in a subplot pursues the destitute count. The star attraction was Tino Pattiera, a famous opera tenor, who was given ample opportunity in this film not only to sing but also to act. Similarly, in the Hungarian version the corresponding actors were well known to their audience: Gyula Csortos as the father; Guyla Gózon as the bailiff; Ernö Verebes as Norden; Lizzi von Balla in the same role; Zsuzsa Simon, in her acting debut, as Ellen; and György Tarján, a young tenor, as the count.

Eine Nacht in Venedig had its premiere in Germany on 21 March 1934 at the Primus-Palast in Berlin and in Austria in early February 1934. The film, which was distributed in Austria under the title *Ein Mädel – Eine Nacht (A Girl – A Night),* must have been very popular because, according to an announcement in a film journal, it was shown in eight Viennese movie houses simultaneously.[59] With its well-known cast, it is likely that it was very popular in Germany as well. The few film critics who commented on the film were somewhat more discriminating. They did approve of the individual performances of some of the actors as well as the sound and photography, but they criticized the script for deviating too much from the operetta by Johann Strauss. Wiene was faulted for not providing sufficient motivation for the roles and for his handling of the actors altogether. By contrast, Wiene's earlier sound film operetta, *Der Liebesexpress,* which was also set in Berlin and Venice, received much more acclaim.[60]

ULTIMATUM   Between *Eine Nacht in Venedig* (1934) and *Ultimatum* (1938) Wiene did not complete any films either as a scriptwriter or as a director. Although it cannot be established precisely when his exile from Germany began, it is clear that he made no more films in Germany after *Taifun* in 1932/33. Upon completion of *Eine Nacht in Venedig,* Wiene moved to London and later to Paris. In both cities he tried to establish himself as a filmmaker and producer, but most of his endeavors failed, undoubtedly due to the problems faced by an exile at that time.

It is all the more surprising then that in 1938 Wiene began shooting a film with two internationally known stars. Dita Parlo, a native German, was known in her country as well as in the U.S.; in France she was one of the most popular actresses. In the lead male role was Erich von Stroheim, whose fame as a director and actor was already legend by then. *Ultimatum* was already the third film in which he appeared together with Dita Parlo, after *Mademoiselle Docteur* (France, 1937; directed by Edmond T. Gréville) and especially after the sensational success of *La Grande Illusion* (France, 1937; directed by Jean Renoir).

The executive producer of *Ultimatum* was Charles-Georges Horset. In the credits listed on the print that is preserved by the Cinémathèque Municipale de Luxembourg, the film is presented as a "Robert Wiene Production," implying that the director participated in some way in the production process. According to the announcements publicizing the film in *La Cinématographie Française,* Pan Production is also cited as the production company; unfortunately, it cannot be clarified anymore whether it is in any way related to the Viennese Pan Film or the Berlin Paneuropa of earlier days.[61] The script was written by Léo Lania and Pierre Allary and was based on the novel *Tage vor dem Sturm: Roman aus den Juliwochen 1914 (Days before the Storm: A Novel from the July Weeks of 1914)* written by Ewald Bertram.[62] The French dialogues were composed by Alexandre Arnoux, who was to write a very moving obituary on Wiene after his death on 15 July 1938. After Wiene's death, a few days before the conclusion of the shooting of *Ultimatum,* Robert Siodmak completed the film, and it premiered during the last week of October 1938.

The action of the film begins during that critical period between the assassination of the Archduke Francis Ferdinand by Serbian nationalists on 28 June 1914 and Serbia's rejection of the abhorrent

Ultimatum Director: Robert Wiene (1938) – Dita Parlo, Bernard Lancret

Austrian "ultimatum" on the threshold of World War I. Nevertheless, *Ultimatum* is not a war film but a film that shows how war damages the lives of ordinary people.

The young Austrian woman Anna (Dita Parlo) is happily married to the Serbian officer Stanko Salic (Bernard Lancret). Though she has gladly taken on Serbian citizenship, she has retained her love for her native Austria. Immediately after the assassination of the archduke, Stanko is summoned by his superior officer Colonel Simovic (Erich von Stroheim) for an espionage assignment against Austria. Soon thereafter a mutual friend of Anna and Stanko, the Austrian journalist, Karl Burgstaller (Abel Jacquin), telephones and urges Anna to meet with him in a park. There he warns her of the imminent danger of war and urges her to return to her family in Vienna. Anna gives Burgstaller a letter, presumably a private communication to her parents. A spy in the employ of Colonel Simovic observes this meeting and in his report calls attention to the letter, the contents of which are unknown to him. As a consequence, Simovic suspects Burgstaller and probably also Anna of plotting against the Serbian cause.

While Stanko is at home preparing his departure for his secret mission, Anna informs him that Burgstaller has telephoned and that he is in Belgrade as a corespondent. Stanko, who knows that Burgstaller is in the Austrian intelligence service, explodes in anger over his former friend, now his enemy. Indeed, soon there is a confrontation between the two intelligence officers as they meet on the Austro-Serbian border where Stanko is pursuing his mission to blow up an all-important bridge. They struggle, and, though Burgstaller lets Stanko escape, he is soon wounded by an Austrian patrol and arrested.

Back in Belgrade Anna has a meeting with Colonel Simovic, who informs her that her husband has been wounded and arrested as a spy. In doubt about her allegiance, Simovic questions her and though she professes her innocence has her arrested. Burgstaller visits Stanko in the army hospital, ostensibly to cross-examine him but in actuality to persuade him to save Anna by letting her return to Vienna. The embittered Stanko, by then a hot-headed nationalist, rages against Burgstaller in whom he sees only an enemy of Serbia.

Burgstaller, against the orders of his superiors, returns to Belgrade to plead with Simovic for Anna's release, offering himself in her place. Recognizing in Burgstaller a man of honor, the colonel accepts; Anna, however, does not. Burgstaller pretends that it was he who was responsible for her husband's arrest. The ruse has its effect and Anna agrees to be repatriated. At this point Simovic learns that Russia supports the rejection of Austria's ultimatum and guarantees Serbia's sovereignty. Knowing the implications of this development, the crippled colonel painfully raises himself on his crutches and says, "This means war."

The desperate Stanko makes one last attempt to gain his freedom and is badly wounded. While Anna rushes to her husband's bedside, Burgstaller is summoned to Simovic's office to be informed by the colonel that he will be freed to reciprocate the generosity of the Austrians who have released a Serbian general. Simovic and Burgstaller solemnly shake hands and part in mutual respect.

At the hospital Stanko, feverish, still thinks of his mission. Just before he dies he hears the explosion that destroys the bridge. Inspired by the thought that his mission has been completed after all, he dies with the awareness that he is the first one to sacrifice his life for his fatherland. While Anna's poignant screams are heard, a montage of marching troops and newspaper headlines announcing the war whirl around the screen.[63]

The French reviewers were mostly positive in their evaluations of *Ultimatum*, though there were a few dissenters:

> The subject of *Ultimatum* is excellent. The same goes for the technical realization. The signatures of Robert Wiene and Robert-Paul Dagan – without doubt the best of the French assistants – are recommendation enough without my having to dwell on them. The photography under the supervision of Ted Pahle is excellent (mostly in yellow to better characterize the era and to allow the insertion of film clips of current events;

this is very effective). Borchard's music is very skilled; and I will note here the return to remarkable musical effects.[64]

With its blend of political and personal fates, the plot was narrated in great detail in the reviews, and *Ultimatum* was unanimously judged to be an important film. Although there was some confusion about the film's attitude toward war, all were agreed that the human aspects of the film were central to the plot.

The reviews of *Ultimatum* in the United States, where the film was released on 3 February 1940, provide a wider spectrum of opinions, some lauding the film and others charging that it was a throwback to silent film techniques. As far as the contents were concerned, there is again confusion as to whether the plot makes it a war film, a spy story, or a human-interest melodrama. One of the most thoughtful viewers of the film summarizes the essence of the plot as follows:

> It is an eloquent document, one imbued with much of that tensity fomented by the assassination of Archduke Francis Ferdinand in 1914. There is no actual war in the film, but the threat of war and those anxious days before the Russian Bear nodded provide a suspenseful background for a thrilling story of espionage. War is descried, not by a resume of its horrors on the battlefield, but from the standpoint of men and women embroiled in its tragic shadows. Friendly peoples suddenly at war! Where once they sang and danced and intermarried, they now look with suspicion and enmity upon their neighbors across the Danube.[65]

Ultimatum, then as well as now, brings to mind a comparison with Jean Renoir's *La Grande Illusion* (1937), as it is expressed in the following comments by an American reviewer in 1940:

> *Ultimatum* in many respects is similar to the prize winning French production of 1938 [sic], *Grand Illusion*. In both pictures Erich von Stroheim and Dita Parlo portray in feature roles the maimed army officer and the girl that was left behind. Both pictures show the effects of war on persons who come in contact with it. And both pictures emphasize the individual ability of the players, with the World War motif secondary to the story of their lives.[66]

From today's point of view, one must bear in mind that *Ultimatum* was made on the eve of World War II about a story that happens just as World War I broke out. In this historical perspective it should also be remembered that the film was made a few months before the Munich Pact, which is now understood as the culmination of the West's appeasement of Hitler. Does *Ultimatum*, like Renoir's *La Grande Illusion*, reflect the policy of appeasement as practiced by the Popular Front government that led France since 1936?[67] The spirit of appeasement that circulated among French intellectuals during the 1930s toward a Nazi Germany that advocated rearmament, an ideology of its own superiority, and an aggressive nationalism is incomprehensible even today. A passage from Richard Roud's biography of Henri Langlois sheds some light on this. Roud had interviewed the French filmmaker Georges Franju about the election of the German Frank Hensel to the presidency of the International Institute of Film Archives in 1938:

> It may seem odd – it certainly did to me – that such politically "progressive" people as Langlois, Vaughan, Iris Barry, and especially Franju himself would accept so lightly a German as president, and even the presence of the Reichsfilmarchiv, as late as 1938 when surely, I said to Franju, all right-thinking people were, if not anti-German, at least anti-German government, anti-Nazi.
>
> "Oh," said Franju, "that was no problem in 1938. You know, in those days, it was the Left that was pro-German in France. Those who were most virulently anti-German were on the right! The Popular Front was all for peace. Hitler was seen wearing a white tuxedo – and people said, 'That's a good sign, he's going to calm down and leave us in peace.'"
>
> … Franju's views can be corroborated by many: even Simone de Beauvoir and Jean-Paul Sartre, pedaling their way across France on bicycles, refused to believe there was any real threat from the other side of the Rhine.[68]

The climate of opinion that is revealed here also explains the politically and historically naïve pacifism of Renoir's *La Grande Illusion*. The exile Wiene could not possibly share such a point of view. Although his *Ultimatum* has some things in common with Renoir's film, it must be kept in mind that Wiene's work contains a concrete warning that war is inevitable if one side aggressively advocates it – just as in the conflict between Austria and Serbia a mere twenty-five years before. Only in this sense is *Ultimatum* an antiwar film.

Whereas the setting of *La Grande Illusion* is 1916 when the war is at a stalemate, *Ultimatum* is set against the crisis immediately preceding the outbreak of the war on 28 July 1914. Surprisingly, the film begins with the exposition of fraternal harmony. Hungarian and Serbian peasants are shown performing their traditional dances at a wedding; two of the main characters – the Austrian Anna and the Serbian Stanko – live happily married in Belgrade; and Stanko and his friend and subsequent enemy, Burgstaller, had been classmates at an Austrian military college. Historically, however, this idyll puzzles. After all, Austria and Serbia had been in conflict for many decades even before World War I. The purpose of this constructed idyll is to highlight the film's main theme, as it is stated in the opening title:

Political crises destroy normal relationships, both between nations and individuals. This story tells how such a crisis affected the lives of ordinary people in 1914. The action takes place in Belgrade, a Serbian city, and Semline (a frontier city of Austria-Hungary). The two cities are separated by the width of the Danube river.[69]

A historic parallel is apparently being implied here, between France and Germany, which are separated by the Rhine and likewise look back on a long history of reciprocal animosities. Wiene's idyll in prewar Belgrade is a commentary on the unrealistic idyll, which his intellectual Popular Front friends and acquaintances in Paris indulged in with their questionable pacifism. Wiene, who had his roots in several European nations and who personally had experienced the aggressive will to power of the new German rulers, could no more believe that a peaceful coexistence between France and Germany was possible then any more than it had been possible between Austria and Serbia in 1914.

Ultimatum Director: Robert Wiene (1938) – Robert Wiene and Alexandre Arnoux during the shooting

However, *Ultimatum* should not be misunderstood as a film that advocates war. Its warning against pacifist illusions in times of imminent war is hidden behind the story of utter humanism in which decent people pursue their private and business interests with kindness and mutual understanding. In this regard, the character of Colonel Simovic stands out especially. A soldier and a patriot, with his striking resemblance to Commandant Von Rauffenstein, in *La Grande Illusion*, he likewise belongs to an older generation of officers.

In an earlier war he was crippled in combat, but he bears no hatred against Serbia's enemies. He embodies the noble soldier whose service to his fatherland has become part of his character. He still serves his country but has not yet lost his humanity in dealing with the enemy. As he frees the Austrian Burgstaller, soon after the declaration of war, he comments, "a nation which does not know how to be humane is not a nation."[70]

At the beginning of the film, a Danube bridge becomes the metaphor for a short phase of a harmonious existence in which cultural differences are no cause for misunderstanding but instead inspire curiosity, interest, and appreciation. When these peasants dance together in the opening sequence, they form two circles, with the Hungarians and the Serbs each dancing according to their ethnic ways, but each in mutual acceptance of their difference and uniqueness. And a little later, just as Anna enjoys seeing herself in Serbian dress, so does her Serbian maid dream of Vienna and sing Viennese songs. Likewise, the life of Anna and Stanko in Belgrade is untroubled. Love and marriage function as the bridge between the two cultures and assimilation takes place only in a playful way. Anna has dressed up in a Serbian folk costume and presents herself to Stanko as "a real Serbian woman." Amused, he answers, "You are the typical Austrian woman!" They spar over this, but their argument concludes with a loving embrace and Stanko's words, "I will love you whatever you are, an Austrian or a Serb. You are adorable."

The news of the assassination brings an end to all this: Stanko, who is sent on an espionage mission to the border, becomes thereby a member of one of the warring parties; Anna begins to feel like an alien in Serbia, and her Serbian maid is harassed for serving in an Austrian household. In the tense phase of prewar politics, Stanko and Burgstaller's friendship is also disrupted when both follow their respective calls of duty. At the peak of international tensions, only Simovic, Anna, and Burgstaller are capable of maintaining their human integrity. In Stanko, however, the chauvinist patriot emerges when he exclaims:

> But he's [Burgstaller] associated with the Austrian armed forces, the intelligence service and he's one of their cleverest and well informed agents. He was sent as a special agent during the Balkan war. Lord only knows what he's up to now. Burgstaller a correspondent? Don't make me laugh! He's a spy! We'll get rid of him sooner or later – wartime makes such things easier. We should have got rid of him before.

In other words, for Stanko war disrupts all previous relationships and social links, and all that matters is victory over the enemy. To be

188 | *Beyond* Caligari

sure, he does not hold Burgstaller's Austrian nationality against him but his established loyalty to Austria's cause. In Anna's case he is convinced that her marriage to him guarantees her loyalty to Serbia. Nevertheless, his passionate patriotism distinguishes him, especially on his deathbed when he revels in the recognition that he is the first to give his life for his country.

On the surface there are a number of similarities between Jean Renoir's *La Grande Illusion* and Wiene's *Ultimatum*. Dita Parlo and Erich von Stroheim star in both films. In both films Stroheim is shown as a high-ranking officer who has suffered mutilating injuries in previous battles, but who is still serving his country as dutifully as possible. Moreover both films are set against World War I and are centrally preoccupied with the issue of humanity in times of war. *La Grande Illusion* seems to suggest that war can be overcome; it "attacks the great illusion that war can be for the good of man."[71] This is the pacifist conception that Renoir, a veteran of World War I, apparently had of war and that he put forth with striking naïveté. At the same time, it is this naïve pacifism that makes *La Grande Illusion* a Popular Frontist film.

By contrast, Wiene – twenty-one years older than Renoir – by birth, upbringing, and career a true descendant of the old Central European culture, who was moreover an exile from Nazi Germany, analyzes his time differently from Renoir. Although humanity and honor are central to *Ultimatum* as well, the film makes it clear in 1938 that war is inevitable. Whereas *La Grande Illusion* suggests that harmony will prevail after war has been overcome, *Ultimatum* maintains that the private harmony of the film's exposition proves to be an illusion that is shattered as nations fight out their political quarrels. Thus, *Ultimatum* by no means advocated an appeasement policy that was part of the Popular Front ideology.

Notes

1. For an analysis of the discussion within the German film industry, cf. Wolfgang Jacobsen, "Wortdämmerung: Auf dem Weg zum Tonfilm," in *Der deutsche Film: Aspekte seiner Geschichte von den Anfängen bis zur Gegenwart*, ed. Uli Jung (Trier: WVT, 1993), 79–90.
2. *Die LichtBildBühne* 23, no. 193 (1930). In the same issue, this journal reprinted its review of Max Mack's *Der Andere* of 25 January 1913, apparently wishing to confirm that Wiene's current film played a similar pivotal role.
3. Quoted from a promotion pamphlet for *Der Andere*, collection of DIF, Frankfurt.
4. *Der Kinematograph* 24, no. 187 (1930): 1f.
5. *Die LichtBildBühne* 23, no. 193 (1930).
6. See Kurt Pinthus, "*Der Andere* einst und jetzt," *Das Tagebuch*, no. 33 (1930): 1323f.
7. *Der Kinematograph* 24, no. 235 (1930).
8. Quoted from a promotion pamphlet for *Der Andere*, collection of DIF, Frankfurt.
9. Ludwig Eisenberg, *Grosses Biographisches Lexikon der deutschen Bühne im 19. Jahrhundert* (Leipzig: P. List, 1903), 1121f.
10. "Literary" film is our translation of the German "Autorenfilm," which refers to films based on scripts written by literary figures, and should not be confused with the contemporary concept of "auteur" films.
11. Censorship card no. 23,882, issued on 13 February 1913 by the Berlin Police Commissioner; SDK Berlin.
12. Although a title of the book by Taine is not given in either the play or the film, it is most probably *De l'intelligence* (published prior to 1866); a German translation was published in 1880.
13. A large file of documentation pertaining to Wiene's *Der Andere* was recently discovered at the Cinémathèque Française in Paris. The file contains the following: Brandt's manuscript, a French translation of the entire manuscript, a French-language list of the film's dialogue, a German-language work schedule for the shooting of the French version, the detailed proceedings of the shooting of the German-language version of the film, and finally, correspondence and contracts relating to the French-language production of the film. We are grateful to the Cinémathèque Française and especially to Dominique Brun for making this material available to us so quickly.
14. "Tonfilm im 'Hippodrome,'" *Die LichtBildBühne* 23, no. 147 (1930): 2.
15. Letter by Terra Film to Albatros on 20 June 1930 in which Terra Film confirms all conditions of the contract, Collection of the Cinémathèque Française.
16. Kurt Pinthus, "*Der Andere* auf französisch," *8 Uhr-Abendblatt*, no. 204 (1930).
17. See Pinthus, ibid., and "*Der Andere* in französischer Fassung," *Der Kinematograph* 24, no. 205 (1930).
18. *Der Andere* appeared with the title, *The Man Within*, and the French version with the title, *L'Autre* and *The Other One*.
19. Francesco Savio, *Ma L'Amore No: Realismo, Formalismo, Propaganda e Telefoni Bianchi nel Cinema Italiano di Regiome (1930–1943)* (Milan: Casa Editrice Sonzogno, 1975), 67. We owe thanks to Roberto Radicati of the Museo Nazionale Del Cinema, Turin, Italy, for this information.
20. Raymond Chirat, *Catalogue des films français de long métrage: Films sonores de fiction 1929–1939* (Brussels: Cinémathèque Royale, 1981), entry number 873.
21. House program of Emelka Film Company.
22. *Der Kinematograph* 25, no. 104 (1931).
23. *Die LichtBildBühne* 24, no. 108 (1931).
24. "The Greenbaum-Emelka Film *Der Liebesexpress (The Love Express)* has been shown at the Monroe Theater in Chicago with next to unparalleled success, and

that in the original German version. The film has received an excellent press."
Der Kinematograph 25, no. 156 (1931).

25. *Variety*, 28 July 1931.
26. Herbert Holba, Günter Knorr, and Peter Spiegel, *Reclams deutsches Filmlexikon: Filmkünstler aus Deutschland, Österreich und der Schweiz* (Stuttgart: Reclam, 1984), 408f.
27. For this plot summary we draw on *Illustrieter Film-Kurier* 13, no. 1608 (1931), as well as on our screening of the film.
28. *Die LichtBildBühne* 23, no. 308 (1930): 3.
29. *Die LichtBildBühne* 23, no. 310 (1931): 3.
30. A program brochure for the screening of the film in December 1932 gives only the German actors as the cast and indicates that the film was dubbed: "A film entirely spoken in French, based on the procedure of Dr. S. Keisermann." This brochure is available in the files of the Bibliothek de l'Arsenal, Paris.
31. *Paimanns Filmlisten* 16, no. 801 (1931): 92.
32. Minutes of the Proceedings of the Censorship Board, no. 2793 of 10 June 1931, available in the collection of DIF.
33. *Der Kinematograph* 25, no. 172 (1931).
34. See *Der Kinematograph* 25, no. 144 (1931); *Der Kinematograph* 25, no. 157 (1931).
35. *Der Kinematograph* 25, no. 144 (1931).
36. *Die LichtBildBühne* 24, no. 150 (1931): 2.
37. See Holba, Knorr, and Spiegel, *Reclams deutsches Filmlexikon*, 409.
38. All reference works draw their information about *Taifun* from Alfred Bauer, *Deutscher Spielfilmalmanach, 1929–1950* (Berlin: Filmblätter Verlag, 1950), 251 f.
39. Our sources for the plot summary are the screening of the film at the Czechoslovakian Film Archive in Prague, the original film script at SDK in Berlin, and the minutes of the Proceedings of the Censorship Board, no. 6593 of 3 May 1933, available at DIF, Frankfurt a.M.
40. *Das Film-Atelier*, nos.1–3 (1933).
41. *Die Filmwoche*, no. 8 (1933): 240–41.
42. Minutes of the Proceedings of the Censorship Board, no. 6593 of 3 May 1933, 6.
43. Ibid., 8.
44. See *Illustrierter Film-Kurier* 16, no. 2148 (1934).
45. *Der Kinematograph* 28, no. 144 (1934).
46. *Berliner Morgenpost*, 29 July 1934.
47. *Das Film-Atelier*, no. 14 (1934); similarly, the film's crew receives no mention in *Illustrierter Film-Kurier* 16, no. 2148 (1934), or in the film program issued by Terra, the distribution firm.
48. *Der Film-Kurier* 16, no. 175 (1934).
49. The Reich Film Archive catalog entry number 0383 *(Taifun)* and 0552 *(Polizeiakte 909)*.
50. *Filmkultura* 6, no. 9 (1933): 9.
51. Bauer, *Deutscher Spielfilmalmanach*.
52. *Filmkultura* 6, no. 9 (1933): 11. For all translations into English from Hungarian sources we give thanks to Agota Ivanics and Evike Czak.
53. *Filmkultura* 6, no. 10 (1933): 9; our italics.
54. *Filmkultura* 6, no. 11 (1933): 8.
55. Conversations with Zsuzsa Simon in Budapest on 23 October 1987, with György Tarján in Budapest on 13 December 1987, and with Géza von Cziffra on the telephone on 28 December 1987.
56. Géza von Cziffra, *Ungelogen: Erinnerungen an mein Jahrhundert* (Munich: Herbig, 1988), Illustration no. 4, 112–13.
57. We are grateful to Zsuzsa Simon for this program.
58. Agota Ivanics, in a typed manuscript prepared for our purposes in the library of the Magyar Filmintézet in Budapest.

59. *Mein Film*, no. 422 (1934): 16.
60. See *Paimanns Filmlisten* 19, no. 931 (1934): 16; *Die LichtBildBühne*, 22 March 1934, p. 3.
61. Between 22 June and 11 November 1938, *La Cinématographie Française* printed at least five full-page announcements for *Ultimatum* on either the front or the back covers.
62. Ewald Bertram, *Tage vor dem Sturm: Roman aus den Juliwochen 1914* (Berlin: Ullstein, 1933).
63. The summary is based on our screening of the film.
64. Robert Chazal, in the file of clippings on *Ultimatum* at the Bibliotheque de l'Arsenal, Paris; the print we had at our disposal, as well as another extant print that is held by the Cinématèque Française, is black and white. Stock footage of historical events is missing from both prints. No other review makes mention of the devices described by Chazal.
65. Dorothy Masters, in the file of clippings on *Ultimatum* at the Theater Collection of the New York Public Library.
66. From the file of clippings on *Ultimatum* in the library of the Academy of Motion Picture Arts and Sciences, Hollywood, California.
67. Christopher Faulkner, *The Social Cinema of Jean Renoir* (Princeton, N.J.: Princeton University Press, 1986), 78–99, describes *La Grande Illusion* as a film that expresses the ideology of the Popular Front. To be sure, Faulkner does not use the word "appeasement," but that is precisely what the Popular Front practiced.
68. Richard Roud, *A Passion for Films: Henri Langlois and the Cinémathèque Français* (New York: Viking, 1983), 35f.
69. The print available at the Cinémathèque Municipale de Luxembourg begins with a credit sequence from the English-language version of the American distributor J. H. Hoffberg. In this print, however, there are no more English titles after the credit sequence, and all dialogues and inserts thereafter are in French.
70. For this and all subsequent quotations from the film, we draw on the English translation of the transcript of the dialogue by Sherry Vosburgh, Library of BFI, London.
71. Faulkner, *Social Cinema of Jean Renoir*, 84.

FILMOGRAPHY

Films are listed in chronological order according to the dates of the premiere and, where this information was not available, according to the censorship dates. If neither of these dates was available, the chronology follows the first reviews in the press.

The filmographies of Gerhard Lamprecht and Alfred Bauer are the foundation for this Wiene filmography. Their data were corrected or supplemented by the contemporary press as well as more recent publications (see bibliography). Nevertheless, incompleteness in the filmographic data is unavoidable.

Abbreviations

AS	Artistic Supervisor
C	Cast
CE	Censorship Edict
CE2	Second Censorship Edict
CM	Cinematography
D	Distributor
DIR	Director
ED	Editing
EP	Executive Producer
FR	Film Reviews
M	Music
P	Production Company
PR	Premiere
S	Studio
SD	Set Design
SND	Sound
SW	Scriptwriter

A: Austria; G: Germany; F: France; H: Hungary

Die Waffen der Jugend (The Weapons of Youth) [G 1912]

PR	10 January 1913
DIR	Friedrich Müller? Robert Wiene?
SW	Robert Wiene
CM	Charles Paulus
P	Komet Film Compangnie, Paulus u. Unger, Berlin
S	Komet Film Atelier, Müllerstrasse 182, Berlin
CE	Berlin, December 1912; 2 reels, 615m
C	Gertrud Gräbner, Curt Maler, Hans Staufen, Conrad Wiene

Er rechts, sie links (He This Way, She That Way) [G 1914]

PR	prior to 6 January 1915
DIR	Robert Wiene
P	Messter-Film G.m.b.H., Berlin
D	Hansa Film Verleih G.m.b.H., Berlin
S	Messter Film Atelier, Berlin
CE	Berlin, June 1914; 3 reels; prohibited for youth; prohibited for the duration of the war
CE2	B.3840, 27 July 1921; 3 reels, 922m; prohibited for youth
C	Max Zilzer
FR	Der Kinematograph 9, no. 419 (1915): 24

Arme Marie (Poor Marie) [G 1914]

PR	April 1915 (our source: 7 May 1915)
DIR	Willy Zeyn (Lamprecht: maybe Max Mack)
SW	Robert Wiene (and Walter Turszinsky?)
CM	Hermann Böttger
P	Projektions AG "Union" (PAGU), Berlin
S	Union Atelier, Berlin-Tempelhof
CE	Berlin, 10195/15; 4 reels; prohibited for youth
C	Hanni Weisse, Ernst Lubitsch, Felix Basch, Friedrich Zelnik
FR	Bild und Film 4, no. 12 (1914–15): 265

Fluch der Schönheit/Seine schöne Mama (The Curse of Beauty/His Beautiful Mom) [G 1915]

PR	Birett: 28 May 1915; Lamprecht: August 1915
DIR	D. I. Rector (Erich Zeiske, director of Bioscop)
SW	Walter Turszinsky, Robert Wiene
CM	Hermann Böttger
SD	Robert A. Dietrich
P	Deutsche Bioscop G.m.b.H., Berlin
S	Bioscop Atelier, Neubabelsberg
CE	Berlin, 10224/15, 5 reels, 1676m; prohibited for youth

C	Maria Carmi, Hans Mierendorff, Rudolf Essek, Emil Albes, Hugo Flink, Hans Swoboda, Alvine Davis, Klaus Reinwald
FR	*Die LichtBildBühne* 8, no. 20 (1915): 22

Die büssende Magdelena (Penitent Magdalena) [G 1915]

PR	October 1915
DIR	Emil Albes
SW	Walter Turszinsky, Robert Wiene
P	Deutsche Bioscop G.m.b.H., Berlin
S	Bioscop Atelier, Neubabelsberg
CE	Berlin 10256/15, September 1915; 3 reels, 1300m; prohibited for youth
C	Thea Sandten, John Gottowt, Karl Hannemann
FR	*Die LichtBildBühne* 8, no. 38 (1915): 22

Der springende Hirsch oder Die Diebe von Günsterburg (The Jumping Stag or The Thieves of Günsterburg) [G 1915]

PR	November 1915
DIR	Robert Wiene? Walter Turszinsky?
SW	Walter Turszinsky, Robert Wiene
P	Deutsche Bioscop G.m.b.H., Berlin
S	Bioscop Atelier, Neubabelsberg (May–June 1915)
CE	4 reels, 1421m
C	Vera Witt
FR	*Die LichtBildBühne* 8, no. 49 (1915): 39

Lottekens Feldzug (Lotteken's Campaign) [G 1915]

PR	1915
DIR	Bruno Ziener
SW	Walter Turszinsky, Robert Wiene
P	Frau S. Zadek, Berlin
S	Filmatelier Müllerstrasse 182 (Komet Film Atelier?), Berlin
C	Bruno Ziener, Wanny Ziener

Fräulein Barbier (Miss Barber) [G 1915]

DIR	Emil Albes
SW	Walter Turszinsky, Robert Wiene
P	Deutsche Bioscop G.m.b.H., Berlin
CE	Banned in Germany for the duration of the war
C	Vera Witt

Die Konservenbraut (The Canned Bride) [G 1915]

DIR	Robert Wiene
SW	Walter Turszinsky

P   Messter Film G.m.b.H., Berlin
D   Hansa Film Verleih G.m.b.H., Berlin
S   Messter Film Atelier, Berlin
CE2   B. 3820, 26 July 1921; 3 reels, 1063m; prohibited for youth
C   Margarete Kupfer, Senta Söneland, Bogia Horska, Paul
        Biensfeld, Guido Herzfeld

Frau Eva (Mrs. Eve) [G 1915/16]

PR   prior to 16 February 1916, Berlin, Mozartsaal
DIR   Robert Wiene
SW   Robert Wiene, based on Alphonse Daudet's novel *Fromont
        jeune et Risler senior*
CM   Karl Freund
M   Guiseppe Becce
P   Messter Film G.m.b.H., Berlin
D   Hansa Film Verleih G.m.b.H., Berlin
S   Messter Film Atelier, Berlin
C   Emil Jannings, Erna Morena, Theodor Loos, Alexander von
        Antalffy
        Lamprecht: Emil Jannings' first leading role (he had been an
        extra in *Im Schützengraben*)
FR   *Der Film* 1, no. 4 (1916): 20–27
        Der Kinematograph 10, no. 477 (1916): 10

**Der Liebesbrief der Königin: Intriguenspiel in drei Akten und 475
Küssen (The Queen's Love Letter: A Play of Intrigue in Three Acts and
475 Kisses) [G 1916]**

PR   30 March 1916, Berlin, Mozartsaal (Belach: 30 March 1917)
DIR   Robert Wiene
SW   Robert Wiene
M   Guiseppe Becce
SD   Ludwig Kainer
P   Messter Film G.m.b.H., Berlin
D   Hansa Film Verleih G.m.b.H., Berlin
S   Messter Film Atelier, Berlin
CE   B.4035, 1917; prohibited for youth
CE2   B.2271, 14 May 1921; 3 reels, 1107m; prohibited for youth
C   Henny Porten, Arthur Schröder, Rudolf Biebrach, Frieda
        Richard, Heinrich Schroth, Paul Biensfeldt
FR   *Der Film* 2, no. 14 (1917): 88; *Paimanns Filmlisten* 2, no. 81
        (1917–18): 287

Der Sekretär der Königin (The Queen's Secretary) [G 1916]

PR   prior to 5 April 1916, Berlin, Mozartsaal
DIR   Robert Wiene

SW	Robert Wiene
M	Guiseppe Becce
P	Messter Film G.m.b.H., Berlin
D	Hansa Film Verleih G.m.b.H., Berlin
S	Messter Film Atelier, Berlin
CE2	B.1315, 14 February 1921; 3 reels, 1244m; prohibited for youth
C	Käthe Dorsch, Resl Orla, Margarete Kupfer, Heinrich Schroth, Guido Herzfeld, Alexander von Antalffy
FR	*Der Kinematograph* 10, no. 484 (1916): 28 *Die LichtBildBühne* 9, no. 14 (1916): 44

Der Schirm mit dem Schwan *(The Parasol with the Swan)* [G 1916]

PR	9 April 1916, Berlin, Mozartsaal
DIR	Carl Froelich
SW	Robert Wiene, based on Walter Schmidthässler's comedy
CM	Wilhelm Hechy
M	Guiseppe Becce?
P	Messter Film G.m.b.H., Berlin
D	Hansa Film Verleih G.m.b.H., Berlin
S	Messter Film Atelier, Berlin (Belach: shot between fall 1915 and February 1916)
CE	B.39148, 24 March 1916; 3 reels, 1222m; prohibited for youth
CE2	B.3203, 3 June 1921; 3 reels, 1160m; prohibited for youth
C	Henny Porten, Hans Junkermann, Margarete Ferida, Max Adalbert, Olga Engl, Guido Herzfeld, Franz Gross, Erich Bartels

Das wandernde Licht *(The Wandering Light)* [G 1916]

PR	1 September 1916, Berlin, Mozartsaal
DIR	Robert Wiene
SW	Irene Daland, based on Ernst von Wildenbruch's novella
P	Messter Film G.m.b.H., Berlin
D	Hansa Film Verleih G.m.b.H., Berlin
S	Messter Film Atelier, Berlin (July 1916)
CE	B.39597, 1916; 4 reels; prohibited for youth
CE2	B.3884, 11 August l921; 4 reels, 1478m; prohibited for youth
C	Henny Porten, Bruno Decarli, Theodor Becker, Emil Rameau, Elsa Wagner
FR	*Der Film* 1, no. 33 (1916): 55 *Der Film* 1, no. 35 (1916): 48 *Der Kinematograph* 10, no. 506 (1916): 18 *Paimanns Filmlisten* 1, no. 35 (1916–17): 111

Die Räuberbraut (The Robber Bride) [G 1916]

PR	29 September 1916, Berlin, Mozartsaal
DIR	Robert Wiene
M	Guiseppe Becce
P	Messter Film G.m.b.H., Berlin
D	Hansa Film Verleih G.m.b.H., Berlin
S	Messter Film Atelier, Berlin (August 1916)
CE	B.38778, 1916; 4 reels; prohibited for youth
C	Henny Porten, Friedrich Féher, Artur Menzel, Karl Elzer
FR	*Der Film* 1, no. 37 (1916): 37
	Der Film 1, no. 37 (1916): 50–52
	Der Kinematograph 10, no. 510 (1916): 15
	Die LichtBildBühne 9, no. 39 (1916): 40
	Paimanns Filmlisten 1, no. 41 (1916–17): 137

Der Mann im Spiegel (The Man in the Mirror) [G 1916/17]

PR	prior to 18 October 1917, Berlin, Mozartsaal
DIR	Robert Wiene
SW	Robert Wiene, Richard Wurmfeld
CM	Karl Freund
M	Guiseppe Becce
SD	Ludwig Kainer
P	Messter Film G.m.b.H., Berlin
D	Hansa Film Verleih G.m.b.H., Berlin
S	Messter Film Atelier, Berlin
CE	4 reels
C	Maria Fein, Bruno Decarli, Emil Rameau, Alexander von Antalffy
FR	*Der Film* 1, no. 39 (1916): 36
	Der Film 1, no. 40 (1916): 46
	Der Kinematograph 10, no. 512 (1916): 26–29
	Die LichtBildBühne 9, no. 22 (1916): 47

Lehmanns Brautfahrt (Lehmann's Honeymoon) [G 1916]

PR	prior to 18 November 1916, Berlin, Mozartsaal
DIR	Robert Wiene
SW	Robert Wiene, Arthur Bergen
SD	Rudolf Kainer
P	Messter Film G.m.b.H., Berlin
CE	4 reels (according to an advertisement in *Der Film* 1, no. 38 [1916])
C	Arnold Rieck, Guido Herzfeld, Hella Tornegg, Christel Lorenz
FR	*Die LichtBildBühne* 9, no. 46 (1916): 46

Gelöste Ketten (Unchained) [G 1916]

PR	29 December 1916, Berlin, Mozartsaal
DIR	Rudolf Biebrach
SW	Robert Wiene
CM	Karl Freund
M	Guiseppe Becce
SD	Ludwig Kainer
P	Messter Film G.m.b.H., Berlin
S	Messter Film Atelier, Berlin (Belach: December 1916)
CE	B. 40122, 1916; prohibited for youth
CE2	1921
C	Henny Porten, Rudolf Biebrach, Johannes Riemann, Bruno Decarli, Adolf Klein, Frieda Richard, Olga Engl
FR	*Der Film* 2, no. 1 (1917): 32–34

Feenhände (Fairy Hands) [G 1916]

PR	26 January 1917, Berlin, Mozartsaal
DIR	Rudolf Biebrach
SW	Robert Wiene, based on Eugene Scribe's play *Les doigts de fée* (1858)
CM	Karl Freund?
M	Guiseppe Becce
SD	Ludwig Kainer
P	Messter Film G.m.b.H., Berlin
S	Messter Film Atelier, Berlin
CE	B.40212, 1916; prohibited for youth
C	Henny Porten, Rudolf Biebrach, Frieda Richard, Paul Hartmann, Fräulein Klein, Arnold Korff, Tony Tetzlaff, Claire Reigbert
FR	*Der Film* 2, no. 5 (1917): 26
	Paimanns Filmlisten 1, no. 58 (1916–17): 204

Das Leben ein Traum (Life Is a Dream) [G 1917]

PR	prior to 24 February 1917
DIR	Robert Wiene
SW	Robert Wiene, Richard Wurmfeld
P	Messter Film G.m.b.H., Berlin
D	Hansa Film Verleih G.m.b.H., Berlin
S	Messter Film Atelier, Berlin
C	Maria Fein, Emil Jannings, Emil Rameau, Alexander von Antalffy
FR	*Der Film* 2, no. 9 (1917): 32
	Die LichtBildBühne 10, no. 8 (1917): 38

Die Ehe der Luise Rohrbach (The Marriage of Luise Rohrbach) [G 1917]

PR	prior to 3 March 1917, Berlin, Mozartsaal
DIR	Rudolf Biebrach
SW	Robert Wiene, based on a novel by Emmi Elert
CM	Karl Freund
M	Guiseppe Becce
SD	Ludwig Kainer
P	Messter Film G.m.b.H., Berlin
D	Hansa Film Verleih G.m.b.H., Berlin
S	Messter Film Atelier, Berlin
CE	B.40371, 1917; prohibited for youth
CE2	B.5507, 14 March 1922; 4 reels, 1314m; prohibited for youth
C	Henny Porten, Emil Jannings, Ludwig Trautmann, Rudolf Biebrach, Klara Berger
FR	*Der Film* 2, no. 10 (1917): 39
	Die LichtBildBühne 10, no. 9 (1917): 42 f

Der standhafte Benjamin (Steadfast Benjamin) [G 1917]

PR	13 April 1917, Berlin, Mozartsaal
DIR	Robert Wiene
SW	Robert Wiene
P	Messter Film G.m.b.H., Berlin
D	Hansa Film Verleih G.m.b.H., Berlin
S	Messter Film Atelier, Berlin
CE	4 reels
C	Arnold Rieck, Guido Herzfeld, Martha Altenberg, Agda Nilsson, Magda Madeleine, Emil Rameau
FR	*Der Film* 2, no. 16 (1917): 66
	Die LichtBildBühne 10, no. 15 (1917): 40–46

Frank Hansens Glück (Frank Hansen's Fortune) [G 1917]

PR	prior to 28 May 1917
DIR	Viggo Larsen
SW	Robert Wiene
P	Messter Film G.m.b.H., Berlin
D	Hansa Film Verleih G.m.b.H., Berlin
S	Messter Film Atelier, Berlin
CE2	B.5546, 18 March 1922; 3 reels, 1350m; prohibited for youth
C	Viggo Larsen, Kitty Dewall, Lupu Pick, Leopold Gadiel, Victor Senger
FR	*Der Film* 2, no. 34 (1917): 43
	Paimanns Filmlisten 2, no. 81 (1917–18): 287

Die Prinzessin von Neutralien (The Princess of Neutralia) [G 1917]

PR	1 June 1917, Berlin, Mozartsaal
DIR	Rudolf Biebrach
SW	Robert Wiene
CM	Karl Freund
M	Guiseppe Becce
SD	Ludwig Kainer
P	Messter Film G.m.b.H., Berlin
D	Hansa Film Verleih G.m.b.H., Berlin
S	Messter Film Atelier, Berlin
CE	B.40627, 1917; 1376m; prohibited for youth
CE2	B.2172, 7 May 1921; 4 reels, 1239m; prohibited for youth
C	Henny Porten, Paul Bildt, Hermann Picha, John Gottovt, Julius Falkenstein, Alexander von Antalffy
	Lamprecht: identical with *Die Millionärin*
FR	*Der Film* 2, no. 23 (1917): 56
	Die LichtBildBühne 10, no. 22 (1917): 63

Veilchen Nr. 4 (Violet No. 4) [G 1917]

PR	prior to 23 July 1917
DIR	Robert Wiene?
P	Messter Film G.m.b.H., Berlin
D	Hansa Film Verleih G.m.b.H., Berlin
S	Messter Film Atelier, Berlin
CE2	B.4368, 3 October 1921; 3 reels, 1076m; prohibited for youth
C	Arnold Rieck, Käte Haack
FR	*Paimanns Filmlisten* 2, no. 73 (1917–18): 255

Gefangene Seele (Imprisoned Soul) [G 1917]

PR	31 August 1917
DIR	Rudolf Biebrach
SW	Robert Wiene
CM	Karl Freund
M ·	Guiseppe Becce
SD	Ludwig Kainer
P	Messter Film G.m.b.H., Berlin
D	Hansa Film Verleih G.m.b.H., Berlin
S	Messter Film Atelier, Berlin
CE	B.40770, 1917; 4 reels, 1473m; prohibited for youth
C	Henny Porten, Paul Bildt, Curt Goetz
FR	*Der Film* 2, no. 36 (1917): 76
	Die LichtBildBühne 10, no. 36 (1917): 30
	Paimanns Filmlisten 2, no. 77 (1917–18): 271

Furcht (Fear) [G 1917]

PR	September 1917
DIR	Robert Wiene
SW	Robert Wiene
P	Messter Film G.m.b.H., Berlin
D	Hansa Film Verleih G.m.b.H., Berlin
S	Messter Film Atelier, Berlin
CE2	B.6920, 17 January 1923; 4 reels, 1361m; prohibited for youth
C	Bruno Decarli, Bernhard Goetzke, Mechthildis Thein, Conrad Veidt
FR	*Paimanns Filmlisten* 2, no. 81 (1917–18): 287

Gräfin Küchenfee (Countess Kitchenmaid) [G 1917/18]

PR	18 January 1918, Berlin, Mozartsaal
DIR	Rudolf Biebrach
SW	Robert Wiene
CM	Karl Freund?
M	Giuseppe Becce
SD	Ludwig Kainer
P	Messter Film G.m.b.H., Berlin
D	Hansa Film Verleih G.m.b.H., Berlin
S	Messter Film Atelier, Berlin
CE	B.41312, 1918; 3 reels, 1307m; prohibited for youth
C	Henny Porten, Heinrich Schroth, Martin Lübbert, Ernst Hofmann, Reinhold Schünzel, Paul Biensfeld
FR	*Paimanns Filmlisten* 2, no. 103 (1917–18): 371

Edelsteine (Precious Stones) [G 1917/18]

PR	15 February 1918
DIR	Rudolf Biebrach
SW	Robert Wiene
CM	Karl Freund?
M	Giuseppe Becce
SD	Ludwig Kainer
P	Hansa Film Verleih G.m.b.H., Berlin
S	Messter Film Atelier, Berlin
CE	B.41510, 1918; 4 reels, 1250m; prohibited for youth
C	Henny Porten, Paul Bildt, Paul Hartmann, Hanna Brohm, Theodor Loos
FR	*Der Film* 3, no. 8 (1918): 45
	Paimanns Filmlisten 2, no. 105 (1917–18): 378

Auf Probe gestellt (Put to the Test) [G 1918]

PR	15 March 1918
DIR	Rudolf Biebrach
SW	Robert Wiene
CM	Karl Freund?
M	Kapellmeister Bechstein (Giuseppe Becce)
SD	Ludwig Kainer?
P	Messter Film G.m.b.H. (der Ufa), Berlin
D	Hansa Film Verleih G.m.b.H., Berlin
S	Messter Film Atelier, Berlin
CE	B.41613, February 1918; 4 reels, 1584m; prohibited for youth
C	Henny Porten, Heinrich Schroth, Reinhold Schünzel, Hermann Thimig, Rudolf Biebrach, Kurt Vespermann, Kurt Ehrle
FR	*Der Kinematograph* 12, no. 585 (1918): 28
	Paimanns Filmlisten 3, no. 121 (1918–19): 14

Das Geschlecht derer von Ringwall (The Ringwall Family) [G 1918]

PR	probably prior to 24 April 1918, Berlin, Mozartsaal
DIR	Rudolf Biebrach
SW	Robert Wiene (from his series *Seltsame Menschen*)
CM	Karl Freund
M	Giuseppe Becce
SD	Jack Winter, Ludwig Kainer
P	Messter Film G.m.b.H. (der Ufa), Berlin
D	Hansa Film Verleih G.m.b.H., Berlin
S	Messter Film Atelier, Berlin; location shots: Bavarian Alps near Garmisch-Partenkirchen
CE	B.41750, 1918; 4 reels, 1436m; prohibited for youth
CE2	B. 2175, 17 May 1921; 4 reels, 1349m; prohibited for youth
C	Henny Porten, Kurt Vespermann, Rudolf Biebrach, Bruno Decarli, Heinz Burkart, Frieda Richard
FR	*Der Film* 3, no. 17 (1918): 61
	Der Kinematograph 12, no. 590 (1918)
	Paimanns Filmlisten 3, no. 123 (1918–19): 23

Agnes Arnau und ihre drei Freier (Agnes Arnau and Her Three Suitors) [G 1918]

PR	24 May 1918, Berlin, Mozartsaal
DIR	Rudolf Biebrach
SW	Robert Wiene
CM	Karl Freund
M	Giuseppe Becce
SD	Ludwig Kainer
P	Messter Film G.m.b.H. (der Ufa), Berlin

D	Hansa Film Verleih G.m.b.H., Berlin
S	Messter Film Atelier, Berlin
CE	B.41868, 1918; 4 reels, 1392m; prohibited for youth
C	Henny Porten, Arthur Menzel, Bertha Monnard, Kurt Ehrle, Hermann Thimig, Rudolf Biebrach, Paul Westermeier, Paul Passarge
FR	*Der Film* 3, no. 22 (1918): 69
	Der Kinematograph 12, no. 595 (1918): 26
	Paimanns Filmlisten 3, no. 122 (1918–19): 18

Die Heimkehr des Odysseus (The Homecoming of Odysseus) [G 1918]

PR	25 October 1918, Berlin, Mozartsaal
DIR	Rudolf Biebrach
SW	Robert Wiene
CM	Karl Freund
M	Giuseppe Becce
SD	Jack Winter
P	Messter Film G.m.b.H. (der Ufa), Berlin
D	Hansa Film Verleih G.m.b.H., Berlin
S	Messter Film Atelier, Berlin
CE	B.42511, 1918; 4 reels, 1390m; prohibited for youth
CE2	B.2131, 17 May 1921; 4 reels, 1291m; prohibited for youth
C	Henny Porten, Bruno Decarli, Arthur Bergen, Rudolf Biebrach, Justus Glatz, Joseph Uhl, Marie Fuchs
FR	*Der Film* 3, no. 44 (1918): 109
	Paimanns Filmlisten 3, no. 143 (1918–19): 105

Am Tor des Todes (At the Gate of Death) [A 1918]

PR	probably prior to 30 November 1918, Vienna (W. Fritz: 20 December 1918)
DIR	Conrad Wiene
SW	Robert Wiene
P	Sascha Film, Vienna
CE	4 reels, 1600m
C	Harry Walden, Axel Plessen
FR	*Der Kinematograph* 12, no. 652 (1918): 21
	N.K.R., no. 91 (1918): 53
	Österreichischer Komet, 30 November 1918
	Paimanns Filmlisten 3, no. 143 (1918–19): 105

Die Dame, der Teufel und die Probiermamsell (The Lady, the Devil, and the Model) [G 1918]

PR	17 January 1919, Berlin, Mozartsaal
DIR	Rudolf Biebrach
SW	Robert Wiene

CM	Karl Freund
M	Giuseppe Becce
SD	Kurt Richter
P	Messter Film G.m.b.H., Berlin
D	Hansa Film Verleih G.m.b.H., Berlin
S	Ufa-Messter Atelier, Berlin-Tempelhof, Oberlandstrasse
CE	B.42733, 1919; 4 reels, 1378m; prohibited for youth
CE2	B.2412, 28 May 1921; 4 reels, 1230m; prohibited for youth
C	Henny Porten, Alfred Abel, Ida Perry, Eugen Rex
FR	*Der Film* 4, no. 4 (1919): 36
	Der Kinematograph 13, no. 629 (1919): 39
	Paimanns Filmlisten 3, no. 155 (1918–19): 152

Der Umweg zur Ehe (Detour to Marriage) [A 1919]

PR	31 January 1919, Vienna
DIR	Robert Wiene? Conrad Wiene? Fritz Freisler?
P	Sascha Film, Vienna
CE	1400m
C	Harry Walden, Ernst Arndt
FR	*Paimanns Filmlisten* 3, no. 148 (1918–19): 123 f

Ihr Sport (Her Sport) [G 1919]

PR	12 April 1919, Berlin, Mozartsaal
DIR	Rudolf Biebrach
SW	Robert Wiene
CM	Willibald Gaebel
M	Giuseppe Becce
SD	Ludwig Kainer
P	Messter Film G.m.b.H. (der Ufa), Berlin
D	Hansa Film Verleih G.m.b.H., Berlin
S	Ufa-Messter Atelier, Berlin-Tempelhof; location shots: Krummhübel/Riesengebirge
CE2	B.2063, 28 April 1921; 4 reels, 1355m; prohibited for youth
C	Henny Porten, Georg H. Schnell, Hermann Thimig, Wally Koch
FR	*Der Film* 4, no. 16 (1919): 34
	Paimanns Filmlisten 4, no. 181 (1919): 261 f

Opfer der Gesellschaft (Victim of Society) [G 1919]

PR	prior to 14 June 1919
DIR	Willy Grunwald
SW	Robert Wiene, Robert Heymann
P	Messter Film G.m.b.H., Berlin
D	Hansa Film Verleih G.m.b.H., Berlin
S	Messter Film Atelier, Berlin

CE2   B.1772, 6 April 1921; 5 reels, 1597m; prohibited for youth
C   Conrad Veidt, Vilma Born-Junge, Kurt Brenkendorf,
      Anneliese Halbe, Carl Wallauer, Willy Grunwald
FR   *Der Filmbote*, no. 45 (1919): 32

Die lebende Tote (The Living Dead Woman) [G 1919]

PR   prior to 7 September 1919, Berlin, Mozartsaal
DIR   Rudolf Biebrach
SW   Robert Wiene
CM   Willibard Gaebel
M   Giuseppe Becce
SD   Jack Winter, Kurt Dürnhöfer?
P   Messter Film G.m.b.H. (der Ufa), Berlin
D   Hansa Film Verleih G.m.b.H., Berlin
S   Ufa-Messter Atelier, Berlin-Tempelhof
CE   B.43276, 1919; 5 reels, 1564m; prohibited for youth
CE2   B.1195, 28 January,1921; 5 reels, 1475m; prohibited for youth
C   Henny Porten, Paul Bildt, Carl Ebert, Ernst Dernburg, Elsa
      Wagner
FR   *Der Film* 4, no. 36 (1919): 36–38
      Paimanns Filmlisten 4, no. 183 (1919–20): 271

Ein gefährliches Spiel (A Dangerous Game) [A 1919]

PR   26 September 1919, Vienna
DIR   Robert Wiene
SW   Robert Wiene
P   Sascha Film, Vienna
CE   3 reels, 1300m
C   Harry Walden
FR   *Paimanns Filmlisten* 4, no. 176 (1919–20): 242

Schuhputzsalon Rolf G.m.b.H. (Shoe-Shine Parlor Rolf, Ltd.) [G 1919]

PR   prior to 8 October 1919 (Berlin?), Theater am Moritzplatz
DIR   Willi Halm
SW   Robert Wiene, Margarete Lindau-Schulz
CM   Hans Bloch
P   Rolf Film
C   Rolf Lindau-Schulz
FR   *Der Kinematograph* 13, no. 666 (1919): 26

Die verführte Heilige (The Seduced Saint) [G 1919]

PR   1919
DIR   Robert Wiene
SW   Robert Wiene

P   Stuart Webbs Film Company, Munich
C   Stella Harf, Dr. Mederow, Max Kronert, Ernst Stahl-
        Nachbaur, Georg Schnell, Kurt von Wangenheim

Satanas (Satan) [G 1919]

PR   prior to 31 January 1920, Berlin, Richard Oswald Lichtspiele
DIR   Friedrich Wilhelm Murnau
AS   Robert Wiene
SW   Robert Wiene
CM   Karl Freund
SD   Ernst Stern
P   Vikoria Film Company G.m.b.H., Berlin
D   Phoebus Film Verleih, Berlin
S   Bioscop Atelier, Neubabelsberg
CE2   B.811, 13 December 1920; 6 reels, 2561m; prohibited for youth
C   Conrad Veidt, Fritz Kortner, Ernst Hofmann, Ernst Stahl-
        Nachbaur, Kurt Ehrle, Martin Wolfgang, Margit Barnay,
        Sadjah Gezza, Else Berna, Marija Leiko, Elsa Wagner
FR   *Der Film* 4, no. 46 (1919): 39
        Der Film-Kurier 2, no. 26 (1920)
        Der Film-Kurier 2, no. 28 (1920); Wiene's letter to the editor

Das Cabinet des Dr. Caligari (The Cabinet of Dr. Caligari) [G 1919/20]

PR   27 February 1920, Berlin, Marmorhaus
DIR   Robert Wiene
SW   Carl Mayer, Hans Janowitz
CM   Willy Hameister
SD   Hermann Warm, Walter Reimann, Walter Röhrig
P   Decla Film Gesellschaft, Holz & Co., Berlin
EP   Rudolf Meinert
D   Decla, Berlin
S   Lixie Atelier, Berlin-Weissensee
CE   B.1498, 11 March 1921; 6 reels, 1703m; prohibited for youth
C   Werner Krauss, Conrad Veidt, Lil Dagover, Friedrich Féher,
        Hans Heinz von Twardowski, Rudolf Lettinger, Ludwig Rex,
        Elsa Wagner, Henri Peters-Arnolds, Hans Lanser-Ludolff
FR   *Deutsche Lichtspiel-Zeitung* 8, nos. 12–13 (1920)
        Der Film 5, no. 9 (1920): 42
        Der Film 7, no. 19 (1922): 31–37; essay on Caligarisme
        Der Film 7, no. 22 (1922): 36; essay on Caligarisme
        Der Film 7, no. 26 (1922): 27; essay on Caligarisme
        Der Film 7, no. 33 (1922): 53; essay on Caligarisme
        Film-Dienst 37, no. 13 (1984): 284f
        Filmkundliche Mitteilungen 3, no. 2 (1970): 3

Der Film-Kurier 2, no. 4 (1920): 1; essay entitled
"Expressionism im Film" by Dr. J. B.
Der Film-Kurier 2, no. 50 (1920): 1
Der Film-Kurier 2, no. 51 (1920); review by Martin Proskauer
Der Film-Kurier 2, no. 58 (1920): 1
Der Film-Kurier 3, no. 112 (1921); survey of American reviews
Der Film-Kurier 6, no. 151 (1924); essay about "Caligarisme" in
France
Der Film-Kurier 8, no. 14 (1926); essay on Walter Röhrig as
sole art director for *Caligari*
Filmtechnik, no. 9 (1925): 192; essay by Walter Reimann
Filmtechnik, no. 10 (1925): 219f; continuation of the above
Film und Brettl, no. 21 (1920): 3–5; review by Claus Groth
Die Filmwelt, no. 4 (1924): 10; excerpt from Upton Sinclair's
They Call Me Carpenter
Das Glashaus 1, no. 4 (1920): 5
Der Kinematograph 14, no. 686 (1920): 21
Der Kinematograph 14, no. 696 (1920): 33
Der Kinematograph 17, no. 879–880 (1923): 19f; essay by Alfred
Richard Meyer entitled "Caligaris Fortsetzung" about Upton
Sinclair's novel *They Call Me Carpenter*.
Die LichtBildBühne 13, no. 9 (1920): 16f
Die Neue Schaubühne 2, no. 1 (1920): 103f; review by Ernst
Angel
Paimanns Filmlisten 4, no. 215 (1919–20): 395
Die Weltbühne 16, no. 1 (1920): 347f; review by Kurt Tucholsky

Die drei Tänze der Mary Wilford (The Three Dances of Mary Wilford) [G 1920]

PR	prior to 1 May 1920
DIR	Robert Wiene
SW	Robert Wiene, Johannes Brandt
CM	Willy Gaebel
P	Ungofilm Ges., Unger and Gottschalk, Berlin
CE	B.858, 11 December 1920; 6 reels, 1941m (after censorship: 1928.75m); prohibited for youth (source: Lamprecht) B.43844, 1920; 5 reels, 1897m; prohibited for children (source: Birett)
C	Erika Glässner, Friedrich Féher, Ludwig Hartau, Hermann Vallentin Lamprecht: the sequel to *Die Sünderin* (1919)
FR	*Der Film* 5, no. 18 (1920): 47 *Der Film-Kurier* 2, no. 86 (1920)

Genuine [G 1920]

PR	2 September 1920, Berlin, Marmorhaus
DIR	Robert Wiene
SW	Carl Mayer
CM	Willy Hameister
SD	César Klein; assistant, Bernhard Klein, Kurt Hermann Rosenberg
P	Decla-Bioscop AG, Berlin
D	Decla, Berlin
S	Bioscop Atelier, Neubabelsberg
CE	B.368, 28 August 1920, 6 reels, 2286m; prohibited for youth
C	Fern Andra, Ernst Gronau, Harald Paulsen, Albert Bennefeld, John Gottowt, Hans Heinz von Twardowski, Lewis Brody
FR	*Deutsche Lichtspiel Zeitung* 8, no. 40 (1920): 3f
	Der Film 5, no. 36 (1920): 28; review
	Der Film-Kurier 2, no. 196 (1920): 1
	Freie Deutsche Bühne, 9 September 1920, pp. 58–60

Die Jagd nach dem Tode (The Hunt for Death) [G 1920]

PR	22 October 1920, Berlin, Decla Lichtspiele Unter den Linden
DIR	Karl Gerhardt
SW	Robert Wiene, Johannes Brandt
CM	Paul Holzki
SD	Hermann Warm
P	Decla Bioscop AG, Berlin
C	Nils Chrisander, Lil Dagover, Bernhard Goezke, Kurt Brenkendorf
	The film consisted of 4 parts:
	1. *Die Jagd nach dem Tode*
	2. *Die verbotene Stadt*
	3. *Der Mann im Dunkel*
	4. *Die Goldmine von Sar-Khin*
	The first two parts were written by Robert Wiene and the third and fourth parts by Robert Liebmann.
FR	*Der Film* 5, no. 43 (1920): 41
	Der Film-Kurier 2, no. 238 (1920)
	Der Film-Kurier 2, no. 239 (1920): 1
	Der Kinematograph 14, no. 720 (1920)
	Die LichtBildBühne 13, no. 43 (1920): 34; review by Hans Wollenberg

Das Blut der Ahnen (The Blood of the Ancestors) [G 1920]

PR	prior to 13 November 1920, Berlin, Decla Lichtspiele Unter den Linden
DIR	Karl Gerhardt

SW	Robert Wiene, Johannes Brandt
CM	Willy Hameister
SD	Hermann Warm
P	Decla-Bioscop AG, Berlin
S	Bioscop Atelier, Neubabelsberg
CE	B.300, 26 August 1920; 6 reels, 1900m; prohibited for youth
C	Maria Zelenka, Harald Paulsen, Lil Dagover, Robert Scholz, Lili Alexandra, Josef Rehberger, Jaro Fürth
FR	*Deutsche Lichtspiel Zeitung* 8, no. 30 (1920): 3
	Deutsche Lichtspiel Zeitung 8, no. 46 (1920): 3
	Der Film 5, no. 46 (1920): 33
	Der Kinematograph 14, no. 727 (1920)

Die Nacht der Königin Isabeau (The Night of Queen Isabeau) [G 1920]

PR	prior to 19 November 1920, Berlin, Marmorhaus
DIR	Robert Wiene
SW	Robert Wiene
CM	Willy Hameister
SD	Robert Winckler-Tannenberg
P	Decla Bioscop AG, Berlin
D	Decla, Berlin
S	Bioscop Atelier, Neubabelsberg
CE	B.763, 18 November 1920; 5 reels, 1972m; prohibited for youth
C	Fern Andra, Hans Heinrch von Twardowski, Elsa Wagner, Fritz Kortner, Lothar Müthel, John Gottowt, Albert Lind, Alexander Moissi, Harald Paulsen
FR	*Deutsche Lichtspiel Zeitung* 8, no. 49 (1920): 3f
	Der Film 5, no. 47 (1920): 37
	Der Film-Kurier 2, no. 256 (1920)
	Der Kinematograph 14, no. 723 (1920)

Brillianten (Diamonds) [G 1920]

PR	prior to 11 December 1920, Berlin, Tauentzienpalast
DIR	Friedrich Féher
SW	Robert Wiene, Johannes Brandt
CM	Eugen Hamm
SD	Karl Machus
P	Ungofilm Ges.
CE	B.843, 29 November 1920; 5 reels, 1740m; prohibited for youth
C	Louis Ralph, Erika Glässner, Julius Brandt, Paul Morgan
FR	*Der Film-Kurier* 2, no. 275 (1920): 1

Der Schrecken im Hause Ardon (Panic in the House of Ardon) [G 1920]

PR	prior to 31 July 1921, Berlin, BTL Potsdammerstrasse
DIR	Robert Wiene

P	Stuart Webbs Film Company, Munich
CE	Munich, 4 August 1920
C	Stella Harf, Paul Mederow, Ernst Stahl-Nachbaur; previous title was *Die Welteroberer*
FR	*Der Film* 6, no. 31 (1921): 67

Die Rache einer Frau (A Woman's Revenge) [G 1921]

PR	prior to 15 April 1921
DIR	Robert Wiene
SW	Based on the novel by Barbey d'Aureville
CM	Erich Waschneck
SD	Hans Sohnle
P	Ufa, Berlin
S	Maxim Film Atelier, Blücherstrasse 32, Berlin
CE	B.1733, 6 April 1921; 5 reels, 2065m; prohibited for youth
C	Vera Caroly, Franz Egeneff, Olga Engl, Boris Michailow
FR	*Deutsche Lichtspiel Zeitung* 9, no. 17 (1921): 5
	Der Film 6, no. 16 (1921): 61
	Der Film-Kurier 3, no. 88 (1921)
	Der Kinematograph 15, no. 740 (1921)
	Paimanns Filmlisten 6, no. 275 (1921): 208

Das Spiel mit dem Feuer (Playing with Fire) [G 1921]

PR	prior to 21 May 1921, Berlin, Marmorhaus
DIR	Robert Wiene, Georg Kroll
SW	Based on an idea by Julius Horst and Alexander Engel
CM	Fritz Arno Wagner
SD	Robert Herlth, Walter Röhrig
P	Decla Bioscop AG, Berlin
D	Decla, Berlin
S	Decla-Bioscop Atelier, Neubabelsberg
CE	B.2269, 11 May 1921; 5 reels, 2134m; prohibited for youth
C	Diana Karenne, Wassily Wronsky, Anton Edthofer, Hans Junkermann, Otto Treptow, Leonhard Haskel, Karl Platen, Emil Heyse, Max Kronert, Lucia Tosti, Viktor Blum, Ossip Runitsch, Emil Birron
FR	*Der Film* 6, no. 22 (1921): 35
	Der Film-Kurier 3, no. 117 (1921)
	Der Kinematograph 15, no. 745 (1921)

Das Abenteuer des Dr. Kircheisen (The Adventure of Dr. Kircheisen) [G 1921]

PR	23 September 1921, Berlin, U. T. Kurfürstendamm and U. T. Nollendorfplatz
DIR	Rudolf Biebrach

SW	Robert Wiene, based on the novel *Das Mangobaumwunder* by Paul Frank and Leo Perutz
SD	Hans Sohnle
P	Maxim Film Ges., Ebner & Co., Berlin
D	Hansa Film Verleih G.m.b.H., Berlin
S	Maxim Film Atelier, Blücherstrasse 32, Berlin
CE	B.4153, 31 August 1921; 5 reels, 1453m; prohibited for youth
C	Lotte Neumann, Hermann Thimig, Hans Marr, Mabel May-Yong, Leopold von Ledebur, Albert Kunze
FR	*Der Film* 6, no. 40 (1921): 43
	Der Film-Kurier 3, no. 223 (1921)
	Der Kinematograph 15, no. 763 (1921)

Die höllische Macht (The Infernal Power) [G 1922]

PR	later than 21 December 1922
DIR	Robert Wiene
CM	Julius Balting
SD	Robert Winckler-Tannenberg
P	Lionardo Film, Berlin
CE	B.6862, 21 December 1922; 6 reels, 2142m; prohibited for youth
C	Thea Kasten, Hans Schweikart, Ossip Runitsch, Emil Lind

Raskolnikow [G 1922/23]

	U.S. distribution title: *Crime and Punishment*
PR	prior to 3 November 1923, Berlin, Mozartsaal
DIR	Robert Wiene
SW	Robert Wiene, based on the novel by Dostoyevsky
CM	Willy Goldberger
SD	Andrei Andreyev
P	Lionardo Film der Neumann Produktion G.m.b.H.
D	Bayerische Film G.m.b.H.
CE	B.7047, 9 March 1923; 7 reels, 3168m; prohibited for youth
C	Gregori Chmara, Pawel Pawlow, Michael Tarschanow, Maria Germanowa, Maria Kryshanowskaja, Elisaweta Skulskaja
FR	*Der Film* 8, nos. 43–44 (1923): 24
	Der Kinematograph 17, no. 872 (1923): 7
	Die LichtBildBühne 16, no. 44 (1923): 13
	Paimanns Filmlisten 8, no. 271 (1923)
	Reichsfilmblatt, no. 44 (1923): 14
	Tagebuch 4, no. 46 (1923); review by Kurt Pinthus

Der Puppenmacher von Kiang-Ning (The Doll Maker of Kiang-Ning)
[G 1923]

PR	prior to 3 November 1923, Primus-Palast (but apparently after *Raskolnikow*)
DIR	Robert Wiene
SW	Carl Mayer
CM	Willy Hameister
SD	César Klein, Walter Reger
P	Lionardo Film, Berlin
D	Deitz & Co.
CE	B.7288, 29 May 1923; 5 reels, 1728m; prohibited for youth
C	Werner Krauss, Lia Eibenschütz, Ossip Runitsch, Luzie Mannheim, Julius Falkenstein, Fritz Achterberg, Hans Schweikhart, Georg Jurowsky, Eugen Rex, Alexander Alexandrowski
FR	*Der Film-Kurier* 5, no. 248 (1923) *Die LichtBildBühne* 16, no. 44 (1923): 20 *Reichsfilmblatt*, nos. 45–47 (1923)

I.N.R.I., Ein Film der Menschlichkeit (I.N.R.I., A Film of Humaneness)
[G 1923]

	U.S. distribution title: *Crown of Thorns*
PR	25 December 1923, Berlin, Mozartsaal, Marmorhaus, Schauburg
DIR	Robert Wiene
SW	Robert Wiene, based on Peter Rosegger's novel, *I.N.R.I.* (1915)
CM	Axel Graatkjaer, Ludwig Lippert, Reimar Kuntze
M	Willy Schmidt-Gentner
SD	Ernö Metzner
P	Neumann Productions G.m.b.H., Berlin
EP	Hans Neumann, Hans von Wollzogen
D	Bayerische Film G.m.b.H.
S	Atelier des Grossfilmwerks Staaken, Berlin (90 shooting days between May and September 1923)
CE	B.7877, 15 November 1923; 7 reels, 2782m; approved for youth; O.7877, 19 November 1923; 7 reels, 3444m; approved for youth; rating: educational (20 December 1923)
C	Gregori Chmara, Henny Porten, Asta Nielsen, Werner Krauss, Theodor Becker, Emanuel Reicher, Robert Taube, Bruno Ziener, Hans Heinrich von Twardowski, Emil Lind, Max Kronert, H. Magnus, Walter Neumann, Guido Herzfeld, Wilhelm Nagel, Leo Reuss, Edmund Kandl, Walter Werner, Alexander Granach, Paul Graetz, Mathilde Sussin, Maria Kryschanowskaja, Erwin Kalser, Elsa Wagner, Erich Walter,

Ernst Dernburg, Gustav Oberg, Jaro Fürth, Pawel Pawlow,
Rose Veldtkirch

FR   *Der Film* 9, no. 1 (1924): 19
Der Film 9, no. 19 (1924): 24
Der Film-Kurier 5, no. 91 (1923); advertisement summary of
the frame
Der Film-Kurier 5, no. 97 (1923); advertisement summary of
the film
Der Film-Kurier 5, no. 174 (1923); observations about the
making of the film
Die Filmwoche, 2 December 1923; review by Paul Ickes
Die LichtBildBühne 16, no. 52 (1923): 14 f
Die LichtBildBühne 18, no. 57 (1925): 25
Paimanns Filmlisten 8, no. 400 (1923)
Paimanns Filmlisten 8, nos. 402–403 (1923)

Die Macht der Finsternis (The Power of Darkness) [G 1923]

	U.S. distribution title: *Power of Darkness*
PR	16 June 1924, Berlin, Mozartsaal
	prior to 4 April 1924, Vienna
DIR	Conrad Wiene
SW	Robert Wiene, based on the play by Leo Tolstoy
CM	Ernst Lüttgens, Willy Goldberger
M	Willy Schmidt-Gentner
SD	Andrei Andreyev, Heinrich Richter
P	Neumann Productions G.m.b.H., Berlin
D	Bayerische Film G.m.b.H., Munich
CE	B.7638, 3 September 1923; 5 reels, 2221m; prohibited for youth
	B.8521, 24 May 1924; 5 reels, 2074m; prohibited for youth
C	Peter Scharoff, Maria Germanowa, Maria Egorowa, Maria
	Krischanowskaya, Alexander Wiruboff, Pawel Pawlow, Vera
	Pawlowa, Nikolaj Massalitinoff, Vera Orlowa, Sergej
	Kommissaroff, George Seroff
	Lamprecht: Actors are members of the Moscow Art Theater
FR	*Der Film-Kurier* 6, no. 141 (1924)
	Das Kino-Journal, no. 714 (1924): 61
	Reichsfilmblatt, no. 25 (1924): 15
	Paimanns Filmlisten 9, no. 417 (1924)

Pension Groonen (Boarding House Groonen) [A 1924]

PR	prior to 31 May 1924, Vienna
DIR	Robert Wiene
SW	Ludwig Nerz
CM	Hans Androschin, Günther Krampf
P	Pan Film, Vienna

CE   5 reels, 2000m
C   Anton Edthofer, Karl Forest, Harry Nestor, Claude France,
       Carmen Castellieri, Charlotte Ander, Albert Heine
FR   *Die Filmwelt*, no. 4 (1925): 5f
       Die Filmwoche, no. 46 (1924): 1080–81
       Das Kino-Journal, no. 722 (1924): 15
       Paimanns Filmlisten 9, no. 425 (1924): 116

Orlacs Hände (Orlac's Hands) [A 1924]

       U.S. distribution title: *The Hands of Orlac*
PR   31 January 1925, Berlin, Theater am Nollendorfplatz
       (Preview: 24 September 1924, Berlin, Haydn-Kino)
       6 March 1925, Vienna
DIR   Robert Wiene
SW   Ludwig Nerz, based on the novel by Maurice Renard
CM   Hans Androschin, Günther Krampf
SD   Stefan Wessely, Hans Rouc, Karl Exner
P   Robert Wiene Produktion der Pan Film, Vienna
CE   25 September 1924; 7 reels, 2507m
C   Conrad Veidt, Fritz Kortner, Alexandra Sorina, Carmen
       Castellieri, Fritz Strassny, Paul Askonas
FR   *Der Film-Kurier* 6, no. 204 (1924)
       Die Filmwelt, no. 5 (1925): 9
       Die Filmwoche, no. 35 (1924): 810f
       Die Filmwoche, no. 39 (1924): 913f; interview with Sorina
       Die Filmwoche, no. 41 (1924): 942
       Der Kinematograph 19, no. 938 (1925): 33
       Das Kino-Journal, no. 733 (1924): 29
       Das Kino-Journal, no. 735 (1924): 5
       Das Kino-Journal, no. 738 (1924): 10f
       Die LichtBildBühne 18, no. 6 (1925): 35
       Monthly Film Bulletin 46, no. 546 (1979): 159f
       Paimanns Filmlisten 9, no. 441 (1924): 181
       Reichsfilmblatt, no. 39 (1924): 38f
       Die Weltbühne 21, no. 1 (1925): 286–88

Der Leibgardist/Der Gardeoffizier (The Body Guard/The Guard Officer) [A 1925]

       U.S. distribution title: *The Guardsman*
PR   24 October 1925, Berlin, Marmorhaus
SW   Ludwig Nerz, Robert Wiene, based on a comedy by Franz
       Molnár
CM   Hans Androschin
P   Pan Film, Vienna
D   Phoebus Film AG

S	Listo Atelier, Schönbrunnfilm Atelier
CE	6 reels, 2520m
C	Alfred Abel, Maria Corda, Anton Edthofer, Alice Hechy, Karl Forest
FR	*Die Bühne* 1, no. 4 (1924): 47f; report from the studio during filming, comments on Wiene
	Deutsche Filmwoche, no. 28 (1925): 14
	Die Filmtechnik, no. 13 (1925): 284f
	Der Kinematograph 19, no. 976 (1925): 21
	Das Kino-Journal, no. 751 (1924): 14
	Das Kino-Journal, no. 769 (1925): 20f
	Die LichtBildBühne 18 (1925)
	Mein Film, no. 3 (1926): 2
	Paimanns Filmlisten 10, no. 472 (1925): 81
	Reichsfilmblatt, no. 44 (1925): 35

Der Rosenkavalier [A 1925]

PR	10 January 1926, Dresden, Opera Haus
	16 January 1926, Berlin, Capitol Theater
	30 March 1926, Vienna, Konzerthaus
DIR	Robert Wiene
SW	Hugo von Hofmannsthal, Robert Wiene, Ludwig Nerz
CM	Hans Theyer, Hans Androschin, Ludwig Schaschek
M	Richard Strauss
SD	Alfred Roller, Hans Rouc, Stefan Wessely
P	Robert Wiene Produktion der Pan Film, Vienna
D	Filmhaus Bruckmann & Co. AG, Berlin
S	Filmatelier Wien-Schönbrunn (beginning 18 June 1925), Vienna
CE	23 December 1925; 8 reels, 2996m
C	Michael Bohnen, Elli Felice Berger, Carmen Castellieri, Jaques Catelain, Huguette Duflos, Paul Harmann, Friedrich Féher
FR	*Bioscope*, 15 April 1926, p. 35; interview with Strauss
	Bioscope, 22 April 1926, p. 53; about Strauss
	Die Bühne 2, no. 20 (1925): 38; report on preproduction
	Die Bühne 2, no. 35 (1925): 37–39; report on the making of the film
	Die Bühne 2, no. 43 (1925): 45f; report on the making of the film
	Die Bühne 3, no. 62 (1926): 48f
	Der Film 11, no. 3 (1926): 16
	Der Film-Kurier 7, no. 145 (1925); report on the making of the film
	Der Film-Kurier 7, no. 148 (1925); report on the making of the film

Der Film-Kurier 7, no. 201 (1925); excerpts from scripts
Der Film-Kurier 8, no. 9 (1926)
Der Film-Kurier 8, no. 15 (1926)
Die Filmtechnik 1, no. 13 (1925): 286f; report on the making of
the film
Film-Ton-Kunst 6, no. 3 (1926): 25f
Die Filmwoche, no. 4 (1926): 1, 76–80
Die Filmwoche, no. 5 (1926): 108
Der Kinematograph 19, no. 981 (1925): 15
Der Kinematograph 20, no. 987 (1926): 19
Das Kino-Journal, no. 801 (1925): 8f
Das Kino-Journal, no. 802 (1925): 6f
Das Kino-Journal, no. 818 (1926): 19f
Das Kino-Journal, no. 823 (1926): 10f
Die LichtBildBühne 19, no. 14 (1926): 3f
Mein Film, no. 2 (1926): 5
Mein Film, no. 15 (1926): 2
Paimanns Filmlisten 10, no. 506 (1925): 233
Reichsfilmblatt, no. 2 (1926): 29
Reichsfilmblatt, no. 2 (1926): 36
Reichsfilmblatt, no. 3 (1926): 39
Reichsfilmblatt, no. 3 (1926): 55
Reichsfilmblatt, no. 4 (1926): 20
Reichsfilmblatt, no. 4 (1926): 27
Reichsfilmblatt, no. 24 (1926): 16

Die Königin vom Moulin Rouge (The Queen of Moulin Rouge) [A 1926]

PR	4 October 1926, Berlin, Marmorhaus
	5 November 1926, Vienna
DIR	Robert Wiene
SW	Based on the play *Herzogin Crevette* by Georges Feydeau
CM	Hans Androschin, Ludwig Schaschek
SD	Alexander Ferenczy
P	Robert Wiene Produktion der Pan Film, Vienna
D	Filmhaus Bruckmann & Co. AG, Berlin
CE	6 reels, 2300m
C	Mady Christians, Ly Josyanne, André Roanne, Karl Forest, Paul Biensfeldt, Livio G. Pavinelli
FR	*Die Bühne* 3, no. 92 (1926): 37f; report on the making of the film
	Die Bühne 4, no. 124 (1927): 35
	Die Filmwoche, no. 42 (1926): 1003
	Der Kinematograph 20, no. 1025 (1926): 18
	Das Kino-Journal, no. 843 (1926): 16
	Das Kino-Journal, no. 845 (1926): 15
	Die LichtBildBühne 19, no. 237 (1926): 2

Paimanns Filmlisten 11, no. 547 (1926): 163
Reichsfilmblatt, no. 41 (1926): 26

Die Geliebte (The Mistress) [G 1926/27]

PR	10 February 1927, Berlin, Tauentziehen Palast
DIR	Robert Wiene
SW	Leo Birinski, based on the play by Alexander Brody
CM	Arpad Viragh, Laszlo Benedek; stills by Karl Görge
P	Paneuropa Film G.m.b.H., Berlin
D	Bruckmann
S	Terra-Glashaus and National Film Atelier, Berlin (January 1927)
CE	8 February 1927; 6 reels, 2168m; prohibited for youth
C	Edda Croy, Harry Liedtke, Adele Sandrock, Hans Junkermann, Hedwig Pauly-Winterstein, Eugen Burg, Karl Platen, Paul Heidemann, Olga Engl
FR	*Die Filmwoche,* no. 6 (1927): 137
	Der Kinematograph 21, no. 1043 (1927): 19
	Die LichtBildBühne 20, no. 36 (1927): 2
	Paimanns Filmlisten 12, no. 578 (1927): 59 f

Die berühmte Frau (The Famous Woman) [G 1927]

	U.S. distribution title: *Dancer of Barcelona*
PR	29 October 1927, Nürnberg, Capitol
	7 November 1927, Berlin, Beba-Palast Atrium
DIR	Robert Wiene
SW	Melchior Lengyel, based on his play *Die Tänzerin*
CM	Otto Kanturek
M	Walter Ulfig
SD	Oskar Fritz Werndorff, Emil Hasler
P	Deutsches Lichtspiel-Syndikat
S	Ufa, Berlin (June 1927)
CE	17 October 1927; 6 reels, 2559m; prohibited for youth
C	Lily Damita, Fred Solm, Warwick Ward, Arnold Korff, Alexander Granach, Lissi Arna, Mathilde Sussen, Alexander Murski, Nikolaus Von Lovric
FR	*Die Bühne* 5, no. 175 (1928): 20
	Die Filmwoche, no. 39 (1927): 931 f
	Der Kinematograph 21, no. 1082 (1927): 19
	Die LichtBildBühne 20, no. 267 (1927)
	Paimanns Filmlisten 12, no. 599 (1927): 153
	Reichsfilmblatt, no. 45 (1927): 28

Die Frau auf der Folter (The Woman on the Rack) [G 1928]

	U.S. distribution title: *A Scandal in Paris*
	Austrian distribution title: *Das göttliche Weib*
PR	13 September 1928, Berlin, Marmorhaus
DIR	Robert Wiene
SW	Dr. Arthur Bardos, based on the play by Edward G. Hemmerde and Francis Neilson
CM	Otto Kanturek, Bruno Timm, stills by Rudolf Brix
SD	Oskar Fritz Werndorff, Emil Hasler
P	Felsom-Film für die Deutsche Vereins-Film AG (Defa-Deutsche Fox), Berlin
D	Defa, Berlin
CE	18 May 1928; 7 reels, 2544m; prohibited for youth
C	Lily Damita, Wladimir Gaidarow, Johannes Riemann, Vivian Gibson, Arthur Pussy, Helene von Bolvary, Ferdinand von Alten, Leopold Kramer, and (according to *The New York Times*), Fritz Kortner
	Possibly appeared in Austria under the title *Das göttliche Weib*.
FR	*Der Kinematograph* 22, no. 1156 (1928): 14
	Paimanns Filmlisten 14, no. 683 (1929): 69
	Reichsfilmblatt, no. 37 (1928): 15

Leontines Ehemänner (Leontine's Husbands) [G 1928]

PR	25 September 1928, Berlin, Mozartsaal
DIR	Robert Wiene
SW	Max Glass, based on a comedy by Alfred Capus
CM	Giovanni Vitrotti
M	Guiseppe Becce
SD	Alexander Ferenczy
P	Dr. Max Glass Film G.m.b.H., Berlin
D	Terra Film, Berlin
S	Terra-Glashaus, Berlin
CE	13 August 1928; 6 reels, 2265m; prohibited for youth
C	Claire Rommer, Georg Alexander, Adele Sandrock, Oskar Sima, Truus van Alten, Carl Walther Mayer, Lotte Stein, Luigi Serventi, Alexa von Poremsky, Betty Astor
FR	*Der Film-Kurier* 10, no. 230 (1928); review by Hans Feld
	Der Filmspiegel 9, no. 9 (1928): 3–6; report of first-run movie houses in Berlin, with photos from the film
	Die Filmwoche, no. 40 (1928): 1020
	Der Kinematograph 22, no. 1161 (1928): 3
	Reichsfilmblatt, no. 39 (1928): 11
	Paimanns Filmlisten 14, no. 697 (1929): 114

Die grosse Abenteuerin (The Great Adventuress) [G 1928]

PR   9 October 1928, Berlin, Marmorhaus
DIR   Robert Wiene
SW   Ferdinand Ujheli
CM   Otto Kanturek, stills by Rudolf Brix
M   Werner Schmidt-Boelcke
SD   Oskar Fritz Werendorff, Emil Hasler
P   Felsom-Film der Fox Europa Produktion
      Deutsche Vereins Film AG (Defa-Deutsche Fox), Berlin
      Lamprecht: Felsom Film = Felner & Somlo Film G.m.b.H.
D   Defa, Berlin
S   Location shots in Calais, London, Paris
CE   18 May 1928; 7 reels, 2590m; prohibited for youth
C   Lily Damita, Georg Alexander, Fred Solm, Trude Hesterberg,
      Felix de Pomès, Heinrich Schroth, Paul Hörbiger, Rudolf
      Letinger, Paul Rehkopf
FR   *Der Film-Kurier* 10, no. 242 (1928); review by Georg Herzberg
      Der Kinematograph 22, no. 1167 (1928)
      Paimanns Filmlisten 13, no. 625 (1928): 51
      Reichsfilmblatt, no. 41 (1928): 24
      Die Weltbühne 24, no. 2 (1928): 647–49; review by Rudolf
      Arnheim

Heut' spielt der Strauss (Strauss Is Playing Today) [G 1928]

      Austrian distribution title: *Der Walzerkönig (The Waltz King)*
PR   26 October 1928, Berlin, Primus Palast
DIR   Conrad Wiene
SW   Robert Wiene
CM   Franz Planer
M   Bernhard Homola
SD   Robert Dietrich
P   Felsom-Film der Deutsche Vereins-Film AG (Defa-Deutsche
      Fox), Berlin
D   Defa, Berlin
S   Ufa Tempelhof, Berlin
CE   22 May 1928; 6 reels, 2608m; prohibited for youth; rating:
      educational
C   Imre Raday, Alfred Abel, Lilian Ellis, Hermine Sterler,
      Wilhelm Schmieder, Antonie Jaeckel, Ferdinand Bonn, Trude
      Hesterberg, Jacob Tiedtke, Paul Hörbiger, Eugen Neufeld,
      Jack Mylong-Münz
FR   *Der Film-Kurier* 10, no. 257 (1928); review by Hans Feld
      Der Kinematograph 22, no. 1174 (1928): 17
      Die LichtBildBühne 21, no. 259 (1928): 12
      Paimanns Filmlisten 13, no. 651 (1928): 149f
      Reichsfilmblatt, no. 44 (1928): 23

Unfug der Liebe (Folly of Love) [G 1928]

PR	14 November 1928, Berlin, Mozartsaal
DIR	Robert Wiene
SW	Max Glass, based on the novel by Alexander Castell
CM	Giovanni Vitrotti
M	Guiseppe Becce
SD	Alexander Ferenczy
P	Max Glass Film G.m.b.H., Berlin
D	Terra Film, Berlin
S	Terra-Glashaus, Berlin
CE	6 October 1928; 6 reels, 2088m; prohibited for youth
C	Maria Jacobini, Jack Trevor, Betty Astor, Angelo Ferrari, Ferry Sikla, Oreste Bilancia, Willi Forst
	According to *Paimanns Filmlisten*, this film appeared in Austria under the title of *Der Nachtchauffeur*.
FR	*Der Film-Kurier* 10, no. 273 (1928); review by Georg Herzberg
	Die Filmwoche, no. 48 (1928): 1209
	Der Kinematograph 22, no. 1183 (1928): 14
	Reichsfilmblatt, no. 46 (1928): 22
	Paimanns Filmlisten 13, no. 663 (1928): 199

Der Andere (The Other) [G 1930]

PR	12 August 1930
DIR	Robert Wiene
SW	Johannes Brandt, based on the play by Paul Lindau
CM	Nikolaus Farkas
M	Friedrich Hollaender, Will Meisel, Artur Guttmann
SD	Ernö Metzner
P	Terra Film, Berlin
EP	Max Glass
D	Terra Filmverleih G.m.b.H., Berlin
S	Terra Atelier, Berlin-Marienfelde (*Die LichtBildBühne* 23, no. 135 [1930])
CE	6 August 1930; 2849m
C	Fritz Kortner, Käthe von Nagy, Heinrich George, Hermine Sterler, Ursula van Diemen, Eduard von Winterstein, Oskar Sima, Julius Falkenstein, Paul Bildt, Otto Stössel, Emil Heyse, Hans Ahrens
FR	*Der Kinematograph* 24, no. 187 (1930): 1
	Die LichtBildBühne 23, no. 193 (1930)
	Die LichtBildBühne 23, no. 193 (1930): 2
	Paimanns Filmlisten 15, no. 750 (1930): 122
	Tagebuch, no. 33 (1930): 1323f; review by Kurt Pinthus

Le Procureur Hallers/L'Autre (The Prosecutor Hallers/The Other) [F 1930]

PR	prior to 2 September 1930
DIR	Robert Wiene
SW	Johannes Brandt, based on the play by Paul Lindau; dialogue by Jean Guitton
CM	Nicolas Farkas
SD	Ernö Metzner
P	Films Albatros
EP	Alexandre Kamenka
C	Collette Darfeuil, Suzanne Delmas, Jean Max, Georges Colin, Henry Krauss, Alfred Pallon, Charles Barrois, Florelle, Bill-Bocket
FR	*Der Kinematograph* 24, no. 205 (1930) *8 Uhr-Abendblatt*, no. 204 (1930); review by Kurt Pinthus

Nuits de Venise (Venetian Nights) [F 1931]

PR	prior to 23 January 1931
DIR	Robert Wiene, Pierre Billon
SW	Ladislaus Vajda, Andrée Zsoldos, Alexander Engel
M	Max Niederberger; lyrics by Léo Leliévre fils
P	Sofar
C	Janine Guise, Germaine Noizet, Florelle, Roger Tréville, Lucien Callemand, Max Maxudian, Pierre Nay, E. Danielli Note: previous title: *Huit Jours de Bonheur;* the French version of *Der Liebesexpress/Acht Tage Glück*
FR	*Ciné-Miroir*, 23 January 1931

Der Liebesexpress (The Love Express) [G 1931]

PR	5 May 1931, Berlin, Titania Palast
DIR	Robert Wiene
SW	Ladislaus Vajda, Andrée Zsoldos, Alexander Engel, based on Wilhelm Sterk's and Alexander Engel's operetta *Es lebe die Liebe*
CM	Carl Drews; sound camera, Erich Lange
M	Max Niederberger; lyrics by Robert Gilbert
SD	Ludwig Reiber
P	Greenbaum Film G.m.b.H., Munich/Emelka, Munich
EP	Fred Lyssa
D	Bayerische Film G.m.b.H. (im Emelka-Konzern), Munich
CE	30 January 1931; 2343m
C	Georg Alexander, Dina Gralla, Joseph Schmitt, Angelo Ferrari, Karl Baumann, Therese Giehse, Wilhelm Marx Alternate title: *Acht Tage Glück (Eight Days of Happiness)*
FR	*Der Kinematograph* 25, no. 104 (1931) *Die LichtBildBühne* 24, no. 108 (1931): 2 *Paimanns Filmlisten* 16, no. 777 (1931): 32

Panik in Chicago (Panic in Chicago) [G 1931]

PR	23 June 1931, Berlin, Ufa Palast am Zoo
DIR	Robert Wiene
SW	Friedrich Raff, Julius Urgiss, based on the novel by Robert Heymann
CM	Willi Goldberger; sound camera, Erich Lange; stills, Max Grix
M	Michael Krausz
SD	Robert Neppach, Erwin Scharf
P	Deutsches Lichtspiel-Syndikat
EP	Leo Meyer
D	Deutsches Lichtspiel-Syndikat
CE	4 June 1931; 8 reels, 2109m; prohibited for youth
C	Olga Tschechowa, Hans Rehmann, Hilde Hildebrandt, Lola Chlud, Ferdinand Hart, Ernst Dumcke, Willy Trenk-Trebitsch, Gerhard Bienert, Friedrich Ettel, Franz Weber, Ernst Wurmser, Arthur Bergen
FR	*Der Kinematograph* 25, no. 144 (1931)
	Die LichtBildBühne 24, no. 150 (1931): 2
	Paimanns Filmlisten 16, no. 801 (1931): 92

Taifun (Typhoon) [G 1933]

PR	25 August 1933, Vienna (*Taifun*)
	27 July 1934, Berlin, Primus Palast (*Polizeiakte 909*)
DIR	Robert Wiene
SW	Robert Wiene, based on the play by Melchior Lengyel
CM	Heinrich Gärtner
M	Helmuth Wolfes
P	Camera Film Productions G.m.b.H., Berlin
D	Terra Filmverleih G.m.b.H., Berlin
CE	3 May 1933; 2200m; film was banned
	20 April 1934; 2137m (other source: 2082m); prohibited for youth; film passed censorship under the title *Polizeiakte 909*
C	Liane Haid, Viktor de Kowa, Valeri Inkischinoff, Friedrich Ettel, Paul Mederow, Paul Henckels, Bernhard Goetzke, Veit Harlan, Joseph Dahmen, Arthur Reinhardt, Franz Kleebusch, Herbert Michels, Arthur Bergen, Erni Berti Carstens
FR	*Der Film-Kurier* 16, no. 175 (1934)
	Der Kinematograph 28, no. 144 (1934)
	Morgenpost, 29 July 1934

Eine Nacht in Venedig (A Night in Venice) [G, H 1934]

PR	21 March 1934, Berlin, Primus-Palast
DIR	Robert Wiene
SW	Robert Wiene, based on the opera by Johann Strauss
CM	Werner Bohne

M	Ladislaus Angyal, with themes from Strauss
P	Hunnia Film AG, Budapest and Berlin
S	Hunnia Ateliers, Budapest; location shots in Venice
CE	15 March 1934; 2259m; prohibited for youth
C	Tino Pattiere, Tina Ellers, Ludwig Stoessel, Oskar Sima, Lizzi von Balla, Fritz Fischer

Note: The German and Hungarian *(Égy ej Velencében)* versions of the film were made simultaneously in Budapest and in Venice. The Hungarian version was made jointly by Wiene and Géza von Cziffra. The source for this information is the Hungarian documentation and eyewitness reports. In Austria the film appeared under the title *Ein Mädel – eine Nacht.*

FR	*Der Kinematograph* 28, no. 58 (1934)
	Die LichtBildBühne 27 (22 March 1934)
	Mein Film, no. 422 (1934): 13f
	Paimanns Filmlisten 19, no. 931 (1934): 16

Ultimatum [F 1938]

PR	last week in October 1938
DIR	Robert Wiene; assistant, Robert-Paul Dagan
SW	Leo Lania, Pierre Allary, based on the novel by Ewald Bertram; dialogue, Alexandre Arnoux
CM	Ted Pahle, Jacques Mercanton
M	Adolphe Borchard
SD	Marcel Royné
ED	Tonka Taldy
SND	Emile Duquesne
P	Films Ultimatum, Paris (Gebauer: Pan Film)
	A Robert Wiene Production (Lux-print)
D	Forrester-Parant (France)
	Milo Films (outside France)
	J. H. Hofberg Films (U.S.)
EP	Charles-Georges Horset
S	François-1er, Paris
C	Dita Parlo, Michèle Alfa, Edith Gallia, Erich von Stroheim, Abel Jaquin, Bernard Lancret, Georges Rollin, Marcel André, Aimos, Pierre Nay, René Alié;Robert Siodmak completed the last few shots of the film.
FR	*Ciné-Miroir* 17, no. 709 (1938): 707–08
	Der Film (Antwerpen) 12, no. 36 (1939)

BIBLIOGRAPHY

Archives and Libraries

Bayerische Staatsbibliothek, Munich
Bibliothek der Hochschule der Bundeswehr, Neubiberg
Bibliothek der Johann Wolfgang von Goethe Universität, Frankfurt a.M.
Bibliothek der Universität Wien, Vienna
Bibliothèque d'Arsenal, Paris
Boston Public Library
British Film Institute, London
Bundesarchiv, Koblenz (Nachlass Oskar Messter)
Cinémathèque Francaise, Paris
Cinémathèque Royale de Belgie, Brussels
Deutsche Bibliothek, Frankfurt a.M.
Deutsches Institut für Filmkunde, Frankfurt a.M.
Deutsches Literaturarchiv/Schiller Nationalmuseum, Marbach
Landesbildstelle, Berlin
Library of the Academy of Motion Picture Arts and Sciences, Hollywood, CA
Münchner Filmmuseum, Munich
Österreichische Nationalbibliothek, Vienna
Österreichisches Filmarchiv, Vienna
Sammlung Oskar Kalbus (Bibliothek der Ludwigs-Maximilians
    Universität, Heidelberg)
Staatliches Filmarchiv der DDR, East Berlin (now: Bundesfilmarchiv, Berlin)
Stadt- und Landesarchiv, Vienna
Stiftung Deutsche Kinemathek, Berlin
Theater Collection of the New York Public Library
Theatersammlung der Universität zu Köln, Köln-Wahn
Weidner Library, Harvard University, Cambridge, MA

Periodicals

Berliner Morgenpost
Die Bühne
Cinema & Cinema
La Cinématographie Française
The Comparatist
Deutsche Allgemeine Zeitung
Deutsche Lichtspiel-Zeitung
DIF-Mitteilungen
Der Film
Das Film-Atelier
Der Filmbote
Die Film-Bühne
Film Criticism
Filmkultura
Filmkundliche Mitteilungen
Filmkunst
Der Film-Kurier
Filmschau
Der Filmspiegel
Die Film-Technik
Film-Tribüne
Die Filmwelt
Die Filmwoche
Freie Deutsche Bühne
Das Fremden-Blatt
Griffithiana
Historical Journal of Film, Radio, and Television
Illustrierte Zeitung
Illustrierter Film-Kurier
Der Kinematograph
Das Kino-Journal
Kosmorama
Die LichtBildBühne
Mein Film
Millennium Film Journal
Modern Austria Literature
The Modern Language Journal
National Board of Reviews Magazine
Die Neue Weltbühne
Neuer Theater-Almanach
Neues Wiener Journal
New Comparison
New German Critique
The New York Times

Österreichischer Komet
Paimanns Filmlisten
Reichsfilmblatt
Sight and Sound
Das TageBuch
Variety
Die Weltbühne
Wide Angle
World Film News

Articles and Books

Arnoux, Alexandre. *Du Muet au Parlant: Mémoirs d'un Témoin.* Paris: La Nouvelle Édition, 1946.

Balázs, Béla. *Schriften zum Film. vol. 1: Der sichtbare Mensch. Kritiken und Aufsätze 1922–1926.* Berlin: Henschel, 1982.

Barlow, John D. *German Expressionist Film.* Boston: Twayne, 1982.

Bauer, Alfred. *Deutscher Spielfilmalmanach, 1929–1950.* Berlin: Filmblätter Verlag, 1950.

Belach, Helga. *Henny Porten: Der erste deutsche Filmstar, 1890–1960.* Berlin: Haude & Spener, 1986.

Belach, Helga, and Hans-Michael Bock, eds. *Das Cabinet des Dr. Caligari: Drehbuch von Carl Mayer und Hans Janowitz zu Robert Wienes Film von 1919/1920.* Munich: edition text + kritik, 1995.

Bertram, Ewald. *Tage vor dem Sturm: Roman aus den Juliwochen 1914.* Berlin: Ullstein, 1933.

Birett, Herbert. *Stummfilm-Musik: Materialsammlung.* Berlin, 1970.

_____. *Verzeichnis in Deutschland gelaufener Filme: Entscheidungen der Filmzensur 1911–1920.* Munich: Saur, 1980.

Böhm, Gotthard. "Geschichte der Neuen Wiener Bühne." Ph.D. diss., University of Vienna, 1965.

Braverman, Barnet. "Courage in the Movies: Concerning Dr. Robert Wiene, Creator of the Famous Film, *Dr. Caligari's Cabinet.*" *The Billboard,* 14 November 1925, p. 49, 21 November 1925, p. 49.

Brennicke, Ilona, and Joe Hembus. *Klassiker des deutschen Stummfilms, 1910–1930.* Munich: Goldmann, 1983.

Budd, Michael. "Retrospective Narration in Film: Re-reading *The Cabinet of Dr. Caligari.*" *Film Criticism* 4 (1979): 35–43.

_____. "*The Cabinet of Dr. Caligari:* Conditions of Reception." *Ciné-tracts* 3 (1981): 41-49.

_____. "Contradictions of Expressionism in *The Cabinet of Dr. Caligari.*" *Indiana Social Studies Quarterly* 34 (1981): 19–25.

_____. "Authorship as a Commodity: The Art Cinema and *The Cabinet of Dr. Caligari.*" *Wide Angle* 6, no. 1 (1984): 12–19.

____. "*The Cabinet of Dr. Caligari*: Production, Reception, History." In *Close Viewings: An Anthology of New Film Criticism*, edited by Peter Lehmann, 333–52. Tallahassee: Florida State University Press, 1990.

____, ed. *The Cabinet of Dr. Caligari: Texts, Contexts, Histories*. New Brunswick, N.J.: Rutgers University Press, 1990.

Byrne, Richard B. "German Cinematic Expressionsim, 1919–1924." Ph.D. State University of Iowa, 1962.

Cardullo, Bert. "Expressionism and the Real *Cabinet of Dr. Caligari*." *Film Criticism* 6, no. 2 (1982): 28–34.

Carroll, Noel. "The Cabinet of Dr. Kracauer." *Millennium Film Journal* 1, no. 2 (1978): 77–85.

Chirat, Raymond. *Catalogue des films français de long métrage: Films de fiction 1919–1929*. Toulouse: Cinémathèque de Toulouse, 1981.

____. *Catalogue des films français de long métrage: Films sonores de fiction 1929–1939*. Brussels: Cinémathèque Royale, 1981.

Cocteau, Jean. *Kino und Poesie: Notizen*. Munich: C. Hanser, 1979.

Courtade, Francis. "Biofilmographie de Robert Wiene." *L'Avant-scène du Cinema*, nos. 160–161 (1975): 28–30.

____. *Cinéma expressioniste*. Paris: Henri Veyrier, 1984.

Cziffra, Géza von. *Ungelogen: Erinnerungen an mein Jahrhundert*. Munich: Herbig, 1988.

Dagover, Lil. *Ich war die Dame*. Munich: Schneekluth, 1979.

Echegaray, José. *Wahnsinn oder Heiligkeit*. Translated by Carl Wiene and Gustavo Kirem. Leipzig: Reclam, n.d. [1889].

Edler, Herbert. "Heinz Hanus–Filmschaffender und Begründer einer Berufsvereinigung für Filmschaffende in der ersten Republik: Ein Beitrag zur (Sozial-) Geschichte des österreichischen Films." Ph.D. diss., University of Vienna, 1983.

Eisenberg, Ludwig. *Grosses Biographisches Lexikon der deutschen Bühnen im 19. Jahrhundert*. Leipzig: P. List, 1903.

Eisner, Lotte H. *The Haunted Screen: Expressionism in the German Cinema and the Influence of Max Reinhardt*. Berkeley and Los Angeles: University of California Press, 1973.

____. *Ich hatte einst ein schönes Vaterland: Memorien*. Heidelberg: Wunderhorn, 1984.

Elsaesser, Thomas. "Social Mobility and the Fantastic: German Silent Film." *Wide Angle* 5, no. 2 (1982): 14–25.

Faulkner, Christopher. *The Social Cinema of Jean Renoir*. Princeton, N.J.: Princeton University Press, 1986.

Feld, Hans. "Jews in the Development of the German Film Industry: Notes from the Recollections of a Berlin Film Critic." *Leo Baeck Institute Yearbook 27*. London: Secker & Warburg, 1982.

____. "Carl Mayer–der erste Filmdichter." In *Caligari und Caligarismus*, edited by Walter Kaul. Berlin: SDK, 1970.

Ford, Charles. *Der Film und der Glaube*. Nürnberg: Glock und Lutz, 1955.

Frankfurter, Bernhard, ed. *Carl Mayer–Im Spiegelkabinett des Dr. Caligari: Der Kampf zwischen Licht und Dunkel*. Vienna: Promedia, 1997.

Fritz, Walter. *Die österreichischen Spielfilme der Stummfilmzeit: 1907–1930.* Vienna, Österreichische Gesellschaft für Filmwissenschaft, 1967.

———. *Geschichte des österreichischen Films.* Vienna: Bergland, 1969.

———. "Hofmannsthal und der Film." In *Hofmannsthal und das Theater: Die Vorträge des Hofmannsthal-Symposiums, 1971,* edited by Wolfram Mauser. Vienna: Halosar, 1981.

———. *Im Kino erlebe ich die Welt: 100 Jahre Kino und Film in Österreich.* Vienna: Brandstätter, 1997.

Gerdes, Peter. "*Das Kabinett des Dr. Caligari*: Unlösbarer Konflikt?" In *Expressionismus und Kulturkrise,* edited by Bernd Hüppauf, 245–62. Heidelberg: C. Winter, 1983.

Gesek, Ludwig. *Filmzauber aus Wien: Notizblätter zu einer Geschichte des österreichischen Films.* Vienna: Österreichische Gesellschaft für Filmwissenschaft, 1965.

Gifford, Dennis. *The British Film Catalogue 1895–1970: A Guide to Entertainment Films.* Newton Abbot: David & Charles, 1973.

Grace, Sherrill E. "'Dans le Cristallin de nos Yeux': *Neige Noir, Caligari,* and the Postmodern Film Frame-Up." *New Comparison 5* (1988): 89–103.

Hanus, Heinz. *50 Jahre österreichischer Film.* Unpaged brochure. Vienna, 1958.

Hess, Peter Klauss. *Das Cabinet des Dr. Caligari: Protokoll.* Stuttgart: Focus, 1985.

Hofmannsthal, Hugo von, and Carl J. Burckhardt. *Briefwechsel.* Frankfurt a.M.: S. Fischer, 1956.

Hofmannsthal, Hugo von, and Willy Haas. *Ein Briefwechsel.* Edited by Rolf Italiaander. Berlin: Propyläen, 1968.

Hofmannsthal, Hugo von, and Richard Strauss. *Der Rosenkavalier: Fassungen Filmscenarium Briefe.* Edited by Willi Schuh. Frankfurt a.M.: S. Fischer, 1972.

Holba, Herbert, Günter Knorr, and Peter Spiegel. *Reclams deutsches Filmlexikon: Filmkünstler aus Deutschland, Österreich, und der Schweiz.* Stuttgart: Reclam, 1984.

Jacobsen, Wolfgang. "Wortdämmerung: Auf dem Weg zum Tonfilm." In *Der deutsche Film: Aspekte seiner Geschichte von den Anfängen bis zur Gegenwart.* Edited by Uli Jung, 79–90. Trier: WVT, 1993.

Janowitz, Hans. "*Caligari*: The Story of a Famous Story." Unpublished manuscript, New York Public Library, Theater Collection.

———. "A Chapter about Carl Mayer and His World without Words." Unpublished manuscript, n.d. (after 1947), Janowitz Papers, SDK, Berlin.

———. *Asphaltballaden.* Edited by Dieter Sudhoff. Siegen: Uni-GHS Siegen, 1994.

Jason, Alexander. *Handbuch des Films, 1935/36.* Berlin: Happenstedt, 1936.

Jung, Uli, and Walter Schatzberg. "Robert Wiene's Film Career before *Caligari.*" In *Before Caligari: German Cinema, 1895-1920,* edited by Paolo Cherchi Usai and Lorenzo Codelli, 292–311. Pordenone: Le Giornate del Cinema Muto, 1990.

———. "*Caligari:* Das Kabinett des Dr. Wiene." In *Filmkultur zur Zeit der Weimarer Republik: Beiträge zu einer internationalen Konferenz vom 15. Bis 18. 6.1989 in Luxembourg,* 71–89. Munich: K. G. Saur, 1992.

_____. "Zur Genese eines Filmstoffs: *Der Andere* von Max Mack (1912) und Robert Wiene (1930)." *Filmwärts* 28, no. 4 (1993): 26, 39–41.

_____. "The Invisible Man behind *Caligari*: The Life of Robert Wiene." *Film History* 5, no. 1 (1993): 22–35.

_____. "The Silent *Rosenkavalier*: A Film by Hugo von Hofmannsthal, Richard Strauss und Robert Wiene." *Modern Austria Literature* 27, no. 4 (1994): 77–89.

_____. "Ein Drehbuch gegen die *Caligari*-Legenden." In *Das Cabinet des Dr. Caligari: Drehbuch von Carl Mayer und Hans Janowitz zu Robert Wienes Film von 1919/1920*, edited by Helga Belach and Hans-Michael Bock, 113–38. Munich: edition text + kritik, 1995.

_____. *Robert Wiene. Der Caligari Regisseur*. Berlin, Henschel, 1995.

_____, eds. *Filmkultur zur Zeit der Weimarer Republik: Beiträge zu einer internationalen Konferenz von 15. Bis 18.6 1989 in Luxemburg*. Munich: K. G. Saur, 1992.

Kaes, Anton, ed. *Die Kino-Debatte: Texte zum Verhältnis von Literatur und Film, 1909–1929*. Tübingen: Niemeyer, 1978.

Kasten, Jürgen. *Der expressionistische Film: Abgefilmtes Theater oder avantgardistiches Erzählkino? Eine stil- produktions- und rezeptionsgeschichtliche Untersuchung*. Münster: MAkS Publikationen, 1990.

_____. *Carl Mayer: Filmpoet–Ein Drehbuchautor schreibt Filmgeschichte*. Berlin: Vistas, 1994.

_____. "Besessene und Geschäftemacher: Zur Rezeptionsgeschichte von *Das Cabinet des Dr. Caligari*." In *Carl Mayer: Im Spiegelbild des Dr. Caligari–Der Kampf zwischen Licht und Dunkel*, edited by Bernhard Frankfurter, 136–46. Vienna: Promedia, 1997.

Kaul, Walter, ed. *Caligari und Caligarismus*. Berlin: SDK, 1970.

Kessler, Michael, and Thomas Y. Levin, eds. *Siegfried Kracauer: Neue Interpretationen*. Tübingen: Stauffenburg, 1990.

Ketchif, Nancy. "Dr. Caligari's Cabinet: A Cubist Perspective." *The Comparatist* 8, no. 5 (1984): 7–13.

Klaus, Ulrich J. *Deutsche Tonfilme*. 8 volumes. Berlin: Klaus Archiv, 1990.

Kracauer, Siegfried. *From Caligari to Hitler: A Psychological History of the German Film*. Princeton, N.J.: Princeton University Press, 1947.

Kurtz, Rudolf. "Film und Kultur." *Illustrierte Zeitung* 159, no. 3975 (1919).

_____. *Expressionismus und Film*. Berlin: Verlag der LichtBildBühne, 1926.

Lähn, Peter. "Über die Wacht im Osten ins Caligari-Atelier: Reimanns Weg zum Film." *Walter Reimann: Maler und Filmarchitekt*, edited by Hans Peter Reichmann, 38–49. Frankfurt a.M: Deutsches Filmmuseum, 1997.

Lamprecht, Gerhard. *Deutsche Stummfilme*. 11 volumes. Berlin: SDK, 1970.

Leidig, Prof. Dr. "Die Filmindustrie in der Volkswirtschaft," *Illustrierte Zeitung* 153, no. 3975 (1919): 2.

Levin, Thomas Y. *Siegfried Kracauer: Eine Bibliographie seiner Schriften*. Marbach a.N.: Deutsche Schillergesellschaft, 1989.

Loacker, Armin. "Die österreichische Filmwirtschaft von den Anfängen bis zur Einführung des Tonfilms," *Maske und Kothurn* 39, no. 4 (1993): 75–122.

Minden, Michael. "Politics and the Silent Cinema: *The Cabinet of Dr. Caligari* and *Battleship Potemkin*." In *Visions and Blueprints: Avant-Garde Culture and Radical Politics in Early Twentieth-Century Europe*, edited by Edward Timms and Peter Collier, 287–306. Manchester: Manchester University Press, 1988.

Möller, Thomas. "Ein Blick zurück auf Dr. Caligari: Die Rezeption einer Legende." In *Walter Reimann: Maler und Filmarchitekt*, edited by Hans Peter Reichmann, 66–71. Frankfurt a.M: Deutsches Filmmuseum, 1997.

Pegge, C. Dennis. "*Caligari*: Its Innovations in Editing." *The Quarterly of Film, Radio, and Television* 11, no. 2 (1956): 136–48.

Petro, Patrice. *Joyless Streets: Women and Melodramatic Representation in Weimar Germany*. Princeton, N.J.: Princeton University Press, 1989.

Pinthus, Kurt. "*Der Andere* auf französisch." *8 Uhr-Abendblatt*, no. 204 (1930).

———. "*Der Andere* einst und jetzt." *Das Tagebuch*, no. 33 (1930).

———. "*Der Andere* in französicher Fassung." *Der Kinematograph* 24, no. 205 (1930).

Porges, Friedrich, ed. *Mein Film-Buch: Vom Film, von Filmstars und von Kinematographie*. Berlin: Mein Film-Verlag, 1928.

Pratt, David B. "'Fit Food for Madhouse Inmates': The Box Office Reception of the German Invasion of 1921." *Griffithiana*, nos. 48–49 (1993): 97–157.

Prawer, S. S. *Caligari's Children: The Film as Tale of Terror*. Oxford: Oxford University Press, 1980.

———. "Vom 'Filmroman' zum Kinofilm." In *Das Cabinet des Dr. Caligari: Drehbuch von Carl Mayer und Hans Janowitz zu Robert Wienes Film von 1919/1920*, edited by Helga Belach and Hans-Michael Bock, 11–45. Munich: edition text + kritik, 1995.

Prinzler, Hans Helmut, and Enno Patalas, eds. *Lubitsch*. Munich: C. J. Bucher, 1984.

Prodolliet, Ernest. *Das Abenteuer Kino: Der Film im Schaffen von Hugo von Hofmannsthal, Thomas Mann und Alfred Döblin*. Freiburg, CH: Universitätsverlag, 1991.

Quaresima, Leonardo. "L'atto di nascita' del *Caligari*." *Cinema & Cinema* 18, no. 62 (1991): 19–24.

———. "Die 'Geburtsurkunde' des *Caligari*: Wichtige Dokumente wiederentdeckt." *Filmdienst* 5 (1992): 16–17.

———. "Wer war Alland: Die Texte des *Caligari*." In *Carl Mayer: Im Spiegelbild des Dr. Caligari–Der Kampf zwischen Licht und Dunkel*, edited by Bernhard Frankfurter, 99–118. Vienna: Promedia, 1997.

Regel, Helmut, and Heinz Steinberg. *Der deutsche Stummfilm*. Cologne: Arbeitsgemeinschaft für Filmfragen at the University of Cologne, Winter Semester 1963/64, mimeographed, Deutsches Institut für Filmkunde (DIF), Frankfurt.

Rentschler, Eric. "Reopening the Cabinet of Dr. Kracauer: Teaching German Film as Film." *The Modern Language Journal* 64 (1980): 318–28.

Robinson, David. *Das Cabinet des Dr. Caligari*. London: BFI, 1997.

Rotha, Paul. *The Film till Now: A Survey of World Cinema*. New York: Jonathan Cape & Harrison Smith, 1930.

Roud, Richard. *A Passion for Films: Henri Langlois and the Cinémathèque Française*. New York: Viking, 1983.

Rubenstein, Lenny. "*Caligari* and the Rise of the Expressionist Film." In *Passion and Rebellion: The Expressionist Heritage*, edited by Stephen Eric Bronner and Douglas Kellner, 363–73. New York: Columbia University Press, 1988.

Salt, Barry. "From *Caligari* to Who?" *Sight and Sound* 48, no. 2 (1979): 119–23.

Sarris, Andrew. "The Germanic Factor: Taking Hitler out of Caligari." *Voice*, no. 1 (1979): 49f.

Saunders, Thomas J. *Hollywood in Berlin: American Cinema and Weimar Germany*. Berkeley: University of California Press, 1994.

Savio, Francesco. *Ma L'Amore No: Realismo, Formalismo, Propaganda e Telefoni Bianchi nel Cinema Italiano di Regiome (1930–1943)*. Milan: Casa Editrice Sonzogno, 1975.

Simsolo, Noel. "Autour de Caligari." *La Revue du Cinema*, no. 376 (1982).

Sopocy, Martin. "The Circles of Siegfried Kracauer: *From Caligari to Hitler* Re-examined." *Griffithiana* 14, nos. 40–42 (1991): 61–73.

Spitzmuller, Georges. *Le Cabinet du Docteur Caligari: Ciné-roman fantastique*. Paris: Ciné-Collection, La Renaissance du Livre, 1922.

Strauss, Richard, and Hugo von Hofmannsthal. *Briefwechsel*. Edited by Willi Schuh. Zürich: Atlantis Verlag, 1952.

Surowiec, Catherine A., ed., *The Lumière Project: The European Film Archives at the Crossroads*. Lisbon: Associaçáo Projecto Lumiere, 1996.

Thiele, Jens. "Die dunklen Seiten der Seele: *Das Cabinet des Dr. Caligari* (1920)." In *Fischer Filmgeschichte*. Vol. 1, *Von den Anfängen bis zum etablierten Medium 1895–1924*, edited by Werner Faulstich and Helmut Korte, 344–60. Frankfurt a.M.: Fischer, 1994.

30 Jahre Sascha-Film: Festschrift der Sascha-Film Verleih- und Vertriebs-G.m.b.H. Vienna: Sascha, 1948.

Ulrich, Paul S. *Theater, Tanz und Musik im Deutschen Bühnenjahrbuch*, vol. 2. Berlin: A. Spitz, 1985.

Van Wert, William F. "Intertitles." *Sight and Sound* 49, no. 2 (1980): 98–105.

Vincent, Carl. *Histoire de l'art Cinématographique*. Brussels: Trident, 1939.

Vincke, Kitty. "Anstelle einer Errettung äußerer Wirklichkeit: Entwürfe von Walter Reimann für *Das Cabinet des Dr. Caligari*." In *Walter Reimann: Maler und Filmarchitekt*, edited by Hans Peter Reichmann, 50–65. Frankfurt a.M: Deutsches Filmmuseum, 1997.

Warm, Hermann. "Gegen die *Caligari*-Legenden." In *Caligari und Caligarismus*, edited by Walter Kaul. Berlin: SDK, 1970.

Welch, David. "The Proletarian Cinema and the Weimar Republic." *Historical Journal of Film, Radio, and Television* 1, no. 1 (1981): 3–18.

Wildberg, Bodo. *Das Dresdner Hoftheater in der Gegenwart: Biographien und Charakteristiken*. Dresden and Leipzig, 1901.

INDEX